The Power of Pedagogy

The Power of Pedagogy

Jenny Leach & Bob Moon

SAGE

Los Angeles • London • New Delhi • Singapore

First published 2008

SAGE Publications Ltd
1 Oliver's Yard
55 City Road
London EC1Y 1SP

SAGE Publications Inc.
2455 Teller Road
Thousand Oaks, California 91320

SAGE Publications India Pvt Ltd
B 1/I 1 Mohan Cooperative Industrial Area
Mathura Road, New Delhi 110 044
India

SAGE Publications Asia-Pacific Pte Ltd
33 Pekin Street #02-01
Far East Square
Singapore 048763

Library of Congress Control Number: 2007942661

British Library Cataloguing in Publication data

A catalogue record for this book is available from the British Library

ISBN 978-1-4129-0722-4
ISBN 978-1-4129-0723-1 (pbk)

Typeset by C&M Digitals (P) Ltd, Chennai, India
Printed in India by Replika Press
Printed on paper from sustainable resources

Contents

'We have the obligation to think about the future, precisely because of the type of work we do. Venturing the future is not a risk – it's a necessity of the dignity of human kind.'

Loris Malaguzzi

for my children Matthew and Miriam (JL)
and for my grandchildren Billie, Tyler, Louis, Zoe and Eva (BM)

Acknowledgements

> Our micro cultures of praxis encompass the reference books we use, the kind of notes
> we habitually take, the computer programmes and data bases we rely on and perhaps
> most of all the network of friends, colleagues and mentors on whom we lean for feed-
> back, help, advice, even just for company.[1]

So many teacher educators, teachers and students have influenced the ideas in
this book spanning the sixty plus years in which between us we have both
been immersed in the fascinating work of learning and teaching. Although too
numerous to name everyone, there are a number of friends and colleagues
who we would like to thank who have been particularly important in the
development of the ideas in this book:

— Past and present members of the Centre for Research and Development in Teacher
  Education (CReTE) and the Research Group in International Development for
  Teacher Education Across Cultures and Societies (RITES) at the Open University,
  UK. Also many teachers and students in the CReTE's PGCE Programme (1994 to
  the present). We are particularly indebted to Bob McCormick, Frank Banks, Anne
  Storey and Elizabeth Bird who commented in such detail on the draft manuscript.
  Many of the ideas in this book were originally discussed with the OU's MA Course
  Team for 'Curriculum, Learning and Assessment'. Bob McCormick and Frank
  Banks have worked with us on the research into teacher professional knowledge, as
  discussed in Chapter 7, since 1995.

— Tim Brighouse, formerly Chief Adviser, London Schools.

— Colleagues at the University of Fort Hare, Eastern Cape, South Africa, especially
  Nhlanganiso Dladla.

— Members of the Digital Education Enhancement Project, especially Tom Power,
  Rhodri Thomas, Shumi Makalima, the late Adi Kwelemtini, the staff and students
  at Butterworth High School (especially Vuyo Klaas) and the staff and students at
  Dongwe Combined Primary School (especially Mandla Mquibisa and Andile
  Mbebe).

— Members of the Teacher Education in Sub-Saharan Africa (TESSA) programme,
  particularly Alison Buckler, Claire Hedges, Anne Roberts, Freda Wolfenden, and
  colleagues across the nine participating countries.

– Colleagues from the Programme, Planning and Monitoring Unit, Cairo, especially Nadia Gamal El Din, Atef Ahmed and Mohammed Bondok, and teachers and students in the Educational Enhancement Programme.

– Members of the Albania Education Development Project (AEDP), Tirana, Albania, 1992–2002, especially Zana Lita and the teachers and students in the Kualida Programme.

– Martha Stone Wiske (Harvard Graduate School of Education, Boston, USA); Eileen Sullivan Shakespear (Fenway High School, Boston, USA); Andrea Karpati (University of Eotvos Lorand, Hungary); Irene Bishop (St Saviour and St Olave's School, Southwark, London); Rachel Allard (Greycoats School, Westminster, London); Tom Leach (Brent Primary Care Trust); Eileen Simpson (EAL Service, Edinburgh).

– We would also like to thank Julie Herbert, who assisted in the preparation of the manuscript, and Marianne Lagrange and Matthew Waters at Sage, who helped us to initiate this project and who worked to see it to fruition.

– Jenny would like to thank staff at the Oncology Unit, Addenbrooke's Hospital, Cambridge, who have provided her with new insights into the learning process, as well as enabling her to survive the writing period. Also the family and friends who have remained so supportive of – and interested in – her being able to complete this project.

We would like to thank the following for permission to use illustrations in the text:

Belinda Canham, Headmistress of the Gateway School, London for permission to reproduce the picture of Maria Montessori.

Professor Andrew Pollard of the ESRC Teaching and Learning Programme (TLRP) for permission to quote extracts from TLRP documents.

Sue Ellis, Director, Centre for Literacy in Primary Education, London, for permission to reproduce the Portfolio from the 'Assessing Learning and Communication in Creative Contexts' project. Acknowledgement is also given to the CfBT Education Trust who funded this project and the authors of the template. Further information is available at www.clpe.co.uk.

The British Library for permission to reproduce the Psalter Map.

Miriam Leach for permission to reproduce the drawing in Chapter 6.

The Open University for the description of the Virtual Identities Digital Arts Project in Chapter 6.

Jenny Leach took the photographs on pages 7, 23, 25, 46, 80, 84, 107, 141.

Bob Moon took the photograph on page 165.

AUTHORS' NOTES

(i) We have used endnotes throughout the text, grouped by chapter at the end of the book. Our plan is that these notes should be used integrally and interactively and they serve two purposes. First, to locate our sources and second, importantly, they indicate many further points of departure for those with the commitment, and perhaps the passion, to explore further. (ii) The quotation that opens each chapter is taken from that chapter.

A note from Bob Moon

Jenny Leach died just a few days after completing her final revisions to the manuscript for this book. As her acknowledgement indicates, much of the writing was carried out in parallel with a very brave struggle to overcome illness. This book allowed Jenny to distill a lifetime's experience of action and reflection, and thus stands as testimony to a very special person.

Introduction

The Power of Pedagogy is the product of a fascinating journey. One that we have, both separately and together, been undertaking over the last few decades. A journey involving contact with a wide range of teachers and other educators in many parts of the world.

Our aim in writing this book is to critically explore the multiple theoretical and practical perspectives embraced by the concept of pedagogy. We want to emphasise from the outset that our intention is not to outline or recommend particular practices of learning and teaching; instead our interest is in trying to tease out why pedagogy is situated in educational cultures in the way it is, what function pedagogy serves and the role it can play in our lives as teachers. We hope to draw out from this exploration a new set of tools, concepts and ways of thinking about pedagogy that will be of use to educators, teacher educators and others interested in analysing the processes of learning and teaching.

We might call this process 'going meta'[1] on pedagogy: turning round on the concept in order to consider not only what and why – but more importantly how – we think about learning and teaching.[2] Throughout history, philosophers, educators, scientists, artists and historians have continually considered and reconsidered 'big' questions – about the nature of the world and what makes us human (metaphysics), the nature of thought (metacognition), the role of language in our lives (metalinguistics), and so forth. We believe the time is right for reconsidering some of the big questions about pedagogy. Major changes are taking place in the social world in which we live which impact widely on teachers and their learners. Innovative research on the nature of the human mind and learning is burgeoning. New communication technologies give teachers and their students access to modes of working and forms of relationship that were impossible just a decade or so ago. This new context, we would argue, invites us to re-address fundamental questions about pedagogy.

The sources and ideas we refer to throughout the book have been chosen to support and develop this hypothesis that it is timely to consider new frameworks for talking, practising, knowing, thinking and learning about learning and teaching. We are not intending to cite every possible source on pedagogy – indeed it would be arrogant to attempt to set out, even superficially, the scholarly record on the many themes covered in the pages that follow. Rather, we use our sources in order to create a shared, negotiable language with which to analyse pedagogy. We are hopeful that the themes we have chosen to explore might constitute the outline of a curriculum for teacher learning and development. We also hope that they will facilitate the consideration of new dispositions and tools for thinking that can be used and critiqued by any group of teachers who, like ourselves, are committed to an ongoing inquiry into learning and teaching. By making ways of thinking about pedagogy – be they new frameworks, heuristics, models, concepts, stories, poetry, images – public and communal, we want to make the field accessible and above all inspiring and fascinating to newcomers and more experienced educators alike.

In this sense then, our work is concerned primarily with the interpretation and understanding of pedagogy, rather than with the achievement of knowledge or skilled performance in the complex business of learning and teaching. To help us in this interpretative process we have raided the historical (as much as the contemporary) ideas from previous centuries to rub shoulders with current practices. We agree with Bruner that there is something special about 'talking' to authors who are no longer living but still very present in their texts or legacies of practice. The objective of such encounters is not adulation, but interpretation.

Interpretation has also been aided by our research and practice across a range of unfamiliar settings and cultures. Comparison and contrast can be powerful means of uncovering unconscious, taken-for-granted habits of mind. We argue that explorations of pedagogy in different settings (which for us has included work in Japan, the Middle East, Sub-Saharan Africa, North America, and Western, Central and Eastern Europe) can jolt us out of the familiar mentalities shaped by habitual practices, national obsessions, taken-for-granted discourses and culturally-specific curricula. In this we expect and hope our discussions will provoke debate and perhaps some dispute. Our own journeying with colleagues has shown that conflictual views – expressed in a context of respect, trust and collegiality – are integral to the process of going meta, and whilst in this book we mostly use the shared voice ('we') our own viewpoints and ideas have not infrequently been at odds.

For all these reasons you will not find us commenting on specific national curricula, management strategies, statutory curriculum requirements, or locally agreed 'standards' and assessment protocols (important as these may be), except where they elucidate our interpretation of a particular pedagogic setting. To this end we deliberately juxtapose instances of practice and theory from a range of sectors – adult to pre-school, teenager to trainee teachers, and medics.

Throughout the book we also use many of the interpretative strategies that have surfaced in our exploration of the how of pedagogy – narrative, image, visual and cognitive models, and so forth. But this is neither a 'gotcha' exercise to locate the definitive story on pedagogy, nor a rhetorical attempt to push particular strategies and points of view. We inevitably bring our own selections, predispositions, experiences and values to the debate and are therefore explicit about these in Chapter 2. But we have tried to root our own assertions in the sort of evidence that others, if they wish, can take issue with. In our separate occupations as teachers, as well as in our more recent joint work in the field of teacher education, we have espoused what some might term 'progressive' careers in education. But we are wary of oversimplistic labels. Our recent experience, for example working extensively in Sub-Saharan Africa, suggests that any exploration of pedagogy needs to work independently of taken-for-granted paradigms, such as notions of the 'progressive' and 'traditional', that so often muddy any discussion around the future of learning and teaching.

We try, therefore, in each of the chapters to provide ideas and illustrations, often in the form of vignettes, that demonstrate the widest spectrum of contexts and cultures. Our own experience in schools and universities still shows through, but we feel that any insights gained are applicable to a range of settings. And indeed 'settings' provide our departure point in Chapter 2.

In juxtaposing a wide range of viewpoints we seek to replicate the way professional knowledge and pedagogic expertise are created. When skilful teachers of science or history really engage their students in explorations of issues of climate change or notions of citizenship, these students are learning how to 'think science', 'think history' – science as a way of analysing the world, history as a discipline of understanding and learning from the past and constructing future possibilities, rather than simply knowing what happened. This is as true for primary teachers as for teachers in a university context. Through the explorations encompassed within this book we want to learn how to 'think pedagogy', namely how we might share knowledge, views of learning and thinking, new tools, models and languages, in order to make sense of this exciting, risky and adventurous field of inquiry. How we can push forward and construct future possibilities for real change and transformation in the processes of learning and teaching. In this way we hope to move some way towards understanding the real power of pedagogy.

1

Pedagogy

We start with the premise that good teachers are intellectually curious about pedagogy.

You can reach Reggio Emilia from Bologna in less than an hour. The road traverses the fertile river valley of the Po, following the line of the ancient *Via Emilia*, the Roman road that crossed the region from east to west. This is the route that Bruno Ciari and others would have taken when he returned from the Second World War with a mission to revolutionise the schooling of their home district.

Half a century on, Reggio Emilia has one of the world's most renowned early years systems. Educationalists from all over the world have followed the *Via Emilia* to seek out and wonder at the opportunities provided for the children of that region.

In 1991 *Newsweek* stated that if you had to choose anywhere in the world for your children to begin their schooling then Reggio Emilia would be the best choice. Jerome Bruner, following a visit, wrote:

> I was not prepared for what I found. It was not just that they were better than anything I'd ever seen … What struck me about the Reggio pre-schools was how they cultivated imagination and, in the process, how they empowered the children's sense of what is possible. But the more I observed, the more I realised that this was not coming out of some abstract theory or inspiration about pedagogy. Rather it exposed something deep about Reggio itself, something 'molto reggiano'.[1]

The journalist Furio Colombo provided a further perspective:

> There is a place in the world where the talent, imagination, and professional skill dedicated to industry or science are dedicated instead to young children. A place in which the same people have worked together for years to refine their experience, and the children are stimulated to express every aspect of their unimaginable resource.[2]

Pedagogy, or *pedagogia* in Italian, was at the heart of the reform movement that Bruno Ciari set in train. It therefore seems a good starting point for our exploration of contemporary ideas about learning and teaching, and the relevance of these ideas to teachers in the twenty-first century.

Ciari's first pedagogical experimentation was in the village school at Certaldo, but rapid promotion to becoming Director of the local school district gave him the opportunity to rethink the concept of early years education. An holistic concept of pedagogy was at the core of his thinking. Parents, as well as teachers and children, were seen as central to the educational process. Pedagogy, therefore, went beyond the particular skills of individual teachers. Children were viewed as strong and rich personalities with a natural curiosity to be exploited in the varied settings of school and community life. Co-operation and communication were seen as crucial and buildings and classrooms were built to exploit this. Teachers worked in pedagogic teams with the support of a pedagogical co-ordinator or *pedagogista*. Observation and research and the need for children to engage in a continuous process of discussion, interpretation and presentation of their work were together seen as key to pedagogical success.

Ciari's ideas were sufficiently powerful for Reggio Emilia, subsequently led by Loris Malaguzzi, to set up a network of schools and centres for 0–6 years with the aim 'to promote children's education through the development of all their languages: expressive, communicative, symbolic, cognitive, ethical, metaphorical, logical, imaginative and educational'.[3]

Ciari's vision was strongly rooted in a wider history of ideas about pedagogy and schooling. He had previously met Maria Montessori, who in the early years of the twentieth century had formulated a pedagogy that embraced the total learning environment of the child and classroom. For Montessori the worlds inside and outside the classroom needed to be brought together and understood when nurturing children. Again, pedagogy had to be understood in the total setting of each learner and school. Montessori railed against the classifications and gradings of children that were such a feature of newly emergent, 'free and compulsory', basic education systems. She became convinced that many children who were labelled as 'low ability', or even 'unteachable', could, given the right pedagogic setting, achieve much more than societal expectations suggested. Thus Maria Montessori found practical ways of demonstrating what could be done. As Director of a school for children with perceived learning disabilities, attached to the University of Rome, she showed how those formerly labelled as 'deficient' could compete successfully with their peers in the main school system.

Reggio Emilia represents one starting point for exploring pedagogy, but there are others. In North America, quite some time before Ciari's reforms were taking root, John Dewey was beginning revolutionary work that was a reaction against the traditional US educational framework of memorisation and recitation. Education is not the preparation for life, it is life itself, he argued. Like Ciari and Montessori he also challenged the prevailing orthodoxy that saw little educational future, not as in the context of a largely peasant population, but for students living in a newly industrial age. Using radically new approaches Dewey, with his wife, Alice Chipman Dewey, launched the University of Chicago Laboratory Schools where he was able to actualise his pedagogical beliefs in a series of educational programmes founded on the principles of hands-on learning and exploration. By 1904, after eight years of intense and creative pedagogical work, the Laboratory School had become, many argued, the most interesting experimental venture in American education. It had also become a centre for

Photo: Courtesy Phyllis Wallbank, Principal, The Gatehouse School

Montessori with pupils at the Gatehouse School in London on her last visit to England, in 1951, the year before her death.

other scholars of various fields to meet together to analyse and discuss solutions to the most pressing intellectual and social problems of the time.

For Dewey, the role of the teacher was not to impose on children irrelevant tasks that would be potentially useful a decade later, but instead to identify each child's interest, organise learning activities around its immediate and proximate use, and then step by step move the process in the desired direction. All so-called 'traditional' subjects such as reading, writing, history, spelling, arithmetic and science, were connected with one another. Dewey saw value in the methods of subjects and disciplines, but he also saw motivational energy coming from a cross-disciplinary approach to curriculum design. Dewey himself promoted the idea that intelligence was an instrument for overcoming obstacles in one's life, and so the focus of the Chicago Laboratory School zeroed in on how to close the gap between thought and action. By having such a focus, the school became the centre for Dewey's educational philosophy, set out in works such as *The School and Society* (1899), *The Child and the Curriculum* (1902) and *Democracy and Education* (1916). The teachers of the Laboratory School, Dewey argued, started with question marks rather than fixed answers.

Both Reggio Emilia's example and the work of John Dewey caught the imagination of the world. It is no coincidence that Ciari, Montessori and Dewey all faced controversy and experienced political pressure.[4] Each saw a new approach to pedagogy as representing something much greater than a more effective approach to teaching.

With their vision of teaching came a new view of learners and learning and a new framework within which to conceive the relationship between teacher and learner. In this way they saw pedagogy as going beyond the specific skills of the teacher to embrace the wider purposes and beliefs that surround and impact upon all pedagogic settings. It is this broader vision that we seek to explore.

We start with the premise that good teachers are intellectually curious about pedagogy. Such curiosity requires an examination of values and beliefs as well as the strategies and techniques the teacher deploys. It is this that makes pedagogy inevitably contested, although the forms and strength of such contestation vary over time and in respect of place. In most education systems there are endemic clashes between the perceived polarities of 'traditionalists' and 'progressives' in thinking about pedagogic theories and practices. At times this can generate all the intensity of an ethnic, sectarian clash and such debates can go way beyond the professional world of formal educators. The media in turn recognise that an increasingly literate and knowing populace has an interest in such affairs that were unknown a generation or two earlier. We recognise the validity of the debate here but we would want to question some of the ways in which the terms of reference are set.

A distinction is often made between pedagogy and education.[5] This is more than mere semantics, although the words do have different Greek and Latin derivations. Pedagogy comes from the Greek *paidagogos* (the leading of the child/slave), whereas education comes from the Latin *educare* (to bring up or nourish). The discourse of education, we want to argue, is more likely to be descriptive and normative, whereas pedagogy invites us to recognise the multiple and various dynamics of scenes of learning and teaching. Henry Giroux[6] has pointed up such differences. Highly pragmatic and behaviouristic in both its assumptions and practice, the field of education has historically always viewed theory as something of an unnecessary intrusion. In distinction pedagogy is a mode of engagement with the social process – or rather with social processes. This in part helps explain its relevance to literacy and cultural studies, feminism, philosophy and political theory, where the notion of pedagogy has invited attack particularly from conservative quarters.

This distinction between education and pedagogy has also informed the debate about the place of pedagogy in preparing teachers. More than twenty years ago Brian Simon, the educational historian, wrote a highly influential article under the title 'Why No Pedagogy in England?'[7] Although specifically addressing the English context, his analysis was also highly relevant to North America.[8] In this article he argued that the social class–related reverence for the 'amateur' infiltrated the school system through the public schools in forms that effectively closed out intellectual curiosity around the concept of pedagogy. Simon's critique then explored the wider social and political context in which pedagogy operates. The demise of pedagogy in England – in his terms 'the end of the systematic study of the teaching process' – was signalled, he contends, as early as the 1920s. Its cause he puts down to an increasing emphasis on categorisation and selection and particularly the then ascendancy of psychometric theory and convictions about the measurement of ability. Simon argued for a science of teaching, creating a body of general principles that would inform all the settings in which learning and teaching take place. Here Simon was greatly influenced by Lev Vygotsky, a Russian psychologist whose work only became internationally known in the middle of the last century. For Vygotsky pedagogy had to be oriented not towards the yesterday of development but towards its tomorrow. What the child can do today with adult help, he said, he will be able to do independently tomorrow. And, for Vygotsky, the only good teaching is that which outpaces development.[9]

This resonates with Montessori's or Ciari's idea of refusing to make predictive judgements about children's potential abilities. Brian Simon was a lifelong campaigner against the categorisations of children promoted by many education systems. He was against streaming or tracking and in the English context he was one of the earliest critics of the system of selective secondary schools introduced in 1944.[10]

But Simon also had a rigorous view about the need for structure in learning and he was critical of some progressives who had argued for a pedagogy of individualisation. For Simon, if teaching is based on the idea that each child requires a specific pedagogical approach, then the construction of an all embracing pedagogy, or general principles of teaching, becomes an impossibility.[11] We share this view, not only because of the constraints imposed in many pedagogic contexts by resources, buildings, classrooms and learner numbers, but also because learning and teaching, we believe, are in essence social processes. One learner needs other learners and while individualisation may have a place in building pedagogic settings, it cannot in its own terms provide an effective pedagogy.

We began this chapter with Reggio Emilia. Recently one of our students posed the question, 'If Reggio Emilia is so outstanding, why has it not been replicated, at least across the western world?' This is a good question and, after some thought, we gave two related answers. First, there are other parts of the world that are trying to emulate the world that Ciari and his colleagues created. Individual groups have created schools that have adopted the Reggio Emilia approach.[12] And aspects of the Reggio Emilia approach have been incorporated into the ideas of some school districts.[13] However, the formal structures of schooling are not easy to change. A few years ago Herbert Kliebard looked at the teaching in one mid-western state of the USA.[14] He analysed the curriculum and organisation of the one teacher school that had existed in the early years of that community and he showed how the project-centred model of curriculum and pedagogy, idiosyncratic at times but inspirational in the memories of the children, had given way to an almost industrial approach as numbers boomed and legislation was passed about compulsory schooling. What he demonstrated was that a form of regimentation had come to dominate schooling as the size of provision and its associated bureaucracy had grown. Large-scale school provision seems to militate against considering, let alone incorporating, the central tenets of the Reggio Emilia provision.[15]

We would argue, however, that as school systems grow and expand[16] the need for a humanistic, not mechanistic, pedagogy is becoming even more critical. This may take many forms, as the title of our last chapter, 'Pedagogies', illustrates. However, at its core pedagogy must have the purpose of power for allowing children and others to forge their own ways and identities in our complex, knowledge-rich society.

We are wary of expressing from the outset a hard and fast definition of pedagogy, since we intend this book to unfold some of the debates and practices that over time have informed the development of this complex concept. A range of definitions already exists in contemporary literature,[17] although we have found that those who talk and write most deeply about pedagogy[18] also tend to avoid neat formulations summed up in a tidy phraseology. Nevertheless, we do hope, in the pages that follow, to convey our view of pedagogy as a dynamic process informed by theories, beliefs and dialogue, but only realised in the daily interactions of learners and teachers and real settings.

In the present day our experience as teachers and our engagement with the study of pedagogy have led us to a number of assertions. We want to identify these at the outset in order to make the preconceptions and values we bring to this task explicit and to form the basis for the structure of subsequent chapters.

Our first assertion, explored in Chapter 2 ('Settings') is that any understanding or theory of pedagogy must encompass all the complex factors that influence the process of learning and teaching. Our discourse is, therefore, wide ranging. In creating and sustaining pedagogic settings teachers crucially determine both the nature and quality of learning. Pedagogy is more than the accumulation of techniques and strategies, more than arranging a classroom, formulating questions, and developing explanations. It is informed by a view of mind, of learning and learners and the kinds of knowledge and outcomes that are valued.

Our second assertion is that within any pedagogical setting the mind must be viewed as complex and multifaceted. Within such settings a broad understanding of the human mind and cognitive science, as we understand it today, is a crucial aspect of teacher knowledge and it is this we will be seeking to explore further (see particularly Chapter 3, 'Minds') as we set out our contemporary understanding of learners and pedagogy.

A third assertion is that learning is a social process and thus it follows that any attempt to influence learning has to go beyond the characteristics of any individual learner to embrace all the influences that impinge on learning in their social settings. From this perspective Chapter 4, 'Learning', considers the key notion of participation which emphasises a learner's location and sense of identity in the many overlapping communities and life worlds to which they belong. A social view of learning recognises that learning is ongoing in every aspect of our lives. It takes a broader view of learners' trajectories through the world – their sense of self, where they are coming from, where they think they are going, what sort of person they want to be.

Our fourth assertion is that the development of knowledge is inseparable from the process of participating in a culture of practice and we discuss this in Chapter 5 'Knowledge': the space in which the planned, enacted and experienced come together is at the heart of the science of pedagogy.

Our fifth assertion is that pedagogy needs to imaginatively consider the wide range of tools and technologies, both material and symbolic, that humankind has developed to make sense of and shape the world in which we live. Language, for example, is one of the most fundamental of symbolic tools and its key role in learning is widely recognised. Yet physical artefacts and technologies of all forms are also crucial to knowledge building, as they extend our understanding and impact on the social context of our daily lives and activities. By extension, teachers will create toolkits specific to the purposes they require. Such toolkits can be wide ranging and imaginative, liberating the process of learning, while others can be narrow and inflexible, doing little to extend learners' development. We believe that an explicit understanding of this aspect of human development is critical to any discussion of pedagogy and this is argued in depth in Chapter 6 'Toolkits'.

Our sixth assertion is this. Pedagogy, we believe, must build the self-esteem and identity of learners (see Chapter 7 on 'Identity') by developing their sense of what they believe or indeed hope themselves to be capable of. Our analysis is therefore, as this assertion suggests, going to be forward looking. This book is not a catalogue of the ills of contemporary education, although these do exist. In respect of self-esteem, however, we do share Bruner's view that the management of self-esteem is never simple or settled and schools (and, therefore, teachers) are often rough on children's self-esteem.[19]

Our last assertion, which we revisit in our concluding Chapter 8 'Pedagogies', is congruent with our view about the liberating role of pedagogy: that pedagogic settings should create the conditions for reflection and dialogue as well as productive cognitive conflict. Developing habits of mind that are questioning and critical is central to pedagogic endeavours. Therein lies the power of pedagogy to transform lives.

'Pedagogy must build the self-esteem and identity of learners': teacher educator Dr Nadia Gamal El Din praises Cairo primary students after a public presentation of their learning

2

Settings

Authentic pedagogy is always explicit about vision, values and educational purposes and addresses 'big ideas'.

The setting is a class of nine and ten year olds in Toronto, Canada. The curriculum focus, biology. The classroom has been carefully organised to mirror the way in which the adult scientific research community operates at the University of Toronto's Zoological Department, which is local to the school. Over a ten-week period these young students are given the opportunity to become immersed in a culture of 'scientific inquiry' by their teacher, Beverley Caswell, who has chosen to make the Madagascan Hissing Roach the focus of their research. She has used sustained investigations of this particular roach (ancient in adaptation and evolution) with classes in previous years, as a way of developing scientific thinking. This experience showed the species to be 'interesting and awe inspiring' for the young students involved.

As the weeks unfold, the students take care of and study the roaches. Caswell starts with an introductory lesson to inspect the live animals and hear some facts about them, as well as students taking turns to hold and sketch them. Each child is given their own research journal, which Caswell tells them is what scientists at the zoological department use for observation questions, research notes and experimental designs.

Each student also learns to use the CSILE (Computer Supported Intentional Learning Environment) Knowledge Forum technology as an integral tool for working.[1] Use of this database shows learners' interests and questions falling into specific categories. These are used to inform the creation of small research groups, variously studying perception, learning, communication, evolution and anatomy. A variety of other activities are integrated into the classroom setting, such as the collective composition of a roach song, the design and carrying out of real experiments, and visits to the zoological lab to watch a dissection and meet expert zoologists. Finally each group contributes to the making of a roach documentary video. The reproduction group asks the zoo lab for a female roach so they can film an experiment 'live'; the ecology group films food experiments they have carried out, whilst the evolution group writes a script and dresses like scientists to film their section of the documentary.

Caswell and her co-researcher are explicit about their intention to create a scientific community which can provide learners with a variety of opportunities to reflect on ideas and to hypothesise, and which also allows for multiple ways of developing understanding. They believe that the understanding of 'deep disciplinary content' knowledge can only grow through a combination of individual and group learning activities, as well as through access to a wide range of human and other resources. As the young scientific community develops, both teachers and students become fully engaged and passionate about their new field of study.

What is particularly distinctive about this community is the use of 'public forums', such as authentic research reports and a 'roach video documentary'. These convey to students that a creative process of knowledge building is of value both individually and for the group as a whole. On visits to the zoological lab Caswell observes that the young students are no longer satisfied with superficial answers to questions; instead they want a 'let's discuss our findings and pursue our interest together' approach and to operate as a real scientific community outside, as well as within, the classroom.

This bustling classroom with its whole-group debates, plus its visits to the zoological department and the ongoing use of the Knowledge Forum reflects a 'mutual community' which typically models ways of doing and knowing, and provides opportunities for emulation, offering a running commentary, providing 'scaffolding' for novices, and even creating a good context for teaching deliberately. It makes possible that form of job-related division of labour one finds in effective work groups ... the point is for those in the group to help one another get the lay of the land and the hang of the job.[2]

This unique learning environment that Beverley Caswell[3] created in a primary classroom attached to the Ontario Institute for Studies in Education (OISE) at the University of Toronto evolved over many years. With each new intake of young learners she honed, developed and refined her choices of learning activity – adding richer resources, exploring new technologies that would support learning and trying out different themes that would fire up young people and bring out their best selves. Such daily work was deeply practical, situated in her developing understanding of her pupils over the year together with a longstanding personal experience of the resources (both material and human) that were local to the school. She also needed to relate this to her intimate knowledge of Canada's statutory curriculum requirements.

Beverley also drew profoundly on a framework of ideas – a touchstone of 'deep principles'[4] – that both informed the decisions she made and the way she viewed her pupils and their huge potential for learning. These principles weren't arrived at in a random or solo way. They were inspired by participation in an educational reform programme called Schools For Thought (SFT),[5] that had been designed to apply research findings about the active and reflective or 'constructivist'[6] nature of learning to classroom pedagogy.

One teacher working on the SFT programme said her participation 'prepared me to look at my teaching practices and examine my vision of what this classroom could look like. I'll admit to you that this has been THE hardest thing I've done professionally. Many, many times I wanted to teach the way I already "knew". I struggled (and still do!) with holding onto a vision of what teaching in a constructivist classroom could look like. This vision has not been a part of my teaching culture!'

Pedagogy was being created in these teachers' struggles in their own classroom settings between vision and practice. Discussing the power of art, Simon Schama[7] suggests that 'art should get under our skin'. This, he says, is what all great artistic ideas should do. Crash into our lazy routines. Provide unsettling surprise and shock. In this book we argue that pedagogy needs to have the same power for us as teachers. It's a process that should get under our skin – exciting, inspiring, disturbing and challenging our 'thinking as usual' and day-to-day routines. This chapter focuses on our first assertion (see page 6) that any understanding or theory of pedagogy must encompass all the complex factors that influence the processes of learning and teaching. To help us do this we will be exploring a range of pedagogic settings, such as Beverley Caswell's Toronto classroom, across a range of educational contexts. Many of the themes and practices touched on here will be revisited in the chapters that follow.

By starting with concrete examples of pedagogic settings, we also intend in this second chapter to highlight in particular the complex characteristics of what Bruner refers to as 'proper pedagogy' or what we like to call 'authentic pedagogy'. In so doing we can clarify that ideas about pedagogy – like knowledge in general[8] – are shaped by those who devise them and the values they hold. Our own explorations will be no different. They reflect our own biases, the ideas that have spurred us on – and our own idiosyncratic experiences of learning and teaching. But they are also informed by research and wide-ranging evidence of practices that have made a difference to learners. What we hope to achieve by reflecting on some of the remarkable pedagogic journeys teachers (be they celebrated or unknown) have taken is to develop a new framework, a new language and a set of analytical tools for looking at teaching, learning and teacher education in a fresh and critical way. Our intention is not to promote or analyse discrete learning and teaching strategies, but rather to point to the differing pedagogic choices that individuals and groups of teachers make in their daily work: to get a sense of the way they have designed learning environments, their visions, values and views of knowledge, the roles and relationships they encourage, as well the experiences of learners in such settings.

To begin with we should say a little about the term 'pedagogic setting' already used in the first pages of this book. We have used this term in our research for several years now[9] to denote any identifiable group (a particular primary class, an adult education programme, training hospital, Koranic school or MA/PGCE course, perhaps) for whom teaching and learning are an explicit and overarching goal. The concept serves as a useful unit of analysis at different levels of any educational system – macro/national; institutional/school; individual/class level. It is also applicable to any context, be it a primary classroom in Egypt, a secondary school in London's East End, or an adult professional development programme in rural South Africa. Most importantly the term serves to remind us that such educational communities grow and develop over time, sharing as they do so a past, present and future. In this sense they develop joint learning histories.[10]

We have found Lave's[11] definitions of 'setting' and 'arena' helpful in creating this notion of a pedagogic setting. An 'arena' she defines as a physically, economically, politically and socially organised space in time. In this sense a school, college, hospital, home or workshop is an arena: an institutional framework existing independent of, yet encompassing, the individuals who work there on a daily basis. For those same individuals – for example the midwife in her training hospital, the pre-school child at home, the teenager following a physics course at his local college or the physics teacher responsible for that same course – the institution is a *'setting', a 'repeatedly experienced, personally ordered and edited version of the arena'*. Arena and setting together intersect to create 'context', for, as we will see throughout this book, much of what is traditionally viewed as the context for learning (the physical surroundings and materials used; the social, institutional and personal purposes at play; the people involved and the language used) are themselves an essential part of learning and thus of what is learned.

In using the term, therefore, we seek to emphasise that the goals, activities and discourse of any group of learners are informed by expectations and interactions beyond a single lesson or scheme of work. It is the interdependence of all participants of the group, together with the unique elements of the local context rather than discrete strategies, that make the pedagogic settings we will be discussing in this chapter holistic and exceptional ventures. Participants of any pedagogic setting (for example Beverley, her co-researcher, her young learners, her colleagues and other visitors from the zoological institute and OISE lab school), we would suggest, will create, enact and experience together and separately purposes, values and expectations; new knowledge and ways of knowing; an intimate and idiosyncratic discourse around shared resources, tools and artefacts; a unique set of roles and relationships; as well as the physical arrangement and boundaries of the setting (which in Beverley's case extended well beyond the classroom walls). All of these together and none of these alone.

So while the principles of the Schools For Thought programme were originated by a community of university researchers, authentic pedagogy was being created by teacher participants and their learners through the redesign, over time, of their own classroom settings. What did these principles enable Beverley and other colleagues to do that was new and different? *First*, they encouraged them to think about learners in a new way – as agentive youngsters, curious, inventive meaning makers. *Second*, they gave evidence-based coherence and direction to their intuitive passions for developing young learners to their full potential. *Third*, they inspired and guided a collaboration between a community of teachers, researchers and academics (including co-teaching) jointly committed to honing and improving classroom practice. *Fourth*, and most importantly, they emphasised that learning is not a series of unconnected steps or the planning of day-by-day exercises and activities, but joint engagement in a shared community developed with learners over time.

When you have a new idea, a vision that runs counter to, or is in some way critical of, the status quo, then it can often be seen by others as risky or threatening. Beverley Caswell was fortunate to be supported in her explorations of new ideas about learning and teaching by the principal and staff at OISE's lab school where she worked. Others in the SFT programme, however, often struggled to convince colleagues about the new ways in which they were choosing to work. They learnt that pedagogic change isn't easily won, either personally or institutionally. We need to be blunt here about the potential for pedagogy to rock the educational boat. If as teachers we really want to effect change, then we must expect to be challenged. This means we need to be confident and explicit about the basis of both new and existing practices and Bruner argues the case cogently. In theorising about the practice of education in the classroom or any other setting, he suggests, you had better take into account the 'folk' theories that those engaged in learning and teaching will already have. Any innovations that you, as a 'proper' pedagogical theorist, may wish to introduce will have to compete with, replace, or otherwise modify the folk theories that already guide both teachers and pupils. Your introduction of an innovation in teaching will necessarily involve changing the folk pedagogical theories of teachers – and, to a surprising extent, of pupils as well.[12]

Bruner's counsel (that introducing pedagogic innovation always entails competing with existing, strongly-held, 'folk' theories) was a lesson he had himself learnt through personal experience. In the 1960s, together with a diverse group of scientists, educators, and other specialists, Bruner had led the design of an innovative pedagogic project – Man: A Course of Study (MACOS). Initially designed for middle school and upper elementary settings in north America, MACOS's curriculum activities focused on 'big questions' that would inspire and capture the imagination of young people: What makes human beings human? How did they get that way? How can they become more so? The goals of the programme were that pupils

- have respect for and confidence in their powers of mind and extend that power to thinking about the human condition;

- are able to develop and apply workable models that make it easier to analyse the nature of the social world;

- develop a sense of respect for humanity as a species and gain a sense of the unfinished business of human evolution.

In Bruner's curriculum framework, knowledge is not in the content but in the activity of the person in the content domain, namely the active struggling by the learner with issues is the learning. Thus it was important for Bruner to begin the MACOS curriculum with the unknown as a means of stimulating children's curiosity – in this case, it involved the study of baboon communities and the culture of the Nestlik Eskimos. This unknown was then related to the known: the child's familiar culture (family, school, and so on) in exploring tool making activities, language, social organisations and the like, as a mechanism for understanding both the unknown and the known. Instructional methods included inquiry, experimentation, observation, interviewing, literature searches, summarising, defence of opinion, and so forth.[13]

Teachers were closely involved at all stages of design, writing, and evaluation of this programme and Bruner and his colleagues paid particular attention to aiding them in using this new approach. In addition to extensive workshops, there was a variety of support materials. Video recordings of students participating in sample lessons provided visual images of the patterns of activity that were being sought and highlighted any problems. Model lessons were designed to address particularly difficult concepts; reading material for the teacher provided a 'lively' account of the nature of the unit, discussing the 'mystery' and why it impels curiosity and wonder, and a guide presented 'hints' to teachers as to the kind of questions to ask, contrasts to invoke, and resources to use. Evaluations of the MACOS curriculum indicated that it was successful in promoting inquiry and interpersonal interaction, increasing both the children's confidence in expressing ideas and their ability to attend as well as their enjoyment of social studies.[14] The difficulty came in the acceptance of an inquiry-driven curriculum that did not 'cover the basic content'. Some teachers expressed concern that there was a neglect of traditional skills, and there was a fairly widespread public concern that the students should actually be exposed to diverse perspectives and involved in inquiry that examined the basics tenets of US culture. One of the films produced for the course told the story of an Eskimo village above the Arctic Circle. Among the Eskimo practices depicted in the film was the custom of borrowing someone else's wife to keep you warm on a long journey across the ice if your own wife was not well enough to accompany you. Another was the practice of abandoning grandparents on an ice floe when they became too old to contribute.

Although MACOS succeeded brilliantly in demonstrating cultural differences it was equally effective in arousing public outrage. Despite being based on systematic research and evidence about learning, the MACOS project suddenly found itself at the centre of a political and ideological firestorm. There were protest rallies, public meetings at schools that had adopted MACOS, and vitriolic editorials on the damage MACOS was inflicting by undermining the moral character of America's young people. This prevented its implementation in many schools, and it was eventually withdrawn countrywide, attacked on the floor of Congress, and used to justify a further ban on use of federal funds for curriculum development.[15]

Fierce public controversies and media attention are frequently given to teaching reforms in most countries of the world when pedagogy is contested. Bruner sums up this contested nature of pedagogy well:

> the choice we make about how to develop and sustain pedagogic settings inevitably communicates a conception of the learning process and the learner. Pedagogy is never innocent; it is a medium that carries its own message.[16] For education, in whatever culture, always has a consequence in the lives of those who undergo it. In this deeper sense, then, pedagogy is never neutral, never without social and economic consequences. All school and classroom climates reflect in-articulated cultural values that are never far removed from considerations of issues of equality of opportunity, class, gender and power. And so, however it may be claimed to the contrary, real pedagogy is always political in this broadest sense.[17]

It is for this reason that many of the most inspiring pedagogic movements in education across countries, continents and centuries have seen their most vocal champions – not unlike leading thinkers in the sciences and arts – disparaged, ridiculed, sometimes even banned or imprisoned. Their unequivocal visions for young people simply went against the grain of the times. In the 1920s Maria Montessori, for example, loudly questioned the regimentation of the existing school system in Italy, its low expectations of children from poor homes and the authoritarian approach that was the norm for teachers in the newly established national state system of education. As we saw in Chapter 1, Montessori's pedagogy attracted widespread interest, not least because children were quickly achieving above average results in conventional school tests of the day. Yet as the 1930s saw fascism taking hold in Europe, Maria was expelled from her home country to Holland. Acrid clouds of smoke diffused over city squares in Vienna and Berlin, while triumphant Nazi soldiers burnt her effigy together with the books she had authored.[18]

There are numerous examples of contested pedagogy closer to home, including the contemporary educational scene in England. Tim Brighouse, a great champion of a pedagogy for the regeneration of vulnerable urban school communities, has developed together with colleagues the vision of a transformation within education that will lead to fulfilling and creative lives for all young people. Yet in this inspiring pedagogical project, implemented particularly in inner city Birmingham and inner city London, he has had to battle against public, and sometimes personal, attack.[19] Never afraid to articulate his vision, he also boldly points to the inextricable dance between the educational, the social and political and it is clear that pedagogy, while powerful, never stands free from other, equally big, questions of equality of opportunity.

Taking a critical approach to pedagogic settings – be they primary or secondary school classrooms or teacher training communities – asks a great deal of those who embrace the challenge. Yet research, observation and experience show that the rewards for teachers and learners alike are hugely worthwhile. Exploring pedagogy can embolden teachers, teacher educators and learners to act in ways that make a real difference, inspiring them to new levels of social and cognitive achievements often deemed impossible. Authentic pedagogy regards complexity as fun, ambitiously seeks adventure, and provides a vision to tread where no one else has gone before.

This leads us to articulate two important characteristics of authentic pedagogy. First,

- *Pedagogy is invariably political*

This is not to propose that pedagogy has to 'politicise' education, but simply is to recognise that it is already politicised and that its political side needs to be taken into account more explicitly.[20]

Second,

- *Authentic pedagogy is always explicit about vision, values and educational purposes and addresses 'big ideas'*

The pedagogic settings we discuss in this chapter are all inspired by a vision about the purposes of schooling, promoting a deep and explicit re-conceptualisation of what human beings are capable of achieving (this is not to say they don't also attend rigorously to details, process and discrete strategies). Influential pedagogic movements also always introduce 'big ideas' that help to frame the way we look at learning and teaching in new ways. For Brighouse and his colleagues it is the practice of leadership, collaboration and collegiality within and across communities that is their overarching focus. For the great educator Paulo Freire (who we discuss later in this chapter) it was the idea that learners can be empowered to move out of a culture of 'silence' by learning to 'read the world'.[21] In the case of Reggio Emilia's schools, it is the idea that children are capable and strong and form a triad of protagonists along with the teacher and the parent.[22]

In the next section we look at Reggio Emilia's ideas in more depth.

We oppose
any prophetic pedagogy
which knows everything before it happens,
which teaches children
that every day is the same,
that there are no surprises,
and teaches adults
that all they have to do is repeat
that which they were not able to learn.
(Loris Malaguzzi)

It would be easy to look at 'virtuoso' pedagogic thinkers such as Ciaro, Montessori, Bruner, or Brighouse and feel that pedagogy is only something that academics or exceptional individuals theorise about. Surely it can't be practical in the real, day-to-day business of learning and teaching? After all, many theorists don't actually spend a lot of time teaching in the truly demanding classrooms, do they? They're so busy talking and writing about their ideas.

In fact (as will be illustrated), many celebrated pedagogic thinkers were also great teachers who first developed and honed such ideas in their own classrooms. In any case, to emphasise the achievements of eminent 'names' is to miss a crucial understanding about pedagogy as a process. One only has to get under the skin of groundbreaking pedagogic movements to recognise that authentic pedagogy is only properly realised and created in the messy and often humdrum practices of everyday learning and teaching across a range of particular settings. Chapter 1 opened with an account of the idealistic young Bruno Ciari, who deeply influenced the ideas on which the international and celebrated pre-school communities of Reggio Emilia in Italy were founded. But while the pedagogical theory behind the Reggio approach may have grown from Ciari's ideas, together with those of his colleague Loris Malaguzzi, it took the determined action of a group of working-class women to give the chance for these theories to develop and be sustained in practice. It also required the radical transformation of municipal governance in their region of Italy in the late 1960s and early 1970s.

As one of the early Reggio Emilia pioneers recalls:

> Reggio Emilia was based on a large-scale popular movement. A lot of workers lived in this neighbourhood and women needed a service for their children. The local administration had no money to develop facilities, so the women got organised and decided to find a place to develop the school. This Liberty-style villa was disused. I wanted an excuse to visit such a villa! Once I was in, I took the keys for good and I have never given them back!

> The women raised money for equipment and organised three coach loads to go the Italian parliament. After six months we had our centre for pre-school children. Some of those women are now grandmothers but they are still on the council of the school.

> To understand how the service has developed, it is very important to remember these historical roots, because the schools were the outcome of an alliance between the community and advocates of a pioneering pedagogical approach. Families wanted not just a social service, but an educational service.[23]

So what is so special about Reggio Emilia's pedagogic settings?[24]

First, the physical settings themselves immediately strike you when entering, for the Reggio environment is viewed as the 'third teacher' of the child.[25] If you walk into one of the preschools on any given morning, you will be struck by the beauty and spaciousness of these buildings. Reggio Emilia's classrooms open from a central atrium and are ample, open, and streaming with light. Potted plants and inviting chairs and couches are strategically placed, adding colour and comfort to the surroundings. There are secluded alcoves to which youngsters can retreat, interior gardens and common spaces where the teachers can meet. On neat shelves are stored literally hundreds of materials – from coloured geometric forms to grains of cereal to seashells to recyclable wooden sticks – with which the youngsters may become engaged at some point (or repeatedly) during the year. Everything seems in place and there is no clutter or mess, yet the spaces feel inviting and flexible.

Reggio schools also stand out by virtue of the type and quality of the activities that the children participate in. In each class children spend extended time exploring a theme of interest. These themes are chosen to attract young children specifically, not only because they offer rich sensory stimulation but also because of the intriguing puzzles they raise. Among the many dozens of ideas that have been investigated over the years are sunlight, rainbows, shadows, the city, poppy fields, an amusement park for birds built by the youngsters, a city for ants, and the operation of the school's fax machine. Students are encouraged to approach objects, themes and environments from many angles and to ponder and question the phenomena that arise in the course of their explorations. From this they will end up creating artful objects that will capture their interests and their learning: drawings, paintings, cartoons, charts, photographic series, toy models, replicas – indeed, many representatives of an ever-expanding and unpredictable series of genres.

It is not possible to plan such a curriculum in advance. Rather, the particular reactions of particular children to particular experiences become the bedrock and the driving force of the 'curriculum'. The activities for next week (sometimes even for the next day) will grow out of the results, problems, and puzzles of this week, and the cycle is then repeated so long as it proves fruitful. Children and teachers are continually reflecting on the meaning of an activity, which issues it raises, how its depths and range can be productively probed.

Once the exploration of a theme comes to an end the objects that have been created are placed on display so that parents, other children and members of the community can observe them, learn from them, and appreciate the care with which they have been executed and mounted. Most observers agree that the works are not just cute throwaways by young children. Instead many are substantial and evocative creations.

In such a practice, children are protagonists in the learning process, encouraged to pursue their own passions and interests. Learning is negotiated between the children and their teachers who co-create out of this dialogue an 'authentic' curriculum – that is a curriculum embedded in the lives of the children and respectful of both families and the local context. As in Caswell's classroom (see Chapter 1), learning is viewed as both an individual and shared endeavour. Children complete learning contracts and group and individual projects also enable learning to be pursued over a protracted period of time.

Although the Reggio Emilia activities and associated learner products are significant, Howard Gardner argues that they do not represent the heart of the Reggio enterprise. It is the social dimension of the setting that is paramount.

> The central endeavour consists of the daily interaction among teachers, students, and sometimes parents and other adults from the community; the equally regular give-and-take among the classroom teachers and their specialized colleagues, the pedagogista and atelierista. And, above all, the astonishing documentation of student work undertaken by the instructional staff during the course of each day.[26]

We will see this theme of community and context unfolding throughout each chapter. Indeed we will see that the more teachers are familiar with the social contexts and communities in which they are working, the more rigorous and critical pedagogy becomes. Authentic pedagogy, such practice would suggest, demands a deep re-conceptualisation of the relationship between pedagogic settings and their communities.

These observations lead us to articulate two further characteristics of authentic pedagogy.

- *Pedagogy is a collaborative, iterative process between teachers and learners and other members of the learning community*

- *Pedagogy evolves over time in the ebb and flow of real settings and local contexts*

No one recognised the importance of context and the demands of the real world in creating new pedagogical theory more than the Brazilian educator, Paulo Freire. Freire is one of the most influential thinkers about pedagogy of the late twentieth century. His seminal (1972) work, *Pedagogy of the Oppressed*, sold five hundred thousand copies on its first publication. In this book Freire critiques dominant modes of educational thinking that portray learners as passive in the teaching/learning process, as empty vessels just waiting to be filled by omnipotent teachers. His work has now been translated into all the major world languages and it continues to be read, debated and discussed worldwide, particularly in developing countries where his ideas on dialogue, his concern for the social justice, and his interest in informal adult education are particularly apt.

A native of Brazil and trained as a lawyer, Freire began his working life teaching Portuguese in secondary schools. He moved on to became a gifted adult educator and by the age of 25 was working primarily among the illiterate poor in urban and rural areas. Through this work Freire became passionate about the process of enabling illiterate adults to find a voice, to develop a critical view of the world and their place in it and to give them the self-esteem necessary for learning. A military coup in 1964 put an end to this work and he was briefly imprisoned as a traitor for his educational ideas. Freire was soon, however, able to take up his work again in neighbouring Chile and during a visiting professorship at Harvard University published his first two books, *Education as the Practice of Freedom* and *Pedagogy of the Oppressed*.[27]

Pedagogy of the Oppressed articulates the distinction between 'banking' education and 'problem posing' education. In the former by using the metaphor of 'banking' education, with students as empty bank accounts waiting for the teacher to deposit knowledge, he argues that the relationship between educators and students is 'narrative' in character. The teacher talks about reality as if it were motionless, static, compartmentalised and pre-dictable. The teacher's task is therefore to 'fill' the students with the contents of the narration.[28] By contrast, 'problem posing' education demands dialogue and the relationship between educator and learner becomes one of critical co-investigation.

Freire's pedagogy was initially realised through a series of experimental literacy programmes for peasants in Brazil. This pedagogy of literacy involved not only reading the word, but also 'reading the world' – a process that he believed would lead to the development of critical consciousness (a process he called *conscientização*). Freire's approach requires a dialogic exchange between teachers and students, where both learn, both question, both reflect, and both participate in meaning making. He insisted that the educators involved in these adult literacy programmes should avoid a schooling atmosphere, and instead advocated what he termed *culture circles*. Culture circles emphasised a non-hierarchical, collaborative relationship between teachers and adult learn-ers. It was intended that these circles should foster an atmosphere in which learners' voices and experiences were valued.

This approach to pedagogy begins through practice with the teacher min-gling with the community, asking questions of the people, and gathering a list of words used in their daily lives that have immediacy and personal meaning for them. Use of traditional literacy primers was avoided. Instead, Freire and his fellow educators created context-specific visual aids, such as pictures or slides from the peasants' own experience, thus introducing as they did so the *generative words* that had been gathered, first via discussion and then through written text. Such words were considered generative because of their ability to generate additional words, especially those con-cepts with cultural, social or political significance. 'The words that adults want to learn are such words as "courthouse", "voter registration", "affi-davit" etc. rather than "Jump Spot, Jump!"'[29] Freire argued. Collectively, when written down by the educator, such words served as a text for joint study and literacy practice.

Freire's first opportunity for really significant application of these theoretical ideas came in the early 1960s when, as Director of the Department of Cultural

(Continued)

(Continued)

Extension at Recife University, he was able to oversee a literacy programme in which 300 sugarcane workers were taught to read and write in just 45 days. In response to this experiment, the Brazilian government approved the creation of thousands of cultural circles across the country. Much later, in 1988, his role as Minister of Education for Sao Paulo enabled him to institute educational reform programmes throughout most of Brazil. Many more such radical literacy programmes based on these ideas have been successfully implemented in countries as disparate as Scotland, Uganda, Bangladesh, El Salvador[30] and Southern Africa.[31]

Freire's pedagogy has been influential in part because of the way it places individuals' prior knowledge and experiences at the heart of pedagogy. Although this work has become known as 'critical pedagogy', Freire himself frequently referred to it as a 'pedagogy of knowing', for this radical pedagogy encourages the abandonment of traditional distinctions between knowledge and beliefs.[32]

Critical pedagogy, which emphasises emancipatory potential, also laid the foundations for the development of feminist pedagogy. This strand of thinking emphasises that the feminist classroom is and should be a place where there is a sense of struggle. Most importantly, feminist pedagogy should engage students in a learning process that makes the world 'more real than less real'.[33]

Most importantly, however, Freire's theory of pedagogy has been influential in re-conceptualising thinking about the teacher's role and relationship to the learner. From this standpoint the learning process should be dialectical and embedded in two interrelated contexts. The first is the 'authentic dialogue' between teachers and learners, the second is the social reality in which people exist. The teacher's role, therefore, is to create 'pedagogical spaces' by using their personal passion, domain knowledge and expertise to pose problems in order to help learners analyse their own experiences and thus arrive at a critical understanding of their reality. In his early work Freire utilised a grammar metaphor 'transitiveness' (the learner as subject or object), and posited four stages in this dialogic process: intransitive; semi-intransitive; naive transitive; and critical consciousness. Such an approach highlights the complex role of the teacher as negotiator, mediating between the learner's personal meanings and the culturally established meanings of wider society. Freire resoundingly rejected interpretations of his own work that diluted the teacher's role simply to that of facilitator or presenter of problems. He viewed the teacher principally as an authority, in the sense of being expert, and as such s/he must provide direction. Yet in constructing critical dialogue the role must also encompass that of facilitator. Feminist pedagogy has expanded many of these ideas.

In this sense, Freire's critical pedagogy views the teacher first and foremost as an intellectual, with unique understandings of their subject, of pedagogy and of their learners. He emphasised the key role that teachers must play in educational change and the importance of a culture of research if educational rigour and quality are to be achieved. Teachers are ongoing learners who have access to knowledge about learning that goes far beyond what other 'expert' researchers can produce. Scholar teachers understand that pedagogy needs to be responsive to students' needs and their lived contexts. 'You can't be a teacher if you don't know anything', Freire wrote candidly. 'What the hell are you around for, if you don't know anything? Just get out of the way and let somebody have the space that knows something … No teacher is worth [her] salt who is not able to confront students with a rigorous body of knowledge. That is not to endorse a banking education but to support the idea that teachers often provide students with knowledge that students then react to, reject, reinterpret, analyse and put into action.'[34]

This complex interrelationship between theory and practice is an important idea for pedagogy. Indeed theory enables our deepest intuitions about the learning process to be made explicit. Theatre artist David Diamond comments 'When I first read Paulo Freire, I was stunned and relieved and exuberant, for he was able to articulate what I knew and felt, but did not have the words for'.[35] A tentative relationship between theory and practice must always therefore be allowed. Theoretical frameworks never tell us exactly what to do. There is always an interpretative (or hermeneutic) dimension that disallows any facile relationship between theory and practice. The role of the scholar teacher is to view practice through the lens of the theoretical framework and the theoretical framework through the lens of practice. In this process each is intensified.

Tochan and Munby express this idea well:

> Pedagogy is concerned with our immediate image of the teaching situation. It is live processing developed in a practical and idiosyncratic situation. Didactic goals can be written down, but pedagogical experience cannot be easily theorised, owing to its unique interactive aspects. Though action research and reflection reveal the existence of basic principles, underlying practical classroom experience, no matter what rules might be inferred, pedagogy remains an adventure.[36]

It is from this perspective that we can formulate two more characteristics for authentic pedagogy.

- Pedagogy acknowledges teachers as intellectuals

- Pedagogy is a complex interplay between theory and practice

Decades ago John Dewey wrote about the contextual dynamics that could free teachers from thinking that knowledge simply required passing on to students an agreed curriculum of relatively de-contextualised information.

> An individual is a sophisticated thinker to the degree in which he or she sees an event not as something isolated but in its connection with the common experience of mankind … School instruction is plagued by a push for quick answers. This short circuits the necessary feeling of uncertainty and inhibits the search for alternative methods of solution … Were all (educators) to realise that the quality of mental process, not the production of correct answers, is the measure of educative growth something hardly less than a revolution in teaching would be worked.[37]

This central emphasis on the teacher as intellectual is fundamental to most of the pedagogic practice and theories we have been looking at. Indeed, the Reggio Emilia communities over time developed a statement of teachers' rights that included their right to contribute to the study and preparation of the conceptual models that define educational content, objectives and practices. This, they asserted, takes place through:

- open discussion among the staff, with the pedagogical co-ordinators and parents' advisory councils in harmony with the rights of children and families

- through co-operation on the choices of methods, didactics, research and observation projects

- through a definition of the fields of experience, ongoing teacher self-training and general staff development, cultural initiatives and the tasks of community management

Our next pedagogic setting, this time in England, illustrates the way in which the notion of teacher self-training and general staff development has been integrated within a contemporary urban pedagogy.

At first sight St Saviour's and St Olave's School would seem to be situated in the most unprepossessing of contexts – squashed between a busy flyover, thundering with lorries, cars and taxis, and a block of high rise, inner city flats, close to London's Elephant and Castle. Yet as soon as you enter this secondary school in one of London's most challenging urban settings, you glimpse the 'third teacher' of the Reggio Emilia schools – a light and joyful environment. A central garden bursting with trees, shrubs, occasional seats for the children and a commissioned sculpture by a local artist (representing girls past, present and future) bring a sense of light, peace and airiness to adjoining classrooms. This island of calm and beauty couldn't seem further from the ugliness, debris, constant noise and intense poverty evident at all hours in the surrounding streets. Here you will have students, some of them recent refugees from harsh political regimes, speaking over 50 home languages and going about purposefully, often with fun and enjoyment.

In discussing this particular setting we want to focus on teacher rather than student activity. Tim Brighouse has argued that inner city schools should be committed to research and innovation. It seems guaranteed, he contends, to predispose school staff into being in a place where intellectual curiosity is a legitimate and common currency and where learning is a habit of life.[38] At St Saviour's and St Olave's teachers are being supported in working towards just such a habit of life.

Many of the staff have taken on diverse roles that have increased the opportunities and the contexts in which students have access to them, in which they can be responsive both to students' intellectual and social needs. All the teaching staff have had school-based training in coaching and mentoring and ten members, including the head teacher, have had intensive training at London University's Institute of Education. Teachers are instructors, experts in pedagogy, confidants, counsellors, advisors and mentors, and see themselves as facilitating learning through all of these means. Access is formally structured through the mechanism of academic mentors (both teachers or support staff) and directors of learning. All staff work collegially and some are primarily pastoral leaders (learning mentors). When problems occur between students or something is stolen, someone is there to sit and listen. A cleaner or IT support staff member – without being asked – might also ensure a pupil gets on the bus safely after staying late at school. One pupil, 'Daisy',[39] who had been made homeless at 14, had been suspended 13 times. 'I was a bad angry kid'. Staff at St Saviour's and St Olave's, however, had consistently sought to make sure she felt important and cared for, despite her erratic behaviour. Not only was she supported intellectually, she was also nurtured both emotionally and physically. She brought her

(Continued)

(Continued)

washing to school for it to be done in the school's machine. Every time she fell down a crack she was lifted. Recently *Cosmopolitan* magazine awarded Daisy a 'Fearless Female' award; with huge support she has gained her GCSEs and A Levels and is now reading journalism at university.

The role of the staff members at St Saviour's and St Olave's is shaped by the demands of the work. Recognition of – and respect for – the complexity of staff's many roles within the school community mean more individual control over activity and time, as well as opportunities for innovation and adult collaboration. This approach means organising around the needs and interests of teachers as well as students. It means re-conceptualising teacher roles and teaching work. Teachers work with students formally in regular scheduled classes, but also tutor them in planned and unplanned sessions, sometimes individually, sometimes in groups. Less conventionally, they are invited speakers in one another's classes along with guests from outside the immediate school community. Recently the staff facilitated a joint in service training day – in science, history, technology and ICT – for their peers from all the other schools in the London borough.

Kelly Hall and Kelly Fitzpatrick are young teachers of Design and Technology and History in the conventional sense, but they are also majoring on assessment for learning – doing regular INSET for the whole school. Their interest arose through Kelly Hall's desire to devise learner assessments that would be visible in practical work. Not only do they teach classes, but in addition they are collaborators, curriculum developers, learners reflecting on their work, researchers gathering data for a leadership course, learning analysts solving the learning problems of their students and making curricular and instructional decisions based on their professional judgment, discussion leaders and resources for visitors to the school, and entrepreneurs accessing and mobilising resources for their courses or a colleague struggling with pedagogical issues, as well as sharing expertise with staff, advocates, mediators and counsellors to their students.

The school's head teacher, Irene Bishop, had worked with Tim Brighouse and other London teachers to develop a Chartered London Teacher award which would symbolise and guarantee that teachers such as Kelly H and Kelly F had demonstrated a continued and continuing learning in terms of pedagogy, including:

- curriculum or subject and phase knowledge;

- whole school issues;

- cultural knowledge;

- barriers to children's learning and how they might be overcome.

Tim would argue that cosmopolitan cities make great demands on teachers' learning. Urban teachers need to know a good deal about children's backgrounds, and perhaps learn some of their language as well as understand their faiths and the different histories of their cultures. 'Cultural knowledge' (with all the implications of racial, national and religious prejudices) is key.

Cosmopolitan cities are multi-racial, multi-faith, and multi-lingual. In language lies the key to communication and with learning the understanding and mutual respect which are characteristic of peaceful and coherent, civilised, societies.[40]

Also pre-eminently important in urban schools such as St Saviour's and St Olave's are teachers' understandings of the barriers to children's learning. Young people in big cities, like Daisy mentioned above, can bring much baggage to the school gate, including abuse, violence and caring responsibilities or any combination of all these and more, which in turn can make student less likely – indeed very unlikely – to be able to take full advantage of their schooling. To know a lot about the issues, to truly understand, must be a 'taken-for-granted' exercise in the experienced urban teacher's repertoire. St Saviour's and St Olave's approach testifies to and develops teachers' continually growing knowledge of these matters and crucially supports co-learning with other teachers. For such collegial activity to be a reality rather than mere rhetoric at St Saviour's and St Olave's they need a wide network of support, different alliances, and the kinds of activities staff and students can carry out together.

This urban pedagogy depends on a re-conceptualisation of teachers as learners and leaders, responsive to context and committed to reaching the best of all possible outcomes from learners – teachers as well as students. Such work would seem to highlight two further criteria of pedagogy, criteria that obtain in all the settings that have been explored in this chapter.

- Pedagogy requires teachers to be researchers of their own settings
- Pedagogy seeks to bring out learners' best selves, working with – rather than despite – institutional barriers such as race, class and gender.

Throughout this book we assume that developing a critical approach to pedagogy is as relevant to teacher learning as to young learners. As a final example of a pedagogic setting we now turn to a teacher education programme. We have chosen a radically different context from others in this chapter – the Eastern Cape, South Africa – though elsewhere in the book we will make reference to our research on teacher pedagogy in contexts as varied as the UK, Eastern Europe, and the Middle East.

It was a programme for and of its time … It was developed when policy was not yet fixed and there was time and space for dreaming and doing what you always wanted to do … We wanted to speak into the Eastern Cape context: the rural, underdeveloped, neglected corners of the province. To take this opportunity to transform people's lives … That is what it came down to in the long run.[41]

In May 2005, the University of Fort Hare's Primary BEd Distance Education Programme (DEP) was overall winner in the National Association of Distance Education Organisations in South Africa's (NADEOSA) course awards. What has made this programme's pedagogy so distinctive, attracting international as well as national acclaim?

First, the context in which this teacher education programme was initially conceived and developed was unique. The DEP was originally scoped in the new South African democracy of 1994 as a grandiose idea that would offer a range of primary, secondary and Masters teacher education programmes to one of the most rural and hitherto marginalised communities of South Africa. As it emerged, this was to become the first teacher education programme to respond to South Africa's new Higher Education Policy and it has also remained possibly the most outstanding of all in its dual commitment to quality of teacher pedagogy, linked to a vision to transform rural education.

Second, the DEP's aim to move beyond the narrow limits of most teacher training programmes, by considering schools as a whole as learning communities, is also unique. The imperative to provide qualified teachers was huge at the initial scoping phase of the programme, given that 40 per cent of the 60,000 teachers in the Eastern Cape were unqualified, with most of them mature women. However, this did not deter the programme planners from considering the kind of wider impact that such a programme could have, not only on individual teachers but also on schools and their communities. This vision was at the heart of the programme's pedagogy.

School-based activities have been the greatest hallmark of the programme and the module 'Schools as Learning Communities' has been the one most quoted by teachers as having made a difference to their schools and communities. Elias, currently a second year teacher-learner in Tyutyu Primary School, Bisho, told us that he is one of eight teachers on the Tyutyu School staff who have gone through the programme at different stages, each one supported by Nydni, an *abakwazeli* (or tutor), also on the school staff. The formulation of a school mission statement jointly created among parents, governors and staff, as well as the creation of a school garden by the pupils, were activities carried out as part of his assessed coursework activity. Currently Elias, who was formerly a builder before he became a teacher, is using redundant corrugated iron from another building and together with parents and children is constructing a new classroom during the summer holidays as a response to his studies.

Many teachers' testimonies speak of the programme as 'helping me to see myself being able to make a difference in people's lives. I have been able to be an advocate of change by improving the learners' lives for the better. I have been able to gain strength and to use all available resources, together with other teacher-learners. Although it has not always been easy to introduce change, the support I got from my other colleagues and my fellow teacher-learners gave me the strength to keep going.'

We have been discussing the ways in which pedagogy enables us to 'go meta',[42] to reflect broadly with colleagues on current practices and the potential for change. Exceptional pedagogic frameworks always emerge out of the 'double-bind' of challenges and problems faced. Teacher educators at Fort Hare had the vision to transform rural education, yet the reality they faced was that a great many teachers were unqualified and were also working in challenging and remote conditions. They realised that in order to effect change they would first and foremost need to build teachers' self-esteem and offer them a professional vision – that they could achieve highly, despite desperate circumstances. As in other pedagogies focused on in this chapter, this approach encouraged teachers to step back and get some perspective on the big questions (as well as paying attention to the more mundane aspects of daily practice). What is the role of education in rural communities? What does it mean to say our school is a learning community? How do we promote and in what ways do we hinder learning?

School-based activities in the DEP were not focused solely on 'teacherly' activities, for example how to create a scheme of work, plan resources for a lesson, manage classroom interaction. Such discrete skills were seen as providing scaffolds to enable teacher-learners to address the broader learning needs of students and their schools as a whole. Teacher-learners would painstakingly learn how to plan and develop resources around an activity that was meaningful and relevant to the whole community and thus an authentic life problem. Such as teaching students the science of permaculture[43] by jointly creating a sustainable school vegetable garden that would also act as a model of practice for parents and the wider family. Or ensuring clean water for drinking. Or engaging the whole community in building a new classroom, encouraging the sharing of a wide range of local skills and knowledge with students in the process.

The growth of teachers' confidence that they could be real agents of change, even in the most vulnerable communities, suggests two further characteristics of authentic pedagogy:

- Pedagogy acknowledges the intimate relationship between learning and learners' identity

- Pedagogy must be relevant to all possible contexts

In this sense pedagogy provides concepts and a coherent discourse about learning, together with new ways of thinking and acting. It also provides a framework of techniques and procedures by which practice can be newly and objectively appraised: a toolkit for teachers and learners alike. But no two uses of such a toolkit will ever be the same. Donald Schon[44] has used the term 'indeterminate zones of practice' to signify the uncertainty, complexity, uniqueness and contested nature of practice. Such complexity rejects universal rules about how to practice 'correctly'. Freire knew this when he urged teachers to remake his ideas in praxis, rather than seeking some form of pedagogic 'purity'. He insisted that we critique him and improve on his work. Each new iteration of practice makes theory anew and different interpretations emerge.

In this chapter we have focused particularly on our assertion that 'any understanding ... of pedagogy must encompass all the complex factors that influence learning and teaching'. We have proposed that pedagogy demands a deep re-conceptualisation of what human beings are capable of achieving, the role of the social, political and cultural in shaping learners' identities, the relationship between community and schooling as well as the relationship between teachers and learners. As part of this discussion we have suggested ten criteria of authentic pedagogy which have been illustrated through a range of settings:

Pedagogy:

- is invariably political, although its political nature is rarely taken into account explicitly;

- is explicit about values, vision and educational purposes and addresses 'big ideas' about learning and teaching;

- is a collaborative, iterative process between teachers, learners and other members of the community;

- evolves over time in the ebb and flow of real settings, and is constantly open to change, negotiation and revision;

- acknowledges teachers as intellectuals;

- is a complex interplay between theory and practice;

- requires teachers to be researchers of their own settings;

- seeks to bring out learners' best selves, working with (rather than despite) institutional barriers such as race, gender and class;

- acknowledges the intimate relationship between learning and identity;

- must be relevant to all possible contexts.

These criteria open up a new language with which to consider the processes of learning and teaching, free from the sometimes dominant discourse of standards, effectiveness and performance. It may be that there is no higher obligation for contemporary pedagogy than the re-instatement of big ideas and humanity.

3

Minds

Intelligent behaviour is not characteristically the solo dance of a naked brain.

In the last chapter we looked in some detail at the Schools for Thought programme. Beverley Caswell and her colleagues were attempting to refocus some of the basic assumptions of learning and teaching. First, they explicitly require an active rather than a passive role for the learner. Second, learner potential is seen as flexible and expandable, not finite. This reflects our second assertion that the mind must be viewed as complex and multi-faceted. And third, the pedagogic setting is created as a community of mutual learners with teachers and learners both actively engaged in the process of knowledge construction. These assumptions and consequent practices interrelate. Ideas about potential, for example, influence the process of mutual learning. Such assumptions do not necessarily presuppose specific forms of pedagogy. They do, however, dispose teachers to adopting some approaches rather than others.

We have come to see the set of dispositions that teachers bring to their task as extremely significant with the scope for analysis of these dispositions considerable. We are all born into cultures and communities that harbour, often unspoken, ideas about the world around us. These might relate to gender, class, ethnicity, and age. Most of us remember those moments in growing up where a formerly self-evident truth is brought into question. An important segment of the dispositions we bring to a pedagogic setting is created by assumptions about the nature of the mind, and the way these influence the forms and limits of learning.

Let us take one example from the Schools for Thought model. For Beverley Caswell and her colleagues potential is not fixed. How many times do we see a school aim, or a governmental aspiration, to equality of opportunity that is expressed in terms of a learner or child being able to 'achieve their full potential'? How often do we hear in everyday speech a reference to someone who has not achieved, or has yet to achieve, his or her potential? In both usages the phrase implies a vessel waiting to be filled or filled up. Sometimes the vernacular becomes deterministic: 'She doesn't have the potential to do well in medicine', (or law, or whatever). At various times in history such notions of potential have seemed incontrovertible. A few centuries ago most cotton plantation owners in the southern states of the USA had explicit and implicit views about the inferior intelligence of black slaves, and this perception has rumbled down through the ages in a variety of quasi-academic, political controversies around the treatment of race and intelligence.[1] Social attitudes to disability represent another example. It is only recently that social and educational attitudes to children born with Down's Syndrome have changed. One of us remembers visiting training centres (the word 'school' was not used) in the 1960s, where all the children with Down's Syndrome, and other physical and emotional disabilities, were placed together for mostly practical, vocational classes.

Fixed ideas about potential lie easily within the social categorisations that deeply define social divisions. 'Retarded', 'handicapped', and a multitude of other words create patterns of thought and expectation that, at different times in different places, have deeply influenced educational thought and practice. Over time, however, community folklore can be broken down. Maria Montessori's work with children with learning disabilities is an example of this but one that in its time provoked considerable antagonism. However, potential remains a contested concept. Think, for example, of the many education systems that separate children into different types of secondary schooling according to perceived potential. In England the whole education system was reorganised in 1944 around the premise that the potential for academic or vocational forms of education could be decided around the age of ten or eleven. Although this orthodoxy was challenged and brought down in the 1960s and 1970s, parts of the country still have school structures derived from 1944.[2]

The dispositions[3] that policy makers, teachers and the public at large bring to ideas about potential are derived from habits of mind that have long historical antecedents. Ideas about the way our minds work, for example, have existed from the earliest recordings of human thought and activity. Some have even stood the test of time. The question-and-answer style of interrogation of issues that is often termed 'the Socratic method' goes with the grain of contemporary ideas about the importance of learners verbalising their ideas. In this chapter we want to look at ideas about mental activity and suggest ways in which the dispositions that teachers bring to pedagogic activity can be developed and adapted.

The human mind is fascinatingly powerful and complex. The ability to think and speak in a myriad forms has preoccupied philosophers and scientists across the centuries. In recent years advances in brain science, stimulated by new technological tools, have given a new impetus to the relationship between brain functions and the mind, between consciousness and the ways in which consciousness can grow and evolve. The Dutch novelist Cees Nooteboom, in his novel *All Souls*, captures the sense of wonder around the brain. 'What we want to say is this', his narrator explains: 'Even though you are mortal, even though you are allotted only a finite amount of time and space, the fact that one small brain can ponder eternity, or the past, allows you to lay claim to vast amounts of time and space. That's the mystery. Each and every one of you can, if you wish, colonise any part of the world, any era.

You're the only creatures in the entire universe who can do that, and all because of your ability to think.' Virginia Woolf gave expression to this in describing how she planned her writing. 'I dig out beautiful caves behind my characters; I think that gives exactly what I want: humanity, humour, depth. The idea is that the caves shall connect and each comes to daylight at the present moment.'[4] Would it be too far fetched to suggest that a successful pedagogy is imbued with the same creative spirit?

A deeper knowledge of the concept of mind, and in particular the implications for learning, would seem a central concern for teachers. We believe that an intellectual curiosity around the brain, the mind and learning should be part of the professional development of all teachers. We are cautious, however, about some of the claims now being made for the ways in which such knowledge could be incorporated into thinking about pedagogy. This may change. The history of education in the twenty-first century may turn out to be just like the history of medicine in the nineteenth century.[5] Doctors have always justified their practices by claiming that they understand how our bodies work. Educators, likewise, have presumed to understand how our minds work. Only in the nineteenth century did systematic research dispel some of the myths around medicine. Only in this century is it likely that the fruits of research on the brain will impact significantly on learning and teaching.

Professor Francis Crick, famous as the discoverer of DNA, dedicated the latter period of his life to trying to understand the relationship between the brain, brain activity and the mind, or as he termed it, 'consciousness'.[6] He suggested that 'the astonishing hypothesis is that you, your joys and your sorrows, your memories and your ambitions, your sense of personal identity and free will are, in fact, no more than the behaviour of a vast assembly of nerve cells and their associated molecules'. And this view represents something of a paradox. Just as brain science is giving us more and more insights and information about the workings of the brain[7] so our knowledge becomes even more complex about how this translates into mental activity and the workings of the mind.

The extraordinary capacity of the brain, in particular our ability to think into the minds of others, to process and store intricate, overlapping shoals of knowledge, to retrieve information that has lain inaccessible for decades, is a product of the process of what has been termed 'constructive evolution'.[8]

The very complexity of this, however, gives us few instances where brain science can give a direct message or lesson for educational practice. One of the leading analysts of the relationship between brain science and education, John Bruner, published a seminal article with the title 'Education and the Brain: A Bridge Too Far'[9] in which he argued that we simply do not know enough about how the brain works to draw educational implications from changes in synoptic morphology. For example, we do not know (he suggests) how such change supports learning, and he sees a gaping chasm between our understanding of what happens to our brains as a result of different experiences and what should happen in pre-school or third or any other grade.

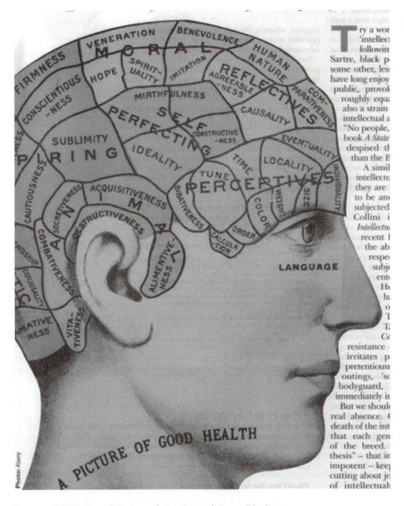

A PICTURE OF GOOD HEALTH

Source: Reeves (2006) *Royal Society of Arts Journal,* June: 50–3.

This conclusion, on which we would concur, might appear disappointing.[10] There has been a huge investment in brain science and yet it has appeared to have few implications for pedagogic practice. We see it differently, however, and for three main reasons.[11] First, contemporary ideas about the brain and the implications for mental activity do, we feel, cast aside some of the old traditional conceptions of mind and intelligence that have so dominated state-sponsored systems of schooling in the late nineteenth and twentieth centuries. Because of the power of these ideas in forming social attitudes to schooling and pedagogy we want to look at these in more detail. Second, brain science is allowing us to debunk more recent ideas that have taken very simplistic understandings of mental activity and raised these to the status of myths. We also want to look at these in detail. Third, a more explicit and less myth-laden concept of mind could lead to a set of dispositions towards learners and pedagogies that we feel goes with the grain of a twenty-first century concept of mind. We turn to the first of these three, what we term 'old conceptions of mind'.

In 1868 a Royal Commission, under the chairmanship of Lord Taunton, reported on a possible future for schools that existed between the expanding elementary or primary school system and the leading public schools of the day.[12] The Taunton Report recommended the establishment of different grades of schools.

> ... we shall call these the Third, the Second, and the First Graded education respectively ... It is obvious that these distinctions correspond roughly, but by no means exactly, to the gradations of society.
>
> First Grade ... This class appears to have no wish to displace the classics from their present position in the forefront of English education.
>
> Second Grade ... though most of these parents would probably consent to give a higher place to Latin, they would only do so on condition that it did not exclude a very thorough knowledge of important modern subjects, and they would hardly give Greek any place at all.
>
> Third Grade ... belongs to a class distinctly lower in the scale ... The need of this class is described briefly by Canon Moseley to be 'very good reading, very good writing, very good arithmetic'.[13]

Taunton unequivocally saw class and educational differentiation as being inextricably linked. There was, after all, a moral and religious underpinning. Only twenty years earlier Cecile Alexander had composed one of the most famous of hymns that is still sung today, 'All things bright and beautiful' with the verse:

> The rich man at his castle,
> the poor man at the gate,
>
> God made them high and lowly
> and ordered their estate.

It was during this period that the first signs of a new discipline – psychology – began to appear, and, particularly with reference to schooling, the linkage of biology, psychology and mathematics psychology began to embrace the elusive but attractive idea of individual measurement, first in terms of physical characteristics and then, increasingly boldly, there emerged the idea of describing mental prowess numerically.

The way this came about provides a fascinating insight into the way social and academic networks, reflecting prevailing social conditions, can emerge.[14] In analysing and interrogating social perceptions of education this is important, particularly in terms of the predispositions that teachers and others bring to pedagogy and learning.

Source: Paul Davis Chapman (1988) *Schools as Sorters: Lewis M Terman, Applied Psychology and the Intelligence Testing Movement 1890–1930,* New York: New York University Press.

Through the first half of the twentieth century in Britain, the USA and Europe, the process of mental testing became increasingly influential. In Britain a number of key figures drove this movement. Francis Galton, the progenitor of the eugenics movement, believed strongly that natural ability like physical characteristics could be seen to follow a normal curve of distribution and those most eminent in society had the highest measure of such ability. Galton also maintained that such ability could be inherited. His work had a profound influence on people such as Charles Spearman, who was the first to suggest that intelligence as a whole could be represented by something he termed the '*g*' factor which could be measured. His work in turn had a strong influence on Cyril Burt (who succeeded him at University College London), who in the 1920s and 1930s developed a range of tests that sought to measure innate ability and would therefore anticipate academic potential.

We now know that some of Burt's research was based on falsified data,[15] particularly where he used studies of twins separated at birth to propose the overriding importance of innate ability over subsequent nurture. However, at the time the perceived science of mental testing was hugely influential in the development of the school systems. In England and Wales, for example, a series of reports that led directly to a series of post-war education reforms gave great prominence to the work of Burt and others. The Spens Report on secondary education, published in 1938, is one example:

> Intellectual development during childhood appears to progress as if it were governed by a single central factor, usually known as 'general intelligence, which may be broadly described as innate all round ability'. It appears to enter into everything that the child attempts to think, or say, or do, and seems on the whole to be the most important factor in determining his work in the classroom. Our psychological witnesses assured us that it can be measured approximately by means of intelligence tests … The average child is said to attain the effective limit of development in general intelligence between the ages of 16 and 18 … Since the ratio of each child's mental age to his chronological age remains approximately the same, while his chronological age increases, the mental differences between one child and another will grow larger and larger and will reach a maximum during adolescence. It is accordingly evident that different children from the age of 11, if justice is to be done to their varying capacities, require types of education varying in certain important respects … [16]

The structure of secondary schooling set out in the 1944 Education Act was derived directly from Spens and the model of mental measurement that was so central to the recommendations made.

Burt's psychology of the twentieth century was mapped, perhaps all too neatly, onto the social structure that Taunton recognised in the nineteenth century. The new science of psychology, particularly in the field of measurement and statistics, went hand in glove with the slow-to-evolve class structure of British society. And Burt himself, in the latter period of his life, was to become increasingly political in aligning himself with traditionalist polemics against the introduction of comprehensive schools in the 1960s.[17]

The impact of this measuring and testing movement in psychology was felt in many parts of the world. In the USA, for example, Lewis Terman had a crucial role in the sort of categorisation of children that the cartoon on page 35 illustrates. Terman was at his most influential in the 1920s when school enrolment in the USA increased from 23.3 million to 28.3 million students. His advocacy of systematic programmes of testing and classification appealed to administrators keen to establish some order in the apparently aimless, even chaotic, expansion of classes. Terman also argued that the preponderance of low scoring children of Spanish, Portuguese and Italian parents in the lower tracks of the school organisation represented a clear sign of genetic inferiority.[18]

It now seems obvious that the quest or search to define intelligence or capture aptitudes held a potentially dangerous potency for policy makers of all types. Such tests, for example, were a neat way of categorising entrants for military service. Some immigrants passing through Ellis Island off Manhattan thus found their entry into the USA depended on their success in passing these newly formulated tests. Our reading of the latest research on brain science and the mind, however, suggests a far more flexible and tentative understanding of ability than that espoused by the deterministic ideas of Spearman, Burt, or Terman.[19]

Burt's ideas in terms of contemporary psychology are a salutary historical footnote. However, we believe that social concepts of ability derived from the early part of the twentieth century, most notably the idea of general ability, still have a strong pull in political[20] and pedagogic debate. In one important sense, ideas about general ability fly in the face of everyday observation. The person who graduates with the highest of honours from Oxford or Cambridge or Harvard or the Sorbonne would not claim a comparable ability in many areas of life that schools seek to develop (the social, sporting, artistic, for example). Terms, however, like 'able', 'less able', and 'average', are scattered across professional and pedagogic discourse with few qualifications (able at what?) and, consciously or unconsciously, a prophetic sense of potential is defined.

Contemporary ideas about the development of abilities differ in many important respects from the overtly simplistic Burtian approach. Perhaps most significantly for an understanding of pedagogy, the exercise of intelligence is not just seen as something that happens inside the head that can be contained within the individual. Rather the function of intelligence, the operation of any ability, crucially takes in social context, not least the network formed by friends and colleagues within which our lives are played out. In this conceptualisation our development and use of abilities need to take account of these wider factors in promoting individual growth – hence the recent use of terms like 'distributed' or 'socially shared cognition' in recent writings in this field. This socio-cultural approach will inform our exploration of pedagogy.[21]

In later editions of his book *Frames of Mind*,[22] Howard Gardner asks the question will intelligence continue to move beyond the brain of the individual, into the realm of the artefacts and context of the wider culture? His answer is yes, although he sees a particular Anglo-American bias that still hankers after the individualistic perspective. Gardner points to other parts of the world (in much of Asia) where concepts of ability and intelligence are very differently brought forth. In Japanese schools, for example, the notion of fixed ability simply does not exist. Children in schools are not grouped by ability because this concept, in the form it takes in Britain and the USA, has not been adopted in Japan.

Howard Gardner's work, spanning more than two decades, has been particularly influential in repositioning teachers' views on intelligence. His theory of multiple intelligences has directly challenged the idea of general ability and intelligence. In a series of books he has suggested that at least seven forms of intelligence can be observed, including the linguistic, narrational, spatial, and logical-mathematical. For Gardner, intelligences are specifically linked to content. He sees human beings as having particular intelligences because of informational contexts that exist in the world – a concept of intelligence that goes beyond the head of the individual to embrace a wider view of knowledge domains with their panoply of associated tools and artefacts. This then provides (as we explore in Chapter 7) the direct link with pedagogy, because intelligences, knowledge and learning become inseparable in any teaching endeavour.

We believe Gardner has been important in providing an alternative model of intelligence to the general version that has so deeply influenced Anglo-American educational culture, and in a form that is accessible to teaching and parents. We are, however, cognisant of those who would criticise Gardner for espousing another overly simplistic theory that fails to respect the complexity of the relationship between intelligence and context.[23] In addition, we are especially concerned about the way some educational practice, supposedly utilising the idea of multiple intelligence, has led to categorisations of children (as for example primarily kinaesthetic, spatial or logical thinkers) every bit as deterministic as those that ideas of general intelligence created.

We have given some space here to ideas about intelligence because we believe new understandings of intelligence need to underpin pedagogic practice. We can also identify other aspects of the brain/mind debate that have implications for pedagogy. One recent publication has examined the term 'neuromyths' in order to identify some ideas that appear to have overstretched the boundaries of evidence.[24] We think that three such myths are particularly relevant to teaching and, therefore, need rethinking. The first is the idea that the brain is divided into left and right, with the left holding more logical, problem-solving functions and the right the seat of more creative actions. This is an idea that has had a long history but it does not represent the much more complex ways in which the brain operates. There does appear to be some localisation of functions in the brain and we think that the frontal cortex of the brain is crucial to problem-solving activities and that this can be impaired by anxiety and fear. However, such areas do not operate in isolation but rather through broader processes occurring across the brain as a whole.

Left-brain/right-brain?

Research on split-brain patients has given us great insights into the workings of the two cerebral hemispheres. This knowledge has infiltrated into mainstream culture, but unfortunately the research has often been overinterpreted with abandon. There is now a widely held belief that the two sides of the brain control different 'modes of thinking' and that each person has a preference for one of these modes, that is, that one hemisphere dominates the other. People are therefore referred to as being 'left-brained', 'right-brained', or even 'whole-brained'. You can even find 'hemispheric dominance inventories' that you can fill in to see whether you are left- or right-brained, and can then do exercises to change this. This is pop psychology but alas not scientific psychology. While it is true that one hemisphere dominates the other in terms of our experience of the world and our actions, both sides of the brain will work together in almost all situations, tasks, and processes. In other words, you are not right- or left-brained. You use both sides of the brain.

It has been argued that education currently favours left-brain modes of thinking – which are logical, analytic, dominant, and accurate – while downplaying right-brain modes of thinking – which are creative, intuitive, emotional, and subjective. While encouraging education to involve a wide variety of tasks, skills, learning, and modes of thinking is a good thing, it is purely metaphorical to call these right-brain or left-brain modes. People with no right hemisphere are not devoid of creativity. People with no left hemisphere, although most will be unable to produce language, can still be analytical. Some will still be able to talk, as language can be housed in the right hemisphere of a small minority (about 7 per cent) of people.

Whether left-brain/right-brain notions should influence the way people are educated is questionable. Most neuroscientists still question the validity of categorising people in terms of their abilities as either a left-brain or a right-brain person. In terms of education, such categorisation might even act as an impediment to learning.[25]

A second myth of particular importance to education and life-long learning is that our brains have optimum moments for development and that missing these can seriously distort mental and educational growth. There is some evidence that for specific areas of our sensory systems (sight, for example) there may be periods of rapid change. Looking at behavioural rather than neuroscientific evidence we have been able to discern a critical period for phonology (beginning with infancy and ending at around age twelve). There is also some evidence to suggest that the knowledge of syntax develops rapidly up to the age of 16. There is no evidence, however, for similar periods in respect of vocabulary. The acquisition of new vocabulary continues throughout our lifetime.[26]

The research record about optimum learning opportunities remains tentative. Popular ideas (myths perhaps) still continue, however, to influence our thinking. Some are a variation on the 'you can't teach an old dog new tricks' way of seeing the world. Neuroscientists today do not, in John Bruer's phrase, 'interpret the critical period phenomenon as a window nature temporarily opens and then slams shut'. What is more accurate is the sense of rather slow, gradual changes in brain plasticity, changes consequent on exposure to the human environment that occur throughout life with perhaps some moments of greater accessibility to change. Our knowledge of such moments, however, only extends to changes in sensory and motor systems and to some extent in language.

A similar sort of critique can be made of attempts to suggest a third myth: that brain science points to the importance of 'enriched environments', for example in early childhood. as a means of encouraging synaptic growth and (by much extrapolation) subsequent educational achievement. Jerome Bruner, in a book review for the *New York Review of Books*,[27] talked of the need to speak out strongly against the all too prevalent false claim that if young children don't embark on a serious learning career by the age of three, then they might fall irreversibly behind.

The Future: Can Education, Neuroscience and Psychology Work Together?

Our burgeoning knowledge of the brain is producing expectations of new educational insights, and many such insights are already beginning to surface. At the same time, neuroscientists are becoming increasingly interested in how the brain functions in complex environments more closely resembling those found in classrooms. Education thus appears set to become an interesting area of challenge for cognitive neuroscience, as it attempts to explore new contexts. Some neuroscientists have even suggested that education might be considered as 'a process of optimal adaptation such that learning is guided to ensure proper brain development and functionality'. This sense of increasing mutual interest underlies calls for a two-way dialogue between neuroscience and education that could helpfully inform both areas. On a broader canvas, the synergy of psychology and education has a very long history – though one which has not been so much in evidence in recent decades.

…

There is also a growing need for collaborations between neuroscience, psychology and education that embrace insights and understanding from each perspective, and that involve educators and scientists working together at each stage. Such collaborations are not straightforward, since the philosophies of education and natural science are very different with various forms of psychology, in a sense, bridging the two. Educational research, with its roots in social science, places a strong emphasis upon the importance of social context and the interpretation of meaning. Natural science, on the other hand, is more concerned with controlled experimental testing of hypotheses and the development of generalisable cause-effect mechanisms. This suggests that collaborative research projects may need to extend the cognitive neuroscience model of brain->mind->behaviour illustrated on page 41, to incorporate processes of social construction pertinent to learning. Although challenging, such interdisciplinary projects may be the most effective way to co-construct and communicate concepts involving neuroscience, psychology and education that are both scientifically sound and educationally relevant.

To interrelate the most valuable insights from cognitive neuroscience and the social science perspectives of education and psychology (represented by arrows), the brain->mind->behaviour model may need to be extended. Even the example of two individuals interacting, as represented here, is suggestive of the complexity that can arise when behaviour becomes socially mediated. Such complexity remains chiefly the realm of social scientists, who often interpret the meaning of such communication in order to understand the underlying behaviour. Cognitive neuroscience has established its importance in understanding behaviour at an individual level but is only just beginning to contemplate the types of complex social domains studied by researchers in social psychology and education.[28]

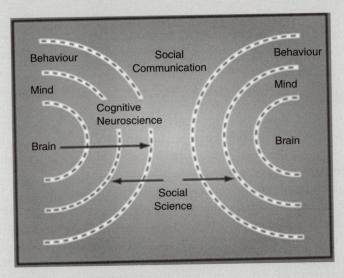

Interrelating cognitive neuroscience, education and psychology

The brain and our minds – our mental functions – are endurably linked but our state of knowledge about that linkage remains fairly primitive. Contemporary brain science does serve to dispel some myths, but it gives us only limited insight into the most important or effective pedagogic strategies. The history of education, particularly mass state education, is replete with periods when deterministic conceptions of 'brain power' or 'mental ability' have loomed large over educational ideas and practices. A number of these, rather like archaeological artefacts, still reside in professional and public thought. Although neuroscience and cognitive psychology may have moved on, such artifices only succeed in cluttering up the contemporary landscape.

That said, we can look with some confidence at the evidence for some tentative links between the science of the brain, neurophysiology and education, with cognitive psychology playing a crucial intermediary role.[29] First, the brain's baseline state is plasticity. Learning something new changes our brains. This plasticity is not confined to childhood and, among teachers for example, supports the notion of continuing and career-long professional learning. Second, the brain becomes 'fine tuned' by experience. And third, in a linked way, the long drawn out development of the brain depends upon a variety of environmental influences among which education can play an important part. All of which tends to give credibility to socio-cultural and social constructivist perspectives on learning, an important point we return to in Chapter 4.

All the issues discussed in this chapter, we would argue, need to be kept under review.[30] They are important to any concept of pedagogy. How we view our minds and intelligence is central to learning and teaching. We believe that any discussion of these themes should constitute an important element in programmes of personal or collective professional development. Awareness of this debate does not lead directly to specific pedagogic practices or strategies, but it does provide a series of dispositions that strongly influence the way we approach learners and the pedagogic settings in which they work. In summary, we would suggest three such dispositions that could be incorporated in any overall framework of pedagogic understanding.

The first, and perhaps the most important, is that ability is not a fixed, singular concept, and potential rather than being seen as finite should be viewed instead as flexible and expandable. School systems, particularly state systems that work on a large scale, have repeatedly produced classifications of children that go well beyond psychological or statistical validity. The evidence here points to the need for a more tentative approach to categorising young learners in any prophetic way.

Second, there is now a strong and convincing argument that the workings of our mind cannot be conceived as being solely 'within our heads'. The way we live and the way we learn depend crucially, as we discussed above, on the interdependence of the development of the mind and our experience of interaction with the environments around us.

David Perkins has characterised this interrelation through the concept of distributed intelligences – the way in which we use physical, social and symbolic aspects of the world around us is crucial to our reasoning.

Distributed Intelligence

Imagine.

You sit at a computer looking at an image of an ensemble of buildings. The buildings surround a plaza. You focus on an arch, the gateway to the plaza. A touch of your finger on the keyboard zooms the arch closer. Another touch pulls the viewpoint back and up for a bird's-eye view.

How does it look? Not welcoming enough, you think. Too severe. You need another possibility.

At this very moment, you are collaborating with a colleague half a continent away. Your two computers are slaved together and you have a voice connection too. 'I don't know about that arch', you say.

'Just a feeling or can you nail down a reason?' your colleague asks.

'I think I can. The arch is too small in proportion to the circle of buildings. Not generous enough. It gives a cramped feel.'

Your colleague agrees, adding 'Let me try another option.' Your colleague makes a few gestures with a mouse. You track the action, seeing what happens. The image reformats into a version with a larger arch.

'Better', you say. 'Definitely better.'

It is usual to ask 'What is intelligence?'… But a somewhat different and equally provocative question asks, '*Where* is intelligence?' The usual answer – when the question is asked at all – is that intelligence rests in the heads of individual human beings. Whether intelligence is a matter of neurons or experience or knowing your way around thinking, or all three as argued here, its home lies under your skull.

Oddly enough, this simple and obvious assumption about where intelligence sits can be challenged. I have urged right along that intelligence consists of whatever factors contribute to intelligent behaviour. In the above story of two architects designing an arch, consider what some of those factors are. The thinking about alternative arches receives support from a computer-aided design system that realizes the designers' conceptions visually and allows them to manipulate alternatives. This system does not do heavy-duty reasoning for them, but it does provide support for two important cognitive functions: memory and visualization, remembering for them their ideas and displaying their ideas realistically. Second, from a social perspective there are two people at work, operating as a team. The intelligent behaviour in question is in an important sense the joint behaviour of tandem minds. Finally, they share a language of options, reasons, and so on, that allows them to articulate to themselves and one another where their thinking stands and where they might take it.

All this has the earmarks of a phenomenon that can be called *distributed intelligence*. The basic idea of distributed intelligence says that the resources that support intelligent behaviour do not lie solely inside the mind and brain. They typically occur distributed throughout the environment and social system in which we operate.

It's useful to think of intelligence as distributed in three ways:

Physical   We rely on physical artifacts as simple as note pads and as complex as computer-aided design systems and beyond to do various kinds of remembering and computing for us.

Social   We do not typically think solo but in teams where different people bring different abilities to the mix and patterns of collaboration move the general enterprise along.

Symbolic   We do not think in bare thoughts but thoughts clothed in symbol systems, including natural languages with their rich vocabulary of thinking-oriented terms and a variety of notational and graphic symbol systems.

Roy Pea of Northwestern University brought this perspective to my attention a few years ago, formulating a version of it. I have written on it myself, as has my Israeli colleague Gavriel Salomon, who has also edited a book on the theme entitled *Distribute Cognitions*. To try to capture the essence of the idea, I like to contrast person-solo with person-plus. The person-solo is the person functioning with mental resources alone – no pencil, no hand calculator, no

(Continued)

(Continued)

partner, and indeed no linguistic or other symbolic resources tuned to the enterprise of thinking specifically, for instance, no terms and concepts like option or reason. Imagine how impaired a thinker this person would be.

The person-plus, in contrast, is the person functioning with such support. The person-plus, not the person-solo, is the typical case. Intelligent behaviour is not characteristically the solo dance of a naked brain, but an act that occurs in a somewhat supportive physical, social, and cultural context. Because of that context, the behaviour proceeds with more intelligence.[31]

This disposition, the social situations of mind, thus leads us to give particular attention to the pedagogic settings in which learning and schooling take place. This is something to which the founders of the pre-school system in Reggio Emilia gave special prominence. Unlocking the creativity of our minds needs the stimulus of rich pedagogic settings.

These dispositions interrelate and overlap and our third flows on from the first two. New learning is possible throughout life. One of the wonders of the human brain is its capacity to continuously grow and evolve and accommodate new challenges. While development of some capabilities, language for example, may be more rapid in our early years, this process cannot be transposed to all areas of intellectual activity. Mass schooling, with its staged and regulated curriculum, finds this hard to accommodate too. The power of pedagogy is to provide a setting in which a curriculum can be revisited and revised. Linear forms of curriculum design give little credence to this need for ongoing opportunities to gain knowledge and skills.

It is in this area that school systems do most damage to self-esteem. Jerome Bruner has pinpointed this as a particular challenge to school systems:

Only two things can be said for certain and in general: the management of self-esteem is never simple and never settled, and its state is affected powerfully by the availability of supports provided from outside. These supports are hardly mysterious or exotic. They include such homely resorts as a second chance, honour for a good if unsuccessful try, but above all the chance for discourse that permits one to find out why or how things don't work out as planned. It is no secret that school is often rough on children's self-esteem, and we are beginning to know something about their vulnerability in this area.

Any system of education, any theory of pedagogy, any 'grand national policy' that diminishes the school's role in nurturing its pupils' self-esteem fails at one of its primary functions. The deeper problem – from a cultural-psychological point of view, but in workaday common sense as well – is how to cope with the erosion of this function under modern urban conditions.[32]

Furthermore, Bruner goes on to argue that schooling has become so preoccupied with 'performance' and with the bureaucratic demands of education as an institution that we have neglected this personal side of education.

Perhaps the biggest challenge for teaching today is to create institutional and pedagogic structures and settings responsive to the unpredictability, creativity and endless potential that the workings of the human mind bring to education.

4

Learning

O this learning, what a thing it is. (Grumio in *The Taming of the Shrew*, Act 1, Scene 2)

Classroom in Albania, pre–1995

Drita grew up in a remote mountain village in northern Albania, the poorest country in Europe.[1] In the mid to late 1980s she attended the local primary school. Her own father had been the head teacher until the year she had started in first grade. He was removed that year by the communist authorities for not conforming to the party line on the curriculum ('use of unsuitable literature'), for 'poor discipline', and for refusing to display Enver Hoxha's image on the classroom walls. A new head teacher, Mr Musai, was forcibly posted to the village from the capital Tirana to take his place.

Like all her classmates Drita learnt by rote, reading sentences aloud from the board in unison with her classmates. Drita had to ask permission to answer a question and the teacher would shout at her if she spoke to a neighbour during lessons. She was very afraid of the head teacher. Once her classmate Ilir was beaten for asking Mr Musai why the local mosque had been pulled down.

Drita learnt to read and write to the texts required – literacy drills were a main focus of the highly structured daily curriculum, alongside political education. Every school text was designed to teach her and her classmates the Marxist-Leninist principles espoused by Albania's communist regime. Storybooks were available but every one carried a communist moral. Instructional resources were scarce. It was hard to find a map in most schools and overseas radio programmes were banned. Children were not allowed to move around the classroom. There were no games, no science, no art activity. Drita learnt the history of the communist party but had a meagre knowledge of the world beyond her local commune of Shkodra. She had only travelled to the town of Shkodra twice with her father and had never been to the capital, Tirana.

She always expected she would farm the land when she finished her primary education. Her *biografi* (the political history of her family over the last two generations, filed against her name with brief examples of her schoolwork) disallowed her from further study, since neither her father nor her uncle had been good communists and one of her cousins was in prison. Now in her late twenties, she is a subsistence farmer selling her produce on market days. However, life for her is broadening in some interesting ways. Four years ago, following the fall of the communist regime and under the auspices of a new Albanian Ministry of Education and UNICEF, an experimental primary school[2] modelled on Reggio Emilia principles was opened in her village.[3] Drita helps the new teachers of this school several days each week, cleaning the new classrooms and setting out resources, reading to small groups of five year olds, and generally helping to support the wide range of learning activities the children are now participating in. In this process she is also learning a great deal herself that is new and hopes eventually to train as a teaching assistant.[4]

In this chapter we explore the central role that views of learning play in the process and practices of pedagogy. In particular we examine our assertion made in Chapter 1 that learning is a social process embracing the individual in varied forms of collective activity. By working in a range of pedagogic settings in unfamiliar contexts and cultures, such as Albania in the mid 1990s, we have become acutely aware of this critical, but often taken-for-granted, dimension of pedagogy. We also found that the issues we were most concerned with in relation to learning and teaching were foregrounded even more clearly through new experiences in hitherto unknown pedagogic settings.

As we emphasised in our introduction, we will not be setting out the complexities of learning theory or citing every possible source on the issues presented in this chapter. Readers interested in bibliographies on learning theory can consult first-hand the very many excellent and absorbing texts in each area.[5] The sources, references and exemplars we use here have been chosen to elucidate key themes that have emerged as we researched the ways in which different views about learning elicit quite different modes of pedagogy. In the culture of classrooms (broadly conceived), whatever the setting, it is teachers'

and learners' implicit, everyday habits and beliefs about learning that bed particular pedagogies down, that make them appear natural and inevitable and
turn them into spontaneous reflexes and responses. What we hope to do in this
discussion is to make the implicit explicit by investigating the iterative and
sometimes contradictory nature of the relationship between views of learning
and pedagogic practices.

Drita's early experience of learning is chilling. Prior to 1990, memorisation,
didactic teaching and the recollection of facts concerning Hoxha's particular
brand of communist ideology formed the modal of pedagogy in Albania.
Young people's identities were moulded by the state. Most expected to be
directed into the military or to work in local co-operatives when they left
school, as attending a high school would require 'a good biography' (that is
one showing you actively supported the regime, regardless of your high score
in school). The teaching role was conceived of as a single omniscient teacher
telling or showing learners the things they in turn had been told in the state's
training workshops.[6] Many teachers told us of the structural relationship of
fear that was engendered between themselves and their learners, 'the system
was designed to make the student fear the teacher, the teacher fear the school
director, the director fear the school inspector and the inspector fear the
ministry'.[7] After the transition to an elected government in the early 1990s a
'depolitisation' or what some called 'disideologisation' process took place, in
which all the 'red threads' of Hoxha's educational and ideological dictatorship
were removed from Albania's school curriculum. Foreign textbooks, such as
English language methods course books, were introduced into schools.
However, since hitherto most foreign books, newspapers and maps of any kind
had been illegal, not only in schools but countrywide, educational resources
were still largely confined to a few state produced textbooks.[8] The issue of
training teachers also remained problematic, as the old methods of teaching
lingered on since teachers had become accustomed to these over time.

We were fortunate to be invited to work with Albanian educators leading
the reform process that followed the collapse of this brutal regime, as they
sought to ensure that children would have new and different kinds of learning opportunities. Their common vision was that learning should enable
young people, for the first time in many decades, to develop to the full; that
learning could equip them with a sense of opportunity to make their mark,
both in their own lives and in their communities; that learning could identify
and fulfill new passions. To this end we supported our Albanian colleagues in
developing a series of professional education programmes (Kualida[9]) that
introduced primary school teachers to new ideas about learning. These innovative programmes, in part capitalising on the ubiquitous medium of state
television, familiarised parents, community leaders and practising teachers
with learning methodologies that had been unthinkable – indeed prohibited –
during the communist regime. How to encourage questioning, how to identify and solve a problem, how to develop and communicate ideas to others,

value self-confidence, engage in the processes of creativity and reflect on the process of learning itself.

Once their borders were open to the wider world, many Albanian educators began to seriously research the relevance of a range of school reform models and new approaches to learning globally. They investigated practices that they hoped might help them to confront constrained habits of mind and could heal the disposition of apprehension and mistrust that the Hoxha era had successfully nurtured in an entire population.[10] Their net of enquiry was cast widely.[11] All the programmes explored had two features in common which were particularly attractive to Albanian reformers given the legacy of their previous regime. First, the programmes are explicit in their commitment to overarching values, namely the right of young people to an education directed towards the full development of the human personality while strengthening a respect for human rights and fundamental freedoms.[12] Second, they are unambiguous about the view of learning that supports the achievement of such goals and from which certain practice and pedagogy follow. They encompass a view of learning as a participative, social process in which teachers, learners, parents and communities share. A process that engenders the experience of belonging to a learning community that permits, indeed encourages, open, critical and creative inquiry without the fear of being judged.

Fenway High School is one example of the many school reform models that have been explored by Albanian educators through visits and discussion with teachers and students.

Situated in an unremarkable building in the Fenway neighbourhood of Boston and backing on to Fenway Park, home to the Boston Red Sox, Fenway High School was originally set up as an alternative academic programme for disaffected students who were failing in the larger public school setting of Boston English High School. Fenway had been a long-time pioneer of the small schools movement. A quarter of a century on, the school had a fully developed mission 'to create a socially committed and morally responsible community of learners, who understand and participate in Fenway's core values[13] as the school grows and changes'.[14]

The desire to build a shared sense of community is not a rhetorical, abstract aim in this particular setting. It is palpable before one even sets foot inside the physical building as students and staff greet each other on the busy sidewalk outside the school reception area, exchanging animated conversations about family, current school projects, or last night's baseball game. If you are a visitor you will be immediately and warmly included in such conversations, for Fenway has a long tradition of welcoming visitors into its community of learners. The school honours and appreciates connections with other educators and members of the local community, indeed any collaborators who are committed

(Continued)

(Continued)

to giving young people a quality education. Staff and students alike are encouraged to find value in the insight, feedback and new ideas that visitors bring. In a very deep sense the physical boundary of Fenway is not demarcated by the busy sidewalk entrance on Ipswich Street or the Red Sox stadium on the other. The city as a whole is viewed, quite literally, as an extension of the school's campus, and the school's many Learning Partners (such as the Museum of Science, Tufts University, and the Darner Farber Cancer Institute) are seen as a vast, ongoing, human resource. This broad view of community ensures that students have the opportunity to participate in real world learning across all types of work and social environments and that the school's practices keep up to date with contemporary, work-place thinking in its main academic disciplines of maths, science and the humanities.

A student mastery and deep understanding of concepts and skills, rather than a broad coverage of content, together guide the formal school curriculum. For instance, in all grades the identification and exploration of central themes and patterns in human history are taught and each year the humanities curriculum is focused on a different theme that is expressed as an 'essential question'. Supporting this inquiry are case studies and readings in the field of history, literature, philosophy, government, religion, sociology and geography. The essential questions in a four-year rotation are: How do you do right in the face of injustice? What does it mean to be human? Who built America? What principles guide the way we govern ourselves? Seniors cover Term 1 and Term 3 on the regular cycle. The second term is entirely devoted to the student's senior portfolio.

If you have the opportunity to attend classes you will be struck by the buzz of excitement, purpose and seriousness about learning. A prevailing sense of self-confidence without arrogance is evident among the students. They will immediately be curious about you, candid in their questioning of why you are there, what interests you, what you might want to know about their school, the kind of work they do, or indeed about themselves. Posters in every room provide a constant aide memoire to this collective sense of adventure and inquiry – summarising the 'Habits of Mind' that Fenway teachers and students have learnt to value, whether they be studying mathematics, science, the humanities or citizenship:

Perspective	Who's speaking? What points of view are given?
Evidence	How do we know what we know? What are our data? What are our sources?
Relevance	Why does any of this matter? How does this relate to us?
Connection	What causes what? How does this connect to what we already know?
Supposition	How might things have been different? What if … ?

The school's advisory system is summarised by Theodore Sizer's assertion that if even one person in a school community knows him/her well enough to care, a student's chances of success go up dramatically. Fenway teachers and their assigned advisory students become friends and allies, interested in one another's lives – in effect, forming a mutual support group. In small groups that can focus on a range of subjects, teachers and students are encouraged to make new connections, and together create a more personalised educational plan. Advisors are the direct link between the school and the home. They maintain regular communication and are the first point of contact for parents. The advisory service can also be a place to prepare portfolios and practise for exhibitions. Students are encouraged to check one another's work and to confront obstacles that limit success.[15] Part of this advisory service, and a requirement for graduation, is that all students perform 40 hours of community service during their time at Fenway. Besides being a requirement by the state and city, Fenway has always believed that community service helps students to understand the needs of the community and to learn about themselves through giving something back to other people.

This particular week students and staff are co-hosting an on-site symposium with the Boston Museum of Science and the Darner Farber Cancer Institute, addressing the overarching question: *Creating American Scientists: What should be done – in and out of the schools?* The objectives of this symposium are a sharing of views on why too few American students, particularly students of colour from urban areas, are becoming scientists and to identify dilemmas in science education and the consequences of not resolving them. The symposium intends to generate a report summarising key points that can inform policy making and practice in Boston's public schools' science education.

Over 100 scientists, policy makers and business people, together with many Fenway students and educators, are involved. To help focus the discussion, participants are grouped into seven professional constituencies[16] working on a common question: *If you had $20 million dollars to improve science education, how would you spend it?* Each table has a group facilitator and a recorder taking notes on a laptop computer. After group debate these notes are entered into a database that makes it possible to categorise them into spending categories (for example, equipment and materials for inquiry-based projects). To further distill participants' responses, spending categories are grouped by target areas (for example, 'schools' or 'community'). The various recommendations for spending in each category are counted and entered onto a spreadsheet entitled Spending Priorities Report and are then debated in plenary session.

A report on the symposium will be circulated among participating institutions and used to inform future thinking about Boston's approach to science education in its public schools.[17]

These two settings – Drita's elementary school and Fenway High – have been deliberately chosen here to reflect deeply contrasting educational practices, albeit focusing on different age groups and cultural and political contexts. They bring into focus what Bruner calls 'antinomies': pairs of large truths about learning that may both be true, but nonetheless contradict each other.

One such antinomy is the tension between 'in the head' and 'social'[18] views of learning. These two very different approaches to learning can be characterised in a number of ways. The main focus of 'in the head', or what some call the 'symbol processing' view of learning, is the individual's mental processes, or a symbolic representation of the mind. Such a view separates the

learner and the learning process from the environment by solely focusing on
internal cognitive mechanisms. 'Social' perspectives, by contrast, view human
development as being inseparable from the physical world and interaction
with others. The main focus of this approach to learning concentrates on the
social structures of the world and how these constrain and guide human
behaviour and development. Such seemingly opposed frames on learning are
embedded in our everyday language. On the one hand we say 'It suddenly
crossed my mind', 'It was difficult to get it into her head', 'I gave him a piece
of my mind', 'Can't remember off the top of my head'. On the other hand we
talk about 'common knowledge', we say 'A problem shared is a problem
halved', we assert that 'Two heads are better than one' and we appeal to 'common sense'. These everyday idioms echo long-standing philosophical disputes,
but they also reflect the productive (if at times bitter) debate between contemporary learning theorists.

Educationalists working for Hoxha's regime espoused the individually focused,
symbol processing view of learning. Learners were seen as empty slates,
essentially imitative beings, learning best by copying the activities of more
expert others, or by memorising by rote carefully selected facts, rules and principles. Students were expected to use an innate intelligence to process the content of exercises and drills. Effective instruction from this perspective entailed a
didactic pedagogy, conceived as a linear process with an identifiable beginning,
middle and end. Learners – whether in remote classrooms in the rugged mountain region north of Shkodra, or packed into learning labs progressively polluted
by the constant emission of toxins from Elbasan's copper and steel factories
south of Tirana – received identical 'lessons' at precisely the same time of the
day and week. The Hoxha regime knew this process must be paid close attention to if it was to maintain its iron hold on the population, and at this it was
highly successful. Prior to transition Albania could boast universal literacy and
universal enrolment in basic education (grades 1–8).[19] Most young people effi-
ciently achieved basic language and literacy skills, a practical knowledge of
working in the fields, and the ability to recite facts from the 'History of the Party
of Labour of Albania', the doctrine of Marxism–Leninism, a distorted history of
Albania and 'moral and political education'.[20] This illustrates the political nature
of pedagogy at its most transparent.

It can be seen how this mode of pedagogy inevitably followed from a particular interpretation of learning. Imitation required that individuals develop
pre-ordained, discrete skills and abilities, rather than an in–depth knowledge
and understanding. Rote learning enabled students to uncritically acquire a
canon of knowledge and to thus mould the so-called 'new man' who was
dedicated to communist ideals and habits of mind. Both processes focused
on the individual and their 'acquisition' of the state's selection of skills and
knowledge.[21] This approach also takes an acquisitional view of learning.
Freire calls this 'banking education';[22] Bruner, 'computational' or 'information
processing'.[23]

At the other end of this spectrum, Fenway's educators explicitly espouse a 'social' view of learning. Learners are seen as inherently agentive, proactive, curious, creative, and seriously committed to ends[24] in the communities in which they participate. From this perspective learning is seen primarily as a social process. Fenway educators believe that students learn best by critically participating in a variety of cultures.[25] Students' knowledge and development in science, for instance, are seen as being inseparable from sustained experience of and interaction with the real world of science and scientists in shared issues and common concerns. Given this very different perspective on learning, Fenway's overarching mode of pedagogy requires a strong focus on the structures of the worlds that Fenway students jointly experience both in and out of school, and how those structures guide, expand or constrain their learning. Learning is seen to exist in the conditions that bring people together. In this sense it does not belong to individual students, but to the various conversations of which they are part.[26] Individually students may spend time trying to learn things, but this phenomenon pales before the fact that, however hard they try, they can only learn what is around them in the culture to be learned. This approach takes a 'participatory' view of learning. Freire calls it 'conscientisation'. Bruner, the 'socio-cultural view of learning'.

We have used these extreme examples to suggest that views of learning and learners logically inform very different practices of pedagogy. Yet such seemingly opposing ideas about of learning – acquisition vs. participation, symbolic processing vs. the socio-cultural, the individual vs. the social – are by no means as discrete as our comparison might suggest at first sight. By looking more closely at the two settings we can see different types of learning occurring side by side. Socio-cultural theories of learning would not have been available to Hoxha's educational policy makers in the 1980s, but nonetheless Drita's experiences illustrated social learning at work. Many kinds of learning were not made socially available to her. For instance, no one she knew ever read a novel or used a map of the world. Drita and her peers were therefore simply unable to conceptualise a world beyond the environs of Shkodra, and instead participated in a form of cultural isolation that made questions about such a world impossible to even formulate. In this sense there was little learning to do. Instead, participation in Hoxha's culture of fear and control, fuelled by a didactic and authoritarian curriculum and the randomness of power, shaped what Drita knew and how she was able to learn while moulding her fragmented understanding of life. In turn this stultified aspects of her emotional development, the way she conceived her own identity and any sense of future possibilities. In Drita's case situated learning is highly evident.

In Fenway, by contrast, the didactic drills and teaching by imitation employed in Drita's classroom are generally seen as unhelpful pedagogy. Nevertheless, as the vignette shows, the school's daily practices involve the regular reinforcement and rote learning of certain habits of mind.[27] It is a matter of emphasis that makes this didactic methodology such a significantly different experience for students. For this constant reinforcement of agreed values and habits of mind is underpinned by extensive opportunities for students to test out, reflect and critically question these habits for themselves in the ambiguous and messy meaning making of the real world.

Some see this complex antinomy between *symbolic* and *socio-cultural* cognition as presenting educators with a 'pedagogical dilemma'.[28] We suggest that these apparently paradoxical views, far from needing to do battle for supremacy, both play a role in our understandings about learning.[29] Indeed Bruner argues that symbol processing is crucial at different points in the learning process (for example, preceding and following interpretative meaning making) and that categorisation systems as the outcomes of such learning are essential to human development. The key issue for our purposes is to broadly understand different approaches, what insights they have to offer and their limitations. What would seem critical for pedagogy is first that views of learning are explicitly acknowledged and consciously reviewed, and second that their relationship to practice is interrogated. We need to inquire what frames of learning dominate in the culture of our classrooms, how do we know, what alternatives are there, can different approaches really be complementary and what is the evidence?

A range of metaphors has been developed that articulates the widely differing roles that practising teachers have identified as supporting their view of learning. The *petrol pump attendant,* who 'fills' learners with 'refined' knowledge delivered by 'textbook tankers'. The teacher as *parent bird* (the *regurgitator*) whereby they interpret and organise learning in digestible chunks for learner 'chicks'. The metaphor of the teacher as *lion tamer* or *sculptor,* moulding learners who are essentially passive in the process into the desired shape. Alongside these are differently focused image – the *watchmaker* (the teacher who sees their role as that of a builder), the *gardener* (where all the growing is done by the plants, namely the learners), and the *sherpa* (acting as 'knowledgeable guide' to explorers of unfamiliar terrain).[30]

In fact it is still rare for institutions or individual teachers to share explicitly a rationale for their particular approach to learning with students and their communities in the way that Fenway does. Research suggests[31] that most educationalists, wherever they are based, practise a kind of 'double think' in relation to their views on learning. They may frequently articulate learning to be a process in which individuals actively create rather than receive meaning, yet everyday practice reveals knowledge transmission of one form or other to be the dominant modus operandi. Such double thinking is strongly reinforced by national educational policies and assessment practices based on the assumption that learning is an individualistic, mental process that takes place independently of social context. Classrooms continue to be arranged so that students focus on their teachers and respond to carefully devised step–by–step exercises, activities and schemes of work exemplified by government guidelines. To assess such learning common standards are devised and regular testing procedures have to be used whereby individual knowledge must be demonstrated and tested in the de-contextualised settings of silent classrooms or imposing examination halls.

We take risks when we critically confront implicit views of learning and when we interrogate the images we hold of ourselves as teachers and match these with learners' perspectives. But if we are interested in the process of change and development, we believe that hard questions need to be raised on an ongoing basis about our shared assumptions concerning the nature of learning. A key implication of any attempt to organise learning differently is that we become reflective with regard to implicit concepts and discourse and the effects of these on the way we design practice. While new perspectives are not recipes, they can act as a guide about what we pay attention to, what difficulties we can expect and how we might approach problems. If we believe that knowledge consists of pieces of information stored in the brain, then it makes sense to package this information in well-designed units, to assemble prospective recipients of this information in a classroom where they are isolated from distractions, and to deliver this to them as succinctly and articulately as possible. If, on the other hand, we accept that learning is primarily a socially situated practice, these traditional models do not look so promising. What might look more promising are inventive ways of engaging students in meaningful practices, of providing resources that can enhance their participation in a range of practices, of opening horizons so they can place themselves on learning trajectories they can identify with, and of involving them in actions, discussions and reflections that make a difference to the communities that they value.[32]

In the remaining sections of this chapter we have identified a number of themes that seem to have emerged strongly in contemporary debates about learning and in the wide range of pedagogic practices we have experienced in different parts of the world. These are by necessity selective, given the huge body of work on learning theory. Our intention in so doing is first to give a sense of the *multiplicity* of ways in which research on learning can challenge and extend educators' understandings. Second, to identify a range of *perspectives* on the learning process and their relationship to pedagogy. Third, by making some comparisons to raise our awareness of *alternative* views[33] and the choices that can be made. We have therefore identified nine themes to explore:

- expectations;
- constructivism;
- intersubjectivity;
- participation;
- distributed learning;
- place;

- narrative;

- affirmation;

- transformation.

EXPECTATIONS

Acquisitional views of learning are frequently coupled to the notions discussed in Chapter 3 – that human ability is pre-wired, fixed, innate. Theories of innate intelligence, as we have seen, propose that individuals differ in the extent of their ability to understand complex ideas, learn from experience and engage in various forms of reasoning. From this perspective the human capacity to learn is implicitly denied, since each individual is seen to be endowed, as it were, with an engine of a given horse power: fixed, unchangeable and measurable, irrevocably setting precise and definable limits to learning and hence to expectations.[34] Such ideas are also implicit in contemporary processes of educational selection and measures of individual achievement, placing a ceiling on teachers' and parents' expectations of students, as well as on students' own perceptions of their ability. McDermott[35] articulates well the impact of differential expectations in the culture of contemporary US practice: 'before any teachers of children enter the schools every September, failure is in every room in America. There is never a question of whether everyone is going to succeed or fail, only of who is going to fail. Because everyone cannot do better than everyone else, failure is an absence real as presence, and it acquires its share of the children.'[36]

A study of creativity by one of us[37] shows that contemporary views that some students are 'gifted' or 'talented' in one particular field or another (such as being a skilful dancer, poet, violinist or mathematician) are underpinned by the notion that such talents are innate, despite no hard evidence to support such a claim. In fact research demonstrates the crucial role of social structuring and expectations for creative learning. A major study of creativity shows that 'all people are capable of creative achievements in some areas of activity, provided the conditions are right, and they have acquired the relevant knowledge and skills'.[38] In a field often regarded as being dominated by the highly individual and creative – namely, Nobel prize winners – Bruner points to research that shows the chance of winning such a prize increases enormously if you have worked in the laboratory of somebody who has already won this accolade. Not solely because of the stimulation, or the 'visibility', but because of shared access to a richer knowledge distribution network. Many of the case studies in this book focus on innovative programmes where young people, many of whom have failed in conventional systems, have reached high standards of achievement when buttressed by consistent structures of intellectual, emotional and social support that were founded on high expectations.

Unfortunately this preoccupation with innate ability has inhibited a more scientific approach to the complex interrelationship between learning and creativity. It has also closed the door on learning for many students, particularly (as discussed in Chapter 3) those from low socio-economic backgrounds. Factors such as technical practice, persistence and motivation[39] for creative learning are largely ignored, factors that in turn depend on supportive learning communities that have high expectations of their members. Achievements in the field of music, for example, have been shown to flourish with encouragement, the personal ownership of musical instruments, early pleasurable (musical) experiences in one's own family or with peers, and the approval of others (either peers or adults). Indeed quite specialised expertise has been shown to emerge very quickly when nurtured in particular groups and communities. In eighteenth century Venice, the orphanage La Pieta established a cultural ambience in which musical expertise was valued and encouraged among all students. Plentiful opportunities for training were made available, thus creating a community with high expectations where a substantial proportion of the orphans became highly accomplished musicians.[40] Similarly, in the Anang Ibibo community in Nigeria many 'aesthetic' areas and creative achievements in music, dance and art have become far more widespread than in the West and are now considered as forming a communal knowledge.[41]

Research by Lucy Green[42] reveals that gendered assumptions, based on the notion of innate predispositions, continue to be re-enacted daily in the music classroom. In a questionnaire distributed to 78 schools in the UK she found that within the music curriculum girls were, almost without exception, reported to sing, play the keyboard and traditional musical instruments and to participate in school concerts. Boys played mainly electric guitars, bass guitars and drums. She comments:

> It was interesting to discover something about teachers' views of students' proclivities in the realm of composition, a curriculum requirement which has only existed in any widespread sense in Britain over the last ten years or so. I found that in teachers' eyes and ears, girls are more conservative at composition, less imaginative, less innovative than boys, who are understood to have all the hallmarks of a sense of aesthetic adventure. In sum, musical girls are understood to be numerous, persevering, but ultimately conservative and mediocre, whereas musical boys are perceived as rare, creative and gifted.[43]

In Chapter 1 we discussed Brian Simon's[44] seminal article 'Why No Pedagogy in England?', in which he points to the inextricable link between prevailing views of differential innate ability, the process of selection and what he sees as the death of pedagogy. If education cannot promote cognitive growth, as such views seemed to suggest, its whole purpose or direction is lost. We agree with Simon that pedagogy needs to start from an opposite standpoint – from what individuals have in common as members of the human species. This common feature is the human capacity to learn, what Amartya Sen calls human 'capability' and

Bruner refers to as 'agency'.[45] Research, scholarship and evidence, such as are discussed in the following sections, together underpin this view. Such a view makes it possible to have high expectations for all learners and to envisage a body of general principles for learning that are relevant for the majority of individuals.[46] The evidence therefore suggests that you can actually build better brains by the kind of intellectual learning they participate in.[47]

CONSTRUCTIVISM

Beverley Caswell (see Chapter 2) acknowledges that constructivism, the theory underpinning the Schools For Thought programme she studied, strongly influenced her view of how students learn. This understanding significantly influenced and changed her practice. The notion of constructivism with its deep roots in ancient philosophy has been informed over time by a wide range of theoretical positions.[48] Jean Piaget and John Dewey were the first major contemporaries to develop a clear idea of constructivism as it might be applied to childhood development and classrooms. For the reformer John Dewey, developing his theoretical ideas in the University of Chicago Laboratory School in the early twentieth century, education depended on action. Knowledge and ideas, he argued, only emerged from situations in which learners had to draw them out of activities that had meaning and importance to them.[49] In the same period, Jean Piaget became particularly influential on thinking about learning in Europe with his views based on a theory of childhood psychological development. To reach an understanding of basic phenomena, Piaget argued that learners need to go through a series of linear stages of development. At the heart of this process is discovery, and understanding is built up step by step through learners' active involvement.[50] To understand is to discover, or reconstruct by rediscovery, and such conditions must be complied with if in the future individuals are to be formed who are capable of production and creativity and not simply repetition. Thus Piaget placed activity and self-directed problem solving at the heart of learning.

From both a Deweyian and Piagetian perspective it is the nature and quality of learning activities and their impact on mental processes that are particularly important. Their work emphasised the need for learners to participate in problem solving and critical thinking about a learning activity that they find relevant and engaging. Learners need to be enabled to construct their own knowledge by testing ideas and approaches based on their prior knowledge and experience, by applying these to a new situation, and then by integrating the new knowledge gained with pre-existing intellectual constructs. Although constructivism embraces many theoretical perspectives on learning and does not of itself suggest a particular pedagogy, it has nevertheless been influential in foregrounding the importance of 'learning by doing and exploration'. While the emphasis remains on learners' internal cognitive processes, this view takes learner agency as a given[51] and has spawned a wide range of pedagogic strategies by which learners can be encouraged and enabled to select and transform information, construct their own hypotheses and be active in their own learning.

In this sense Beverley Caswell's classroom exemplifies a constructivist approach. She has designed a classroom setting where learners are focused on an engaging and absorbing research activity – an exploration of the Madagascan roach. This broad investigation is supported by a wide range of discrete learning activities that she knows from experience will stimulate problem solving and knowledge building (such as reciprocal learning,[52] benchmark lessons,[53] CSILE software, structured lab visits and lab journals). Her students play a central role in controlling aspects of their learning: learning objectives are negotiated with them and their previous knowledge is taken into account. There is a focus on real world problems that learners are encouraged to solve for themselves. Multiple perspectives and representations of concepts and content are presented in the course of this investigation. Problem solving and higher order thinking skills are deliberately facilitated through the careful selection of activities mediated by range of physical and cognitive tools.

This approach to learning impacts strongly on views of the teacher role. By emphasising the interaction between the learner and the activity, the focus moves away from the teacher and the content to learning mechanisms and learners' cognitive processes. From a constructivist perspective, teachers need to adopt the role of facilitator,[54] with the critical goal being to support learners in becoming effective thinkers. Rather than assuming a didactic approach which aims to cover selected subject matter, the teacher as facilitator helps learners to reach the level of understanding. This dramatic change of role implies a totally different set of skills: from the teacher telling, to the facilitator asking; from the teacher lecturing from the front, to the facilitator supporting from the back; from the teacher giving answers according to a set curriculum, to the facilitator providing guidelines and creating activities designed to support and challenge learners' thinking[55] and to arrive at their own conclusions. Beverley Caswell's colleague admitted this changing role was daunting. As von Glasersfeld,[56] a radical interpretator of constructivist conceptions of learning, put it, teachers must play the role of 'midwife in the birth of understanding' as opposed to being 'mechanics of knowledge transfer. Their role is not to dispense knowledge but to provide students with opportunities and incentives to build it up.'[57] This conception of the teacher became highly influential between the 1960s and the late 1970s[58] in many parts of the world and in projects such as the UK's 'Children Learning Science'.[59] It has now re-emerged strongly in contemporary thinking about the role played by teachers in ICT-enriched classrooms, where technology can be seen to facilitate a range of learning mechanisms.

Constructivist ideas have continued to be influential in contemporary thinking about the agency of the learner and the need for educators to think critically about the nature and purpose of learning activities. A new group of ideas was to bring some rather different insights to educational thinking in the late 1970s. These were to provide a clear focus on the relationship between learners and their environment, challenging the singular conception of the teacher as facilitator. Sometimes known by the umbrella term 'social constructivism', this somewhat different frame on learning defines our third theme, *intersubjectivity*, a term used to describe the mutual exchange and understanding that people achieve through communication and their place in learning.

INTERSUBJECTIVITY

Social constructivism largely emerged out of the work of Lev Vygostsky[60] and his colleagues, who emphasised what was at the time a radical and controversial idea: that learning was primarily a socio-cultural process.[61] Meaningful learning, they argued, only occurs when individuals are engaged in social activities. Individual consciousness is built from the outside through our relations with others. From this perspective higher mental thinking is seen to develop through interpersonal communication mediated by shared psychological (language, sign systems and gestures) and physical tools (see also Chapter 7). Vygotsky's particular influence on educational thinking came via his research work on the relationship between thought and language: *thought is not merely expressed in words; it comes into existence through them.* While Piaget had been concerned with learners' qualitative mental shifts in perspective on problems (an *acquisitional* perspective), Vygotsky channelled his energies into looking at the way learners developed the communicative skills and knowledge that allowed them to use the many tools for thinking available in the surrounding culture (a *participative* perspective). Such differing purposes therefore explain their very different viewpoints on learning mechanisms. Piaget saw cognitive restructuring as occurring between equals in peer interactions. Adult 'authority' was seen to hinder this process. By contrast, Vygotsky argued that ideal partners in learning are not equal but that this inequality is of expertise and understanding rather than power.[62] Vygotsky's theory saw instruction (both formal and informal) not only as being central to learning, but as the main vehicle for the cultural transmission of knowledge. Where Piaget looked for confrontation in learning, Vygotsky looked for dialogue. Learners, he argued, need to work with a more skilled and knowledgeable partner in joint problem solving within a 'zone of proximal development' (namely, the gap between learners' unaided achievement and their potential achievement with the help of a skilled partner). Learning then occurs as learners internalise shared cognitive processes – by socially constructing meaning. The process of learning and teaching from this perspective has been powerfully described by Bruner[63] as a forum or dialogue, a constant meeting of minds whereby teacher and learner engage in the negotiation of shared meaning. The language of education, he argued, if it is to be an invitation to reflection and culture creating, cannot be the so-called 'uncontaminated' language of fact and objectivity. It must express a stance and counter-stance and in the process must leave a place for reflection, for metacognition. It is this that permits one to reach the higher ground, this process of objectifying in language and image what one has thought and then turning around on it and reconsidering it.[64]

Social constructivism has been translated into pedagogic principles that are highly varied in practice. Nevertheless, this view of the importance of inter-subjectivity and culture provides a singular take on the interrelationship between learning tasks and learners. The context in which learning occurs, the social knowledge learners bring and the nature of their dialogue and collaboration become critical. Importantly, this perspective also introduces a proactive role for the teacher who must continually model learners' understanding, gauge what 'scaffolding' to provide, and decide how and when to reduce such support. Language and dialogue between teachers and learners play a pivotal role in the learning process. As we can see from the two vignettes below, this view of learning can then be used to underpin quite radically different practices in the classroom.

To encourage students to adopt more sophisticated writing strategies, Scardamalia and Bereiter[65] developed a detailed cognitive analysis of the activities of expert writers. This provided the basis for a set of prompts, or *procedural facilitations*, designed to reduce students' information-processing burden by allowing them to select from a limited number of diagnostic statements. For example, planning for writing was broken down into five general processes or goals: (a) generating a new idea, (b) improving an idea, (c) elaborating on an idea, (d) identifying goals, and (e) putting ideas into a cohesive whole. For each process, Scardamalia and Bereiter developed a number of specific prompts, designed to aid students in their planning as shown below. These prompts served to simplify the complex process of elaborating on writing plans by suggesting specific lines of thinking for students to follow. The process drew explicitly on Vygotskian concepts of modelling, scaffolding and the expert/novice.

PLANNING CUES FOR OPINION ESSAYS

NEW IDEA
An even better idea is …
An important point I haven't considered yet is …
A better argument would be …
A different aspect would be …
A whole new way to think of this topic is …
No one will have thought of …
IMPROVE
I'm not being very clear about what I just said so …

(Continued)

(Continued)

I could make my main point clearer …
A criticism I should deal with in my paper is …
I really think this isn't necessary because …
I'm getting off the topic so …
This isn't very convincing because …
But many readers won't agree that …
To liven this up I'll …
ELABORATE
An example of this …
This is true, but it's not sufficient so …
My own feelings about this are …
I'll change this a little by …
The reason I think so …
Another reason that's good …
I could develop this idea by adding …
Another way to put it would be …
A good point on the other side of the argument is …
GOALS
A goal I think I could write to …
My purpose …
If I want to start off with my strongest idea, I'll …
I can tie this together by …
My main point is …

Scardamalia and Bereiter's pedagogic method proceeds by using a combination of modelling, coaching, scaffolding, and fading. First, the teacher models how to use the prompts, which are written on cue cards, for generating ideas about a topic she is going to write about. Then the students each try to plan an essay on a new topic using the cue cards, a process the students call 'soloing'. While each student practises soloing, the teacher as well as other students evaluate the soloist's performance, by, for example, noticing discrepancies between the soloist's stated goals and their proposed plans. Students also become involved in discussing how to resolve any problems that the soloist could not solve. An assumption of the role either of critic or producer is incremental, with students expected to take over more and more of the monitoring and problem-solving process from the teacher as their skills improve. Moreover, as the students internalise the processes invoked by the prompts, the cue cards are gradually faded out as well.[66]

This approach using modelling and scaffolding remains influential in many classrooms and has, for instance, been incorporated in England's national literacy strategy. In its interpretation of social constructivism it focuses on a quite specific learning mechanism (the use of cue cards) and a discrete learning goal (the writing of opinion essays). In our second example we see a very different approach to pedagogy, also explicitly influenced by social constructivism but with a more open-ended learning activity and a broader learning goal (namely, an understanding of the way in which history is constructed and contested).

Wanda May teaches curriculum history to graduate students in Vermont, Canada. In 'Constructing History in a Graduate Curriculum Class'[67] she describes a new approach she decided to take with this class. The initial task Wanda May presented to her graduate history students at the start of the term was at one and the same time highly specific and yet open-ended and unfamiliar: 'Identify a pattern or theme in curriculum history so that you can represent this theme in a two- or three-dimensional *visual* model'. Note this task is quite different in nature and scope from the highly focused activities designed above using Scardamalia's cue cards.

May's starting point was not the students' acquisition of discrete skills or historical facts, but how she might, over the period of a term, engage their understanding of history and their relationship to the subject matter. She was concerned that 'enduring questions within subjects such as history and philosophy are often presented and perceived by students as privileged, esoteric forms of knowledge, bearing little relation to everyday reality and practice'. Most of her students were teachers of history, so she was keen that they should learn to problematise historical interpretation and understand how history is constructed and contested.

May told students in the first session that they would be using the next few weeks to identify a pattern or theme in curriculum history in order that they could represent this as a visual model. She stressed that they would probably find the assignment challenging and that most likely no two models would be alike. The task created some anxiety for most of the students ('My first response to this historical model is sheer disbelief. Here I am at 41 being asked to do a cut and paste assignment. My secondary response is fear. I'm trying to have faith that this will eventually become clear'). In addition, May was herself uncertain as to whether students might resist the activity. Nevertheless she felt that giving more structure would result in her authoring the history for students and distancing them from their own constructions. The starting point *must* be the learners' own knowledge and narratives in terms of their own readings, responses, biographies and experiences.

More than 75 articles and excerpts relating to curriculum and socio-political forces were provided for the class, including those from authors during certain periods (for example, Dewey to Kliebard, Goodlad to van Manen). Students were asked to read these accounts selectively, choosing what interested them from different periods and perspectives. A wide range of written historical references, time frames, contemporary and historical resources such as art, photographs, scrapbooks and film, music, advertising, people, oral histories and diaries was provided, as well as structures such as discussion groups and seminars to support the task. Structures were also created by the students themselves (namely, home study groups or including family members in their learning). Students then documented their thoughts and feelings in journals as they grappled with the assignment, and as they felt perplexed or stymied they wrote about these dilemmas. They were encouraged to sketch, doodle and

(Continued)

(Continued)

make notes, to 'talk' to their readings. After identifying a pattern or theme and creating their models, students were then asked to write a five-page defence of their creations – how they arrived at their selected images, a brief description of the model, why it was a good interpretation of curriculum history, and a summary analysis in terms of what they had learned about themselves as learners/teachers. One entire session was devoted to ten-minute presentations of the models, which was lively and intense because of the varied interpretations of history that the students had constructed.

In an evaluation of the task, the majority of students reported that they had enjoyed the history module most of all the assignments because of its problem-solving focus and being able to share interpretations. 'As I began to get into this, I found it compelling. It wouldn't let me go. For me this experience has been similar to the eruption of a volcano ... This is almost identical to the process of solving hard, weeklong maths problems we did in graduate school. I wonder if the solution will come in the middle of the night!' The course had required students to engage in analytical and critical thinking. In the assigned task, most students interpreted history as a complex interaction of ideas, events and personal relations. Few interpreted curriculum history as a time-line of disjointed dates, facts and remote events that had little bearing on the present. They developed, May argues, a learning community that continued a conversation 'begun long ago by others'.

May's learning task is highly specific and as the knowledgeable expert she provided numerous scaffolds for the learners. Yet unlike the mechanism provided by the writing cues and the process of constructing a piece of writing, the task puts both the teacher and the students in the role of risk takers. May deliberately created uncertainty and anxiety for her students and herself rather than comfort and familiarity. Her approach is akin to Freire's, where he is chiefly concerned with enabling learners to develop a critical view of the world. He variously referred to his pedagogy as a 'practice of bafflement' and the 'vagabond of the obvious', deliberately creating in the dialogue 'epistemological inquietitude'. In this sense May's pedagogy is explicitly informed by critical pedagogy, including, as she points out, feminist thinking.[68]

From this perspective May's classroom, in line with the ideal of a feminist classroom,[69] is concerned with how students and teachers relate to one another and the materials presented. The personal experiences of students and their instructors are integrated into the course materials, creating an environment where numerous and sometimes contradictory voices are heard. This pedagogical approach requires active student participation and the perception that all participants' voices will be taken seriously – something often denied to female students. Special attention must be paid to voices that are often silenced and opportunities must be given for *all* students to speak and be heard. May adopts pedagogical strategies that invite the participation of every class member present and all class members are expected to 'become self-conscious participants in the process of knowledge construction' and be 'aware of the limitations of their own experience and perspectives and therefore value the perspectives of others'.[70] Moreover, May's commitment to feminist pedagogy means she must reject the positivistic stance of value-neutrality, replacing it with 'passionate scholarship' and 'necessary heresy'.[71] *Every* course participant's voice is presented as both limited and situated but also necessary and equally important in the construction of classroom knowledge. When disagreements arise, instead of smoothing them over or simply dismissing them, further energies must be spent exploring why they exist. The inclusive, feminist classroom is one where there is a shared sense of struggle. Connections and feelings of community often arise out of courses taught using an inclusive feminist pedagogy and this, May argues, is what she is struggling to achieve in her work.

We have seen how social constructivist views focus our thinking on *intersubjectivity*, particularly the interrelationship between teacher (or expert peer) and learner, the environment and joint interpretations of learning tasks. More radical approaches to the social view of learning, however, suggest this paradigm is still too narrow and that it is the learning community as a whole that should be the main focus or unit of analysis. This rather different interpretation of learning as a socially-situated practice has led to a new emphasis on the broader learning trajectories of individuals over time and the place of identity in the learning process. It generates our fourth theme: *participation*.

PARTICIPATION

This radically different view of learning has become highly influential over the last decade, particularly through the joint work of social anthropologist Jean Lave and her colleague Etienne Wenger, who began his career as a teacher and then became a computer scientist (although many others have significantly contributed to this important strand of thinking about learning).[72] In their now classic (1991) monograph, 'Situated Learning', Lave and Wenger argued that many so-called 'social' theories of learning, including traditional interpretations of Vygotsky's work, merely led in practice to 'a small aura of socialness' (group or pair work for example) being put in place essentially to provide cognitive input to individual learners. Such practices, they argue, remain firmly embedded within a symbol-processing paradigm, since their overall purpose is the learner's acquisition of knowledge and the mental internalisation of the cultural given.[73] These interpretations of socialness simply foreground the immediate physical nature of any learning activity (namely, a classroom, science lab or gym/learners/teacher/discrete tasks). A more complex view of the social nature of learning than that simply of locale is required, they say, one which recognises that learning is ongoing in every aspect of our lives and which takes a broader view of learners' trajectories through the world – their sense of self, where they are coming from, where they think they are going, what sort of person they want to be.

This work deeply challenges traditional views of learning as a sequence of discrete pedagogic activities. From this perspective the 'social is primary, the individual secondary in act and time'.[74] Classrooms from this stance are viewed as complex social settings in which learning is jointly constructed, 'stretched over the individual, other educators, learners (and many others), activities, tools and artefacts'.[75] Socially-situated learning focuses on the importance of 'the intricate and variable structuring of the total resources for learning in communities'. The notion of participation is key in this paradigm of learning, emphasising learners' location and agency in the many and varied life-worlds to which they belong.

From such a perspective learning is never a one-person act, instead it is the many communities in which we participate who also learn and develop (whether at work, school, home, or in our civic and leisure interests). In some communities we are core and active members, in others we remain on the margins. When we intensively participate in activity with others this can be an empowering position. If we are deliberately kept – or indeed place ourselves – on the margins of a particular social group, this can be disempowering and inhibit learning in that setting. Paradoxically, by focusing on the structure of social practice and on learners' participation in a range of communities, a more explicit focus on learners is possible and the individualistic emphasis of a cognitive focus, characteristic of most theories of learning, appears to concentrate on the person. However, painting a picture of the person as primarily a 'cognitive' entity in practice promotes a non-personal, decontextualised view of knowledge, skills, tasks, activities, and learning. As a consequence, both theoretical analyses and pedagogical prescriptions tend to be driven by reference to reified 'knowledge domains', and by constraints imposed by the requirements of learning mechanisms understood in terms of *acquisition*. Placing the social world at the heart of the analysis, starting with social practice, and taking participation to be the crucial process might, in contrast, seem to eclipse the person. In reality, however, a focus on social practice requires a very explicit focus on the individual learner, as person-in-the-world, as a member of various socio-cultural communities. Such a focus promotes a view of knowing as activity by specific people in specific circumstances. It looks at the whole person. It implies not simply engagement in discrete activities, but a relation to social communities. It implies becoming a particular kind of person.[76]

A recent research project carried out by the University of Cambridge suggests that students' accounts of school show that while they may spend large amounts of their time in classroom communities, the learning agendas of these settings are rarely important to them. Nor do they see school as relating in any way to their other life worlds (for example peer/family/leisure groups) or to their predominant interests, values and concerns. Many students – especially those who are being seen to 'fail' – simply do not feel themselves to be participating in the same community as their teachers and more highly attaining peers.[77]

The setting below illustrates these ideas. It outlines an educational intervention in Edinburgh to investigate why a group of male bilingual learners felt — and were perceived to be — marginal in their school community. It explores the mechanisms that were put in place to improve the participation structures for these students within the school community and the ways in which students' broader learning trajectories and sense of self were addressed.[78]

The English as an Additional Language (EAL) Service within the city of Edinburgh's council works in partnership with schools, parents, communities and agencies to support bilingual learners' development of English and their access to the curriculum. However, the service also has a remit to promote achievement and inclusion and to address barriers to these. This may involve working with students to promote their self-esteem, confidence and sense of belonging, but it may also involve 'supporting and challenging' schools to identify and address such barriers within educational practice. Eileen Simpson, Principal Teacher at EAL, has a specific remit for this work.

James Gillespie's High School is a multi-ethnic community with complementary aims – to provide a secure learning environment that values and promotes diversity, and in which individual students can fully realise their potential. The school serves a mainly academic and professional community. Twenty five per cent of its students are from minority ethnic communities. A small proportion of these come from non-professional backgrounds.

As part of its ongoing review of learning, the school approached Eileen Simpson concerning a small group of such students (aged 16) approaching their final years at the school. These students had been identified as having, to varying degrees, unrealised potential – 'achieving poorly, lacking confidence, displaying poor, even at times disruptive behaviour, feeling marginalised from school'. In close liaison with the school and students themselves, Eileen collated all the available data on these students' attainments, shadowed them in class, held one-to-one meetings with students and met with their parents (none of whom had any experience of higher education). These parental meetings revealed dated perceptions of many aspects of higher education and a considerable bias against further education as being vastly inferior. Most importantly, parents also indicated a lack of confidence about approaching the school about these issues.

An evaluation of these students' performances in standard tests showed no significant underachievement for any of the boys despite them being perceived – and perceiving themselves – to be 'low attainers'. However, it did show a 'literacy lag' in reading comprehension, which the EAL Service had found frequently undermined bilingual students' progress, and measures were initiated to address this with the students concerned and with later cohorts of students with the same 'lag'.

Following these preparatory activities, a programme was agreed for five of the seven students that would seek to identify factors affecting their behaviour, attainment and motivation, that would support them to address these as appropriate and that would support them individually in taking the next steps. An important additional factor was the offer of collective group work for them and their wider friendship group, in order to give them a voice and

(Continued)

(Continued)

get their perspectives on their situation. Finally, there would be a report on the outcomes.

The individual support was effective in many ways. However, it was the group work process that initiated real and dynamic change.

To facilitate the group work, Edinburgh's Black Community Development Project provided a minority ethnic group worker, Mesfin James, to help Eileen lead the group. Together Eileen and Mesfin adapted a group work model for use in this context.[79] Weekly group sessions lasting 80 minutes were held for the students during the Spring term. In the first session members were invited to consider which issues they wanted to examine; these were then prepared by the staff in a format to facilitate group engagement. The group work was based on: a shared structure of participation, a high priority on confidentiality; and the freedom to express feelings and views within agreed group rules. Students were keen that the school was informed of any key ideas emerging from their discussion and any implications for practice.

The project workers felt this was a group 'waiting to happen'. Participation was active and enthusiastic. 'It was like turning on a tap – they just didn't stop talking.' The students selected wide-ranging issues for discussion: their religion, culture, language, family, race, school experience and 'the future'. Gradually, as the sessions unfolded, they opened up about their daily experiences of 'juggling' two cultures and how the school's expectations sometimes unwittingly placed them in conflict with their families/communities. One particular anxiety was a sense of pressure from the school to go to college rather than pursue higher education as was often desired by parents: 'If the school suggests I leave and go to college, it'll be the end of my life – I'll be working in the take-away 24/7'. Those who needed it were offered ongoing, separate, individual support to discuss the next steps with their parents and to investigate progression routes into further/higher education.

The importance of participation emerged strongly from this innovative work. Not only did the students begin to feel they could fully and actively participate in this small group (which had been given status by being integrated into the school's personal development curriculum), but more importantly from an initial place of alienation and marginalisation, the students also began to feel they could contribute actively to the culture and practices of their school. 'This has made us feel that the school values us, and that our feelings and issues matter. We haven't always felt like this. We haven't felt that we were very involved in the school – we just came, did our work and left. We felt we were sort of on the edge of things. It has made a difference for us to feel that we are playing a bigger part in the school.'

The practical outcomes of the project were in large part the key to a genuine sense of participation. These made concrete the students' belief that they now had a stake in the school community, as well as in their own learning processes. Both these students and other members of the school community had roles to play in responding proactively. The students had an obligation to share their views and say how they thought they could actively play a lead role in school activity. They tentatively presented their views to key staff and also offered to help with anti-racist education for younger students. The school in turn had to take the students' proposals seriously and accept that they had a real – and unique – role to play in contributing to shared values and changing practices. The school showed commitment and courage in remaining open and supportive of this process throughout.

When the school was invited by Her Majesty's Inspectorate of Education (HMIE) to help launch its race equality document 'Making It Happen' at the Sheraton Hotel in Edinburgh, the Head asked Eileen and the students to do the presentation. With support, the students put together a PowerPoint presentation, and three representatives spent many hours rehearsing their talk. 'Before the workshop', Eileen said, 'the high profile professionals in the audience were looking askance at these three guys who had roamed around during the break, exhibiting bravado, grazing all the food. Once on the platform though they were really nervous. But they suddenly began to speak to the large audience with such intense and serious conviction that there was an electric silence in the room. The content was of high quality, very hard-hitting and extremely pertinent to participants. The last student to speak concluded unrehearsed, in vibrant Scots-Bengali vernacular, 'That's the end of our presentation, have yous any questions?'

'Needless to say there were many questions, plus a great deal of praise and numerous invitations to repeat the performance for other education professionals. One enterprising Youth Work Manager even jokingly offered to become their agent. The effect on all three was salutary ... the growth in self-esteem and confidence was visible, and was sustained on their return to school.'

The group's final report was hard hitting and honest, under such headings as 'Our views on religion'; 'Our experiences of racism and Islamophobia'; 'Language issues'; 'What we feel about teachers' attitudes'; 'Parents' vs. students' expectations'. The students presented it formally to the school's senior management team and senior support staff. The school in turn responded immediately to certain aspects of the report, while others (including the issue of reading comprehension and parental awareness and participation) were followed up in response to Eileen Simpson's summary report on the research project, 'Juggling Two Cultures'.[80] The group had been empowered to effect change for themselves and their school, as this excerpt from their PowerPoint presentation shows:

Changes in the school	Changes in us
Standard letters for cultural absences	More confidence and self-esteem
Racism dealt with differently	Clearer ideas and more understanding
Staff listening – some changes	Feeling valued/more part of the school
Involving us more	Wanting to give something back.

A number of pedagogic principles can be derived from the vantage point of a participatory view of learning, which are all notable in this vignette:

- Learners take charge of their own learning.
- Teachers are model learners.

- The school embraces learners' other communities, rather than setting up conflicts of identities.

- The curriculum builds on diversity and is embedded in meaningful activity; there are no artificial boundaries between subject matter and the social contexts in which it is useful.

- The curriculum is transparent; learners know where the curriculum is going and why, what there is for them to learn and what they will be able to do with it.

- The curriculum supports a view of learning as 'deepening', rather than accumulating, understanding.

- Grouping is according to task; 'class' size has no meaning in the abstract, since different activities call for different size of groups.

- Community resources for learning are taken advantage of.[81]

In our research, we have used the ideas of participation[82] within a community of practice to describe and analyse the process of teacher learning and development. We argue that it is gradual and highly-structured participation in the practice of teaching, rather than the internalisation of discrete, prescribed teaching skills and competences, that enables new learning and professional knowledge. Developing as a teacher, in common with any other practice (belonging to a family, or being a member of a religious group or sports team for example), evolves as a history of learning shared with other members of the teaching community. In this sense learning is neither specifically personal nor solely collective, for participation does not refer simply to discrete teaching activity but to the more encompassing processes over time by which we construct our identities in the varied communities to which we belong – be they teacher of science/form tutor/teacher governor (or all of these).

We have illustrated this analysis of teacher learning through the case study of a state school setting that focuses on a mature trainee English teacher, Lucy, in her final work placement.[83] This case study presents the student's own selected reflection on her first experience of teaching an A-level English group, as she begins to combine different elements of professional knowledge in her work. Her account is juxtaposed with data drawn from college assignments, in order to illustrate the wide variety of knowledge she is synthesising from different aspects of her experience in a range of groups (for example, PGCE community, university's subject faculty, school's English department, community local to the school, and so on), as she learns what it means to participate in the daily practice particular to the English department in which she has been placed.

Teaching A-level English for the first time

Change is an inevitable outcome of the deep link between learning and communities. Shared participation is the stage on which the old and the new, the known and the unknown, the established and the hopeful, act out their differences and discover their commonalities, manifest their fear of one another, and come to terms with their need for one another. Since communities are always in motion, change is a fundamental property of their activities. Every teacher can to some degree therefore be considered as a 'newcomer' to the future of a changing professional practice.[84]

'I had this sixth form ... an exam class.

Their set book for this part of the term was Chaucer's 'Prologue' ... I hadn't done Chaucer for about ... since ... 1975 and er I thought 'Gosh! I can't remember this book', the idea of going back to study and look at the background information ... and all that ... and the idea of having to experiment with a sixth form class was a new experience I was trying to look for.

'And based on that what I did first was to try to find out what kind of students they were ... what level they were at ... what was the method of teaching the sixth form?

'So **what my mentor and I** decided to do was to go about it in a fun way. **We decided** that my first lesson was going to be a kind of ... group work, all the lessons were group work except for when they were going to write, and **we decided** that **we should ask them** to plan a modern pilgrimage, just kind of break them into the idea of pilgrimages and the motive behind pilgrimages.

'I asked them to come together in groups of fours, think of characters within this country for example who might go on a protest – animal rights, or something like that, characters within the groups, the genuine ones and the ones with different motives, then draw the characters, what they're wearing and why they think they're wearing this outfit and give them dialogue. So **we did that** and they presented it to the class and it really was very good!

With that I was now able to come into Chaucer and talk about Chaucer as a person, who he was, his background and then what the society was then, in medieval times, and ... what I felt Chaucer's motive was in writing the General Prologue and that kind of, the kind of activity they'd done gave them the basics and they were able to look at ... in that light without just looking at it in terms of the text book, but looking at it in terms of life itself and how they can actually assimilate what's been happening in this present life and what's been happening in medieval times. It was quite successful because after the first lesson, there was a parents' evening. I didn't even know what had happened and when I came back the following day my mentor said to me 'What did you teach them? Show me what you did'. And the kids had gone to tell their parents that they had a very exciting lesson on Chaucer.

(Continued)

(Continued)

Whan that April with his showres soote
The droughte of March hath perced to the root
And bathed every veyne in swich licour
Of which vertu engendered is the flour;
When Zephirus eek with his sweete breath
Inspired hath in every holt and heeth
The tendre croppes, and the yonge sonne
Hath in his ram his halve course
And smale fowles maken melodye

That slepen al the nyght with open Ye
and (So pricketh hem nature in hir courages);
Thanne longen folk to goon pilgrimages."
from Chaucers' *Prologue to the Canterbury Tales*, originally studied at
university twenty years earlier.

'My mentor's an extremely imaginative person, don't know how she
gets all the ideas, and it just comes like that, I get my ideas basically
from her and from ... classes I observed during my teaching practice.
So my mentor was really quite instrumental towards all the ideas
I had.' *Interview*

'Vygotsky's theory of social constructivism emphasises 'human
potential and educability' which does not recognise any notion of
absolute imitation. This theory emphasises "the crucial role of human
culture in the development and direction of learning" ... there is great
emphasis here on the role of language in learning.' *Final written
assignment of PGCE course*

'My partner school is situated at the edge of Coventry. A high
percentage of children come from the neighbouring council estates
but also from the privately owned housing around the area. Asian
Moslems and Brethren children from the city centre attend because
their parents prefer a single sex school.' *PGCE written assignment* ...

'Then after that, **we did** ... **we took** the first 42 lines which was
introduction, basically and did it **together as a group** so they could
have that sense of security ... because I wasn't feeling too secure myself
... (laughs) ... so it was kind of a **'get it together'** and then we did the
translation **together**. And **I** introduced them to reference books that
they could use. After that **I** gave them homework, that they were to go
back and use the CD-ROM, use the library, and do research into
Chaucer's background – the historical perspective, sociological and
geographical ... They went and did a lot of research ... because without
that most of the information would be lost to them and they would not
be able to understand and empathise with what Chaucer was trying to
do and what society was like then. And that was quite good as well!'

'By the time they came back, **I** had found a tape, a tape of 'The Canterbury Tales' and **I** thought 'this is good', it's going to take the pressure off me because I don't know how to pronounce this and the kids are now going to listen, get the meaning without worrying about the pronunciation! **We would** have spent so much time on ... that would have done them in actually in terms of their confidence ... and that worked ... **we listened** to the tape (which was very funny because of the pronunciation) and then we **stopped** it intermittently to discuss the issues and then **we went back** to their groups and started sketching. Sketching the characters **as we read** them ... the picture that came to them and how they saw those characters and they were able to present it together as a kind of display to the class ... And that was how **we did it.**'

'Teachers in T School's English Department share knowledge with other members of staff. There are regular INSET programmes for staff and special provision is made to newly qualified staff to enable them to develop confidence and versatility – they have quite a number of resources in the department. I looked through them and picked out what I thought was going to be useful to me.' *Written assignment*

'Even the map for the route to Canterbury ... that I gave to the students, somebody in the department gave me that too.' *Interview*

'At T School, in English lessons, students are often placed in a variety of contexts in which they are speaking and listening, reading and writing contemporaneously ... the department recognises the central importance of speaking and listening which, in real life are the most used elements of language. In most of my lessons speaking preceded writing and reading.' *Final written PGCE assignment*

As a pre-service teacher, Lucy[85] is a newcomer being inducted into a setting that structurally and explicitly supports her interaction with 'old timers' (other professionals, students, parents and particularly her mentor). Newcomers can often be prevented from the vital 'legitimate peripheral participation'[86] that supports learning by not being given *productive access to activity in the community of practitioners or if the meaning of such activities is not made transparent.*[87] Lucy's account in our view demonstrates 'productive access', illustrating ways in which the practice of English teaching is made fully transparent to her. The pronouns 'I' and 'we' that she uses as she talks about her planning and teaching have been deliberately highlighted in the transcript above. Lucy moves imperceptibly between them. Sometimes the 'we' refers to herself and her mentor, indicating the ongoing importance of collaborative planning despite her growing confidence in solo teaching. At the beginning of the transcript it would appear as though she co-taught the first lesson with her mentor: 'What **my mentor and I** decided to do was ... so **we** did that'. It is only when she

notes that her mentor 'asked me "What did you teach them?"' that it becomes
clear that although Lucy was teaching alone, she felt it was also a joint activity.

Lucy provides clear evidence that the English department operates explicitly as a community that is jointly committed to shared purposes and values
and joint problem solving. Experienced and new members of staff are encouraged to share materials, feedback from courses, and exchange views on the
subject of 'English', as well as support one another in planning new curriculum
practices. They also struggle together over problems faced in the classroom.
Because the experienced teachers also see themselves as learners, Lucy is thus
able to see departmental practice as an ongoing pedagogical 'adventure'[88] of
research and critical inquiry. In the final sentence of her account, and the second time she uses the phrase 'that's how **we** did it', she emphatically gathers
together the community of practice in which she has been participating. The
phrase draws together herself both as teacher and learner, her students, other
members of the department and of course her mentor. Such a process critically extends the role of teacher or mentor well beyond that of facilitator or
coach, with the quality of the participation structures put in place a key
dimension of the pedagogy.

In her rich, if incomplete, attempt to articulate this process Lucy nevertheless clearly illustrates the way in which her learning is maturing. This is a
unique process of participation, which is not abstract and internal, but instead
is concrete, social and dynamic, as well as inherently fraught with challenge
and dilemmas.[89]

DISTRIBUTED LEARNING

Research shows that today's most successful communities – be they businesses,
hospitals, marketing projects or English departments like Lucy's – have one
thing in common. They know how to transform individual expertise into collective knowledge. They are places where each individual contributes their
particular expertise to a shared learning history. The creation of new knowledge is everyone's most important work: joint learning leads to innovation and
growth as well as creativity and the development of self-esteem on the part of
individuals. Researchers often refer to this as *distributed learning*.[90] Indeed,
Chris Dede predicts that distributed learning and knowledge-building communities will be the new paradigm of twenty-first century education.[91] It is
an integral aspect of a socially-situated view of learning and is our fifth theme.

Members of real communities always have well-defined roles and responsibilities, which are related to and also serve to develop their particular interests
and expertise. This sense of expertise fuels individuals' commitment to a
shared enterprise that is so crucial to successful communities and innovative
forms of learning.[92] We saw what impact the recognition of unique expertise
had on learners' self-esteem in the Edinburgh case study detailed earlier. The

vignette that follows illustrates this frame on learning in the context of a large teaching hospital in the UK where staff were faced with a unique medical problem.

Vicki Save,
Consultant Histopathologist

Moira Howley,
Senior Sister

Rebecca Fitzgerald,
Honorary Consultant
Gastroenterologist

Kevin Gunnee,
Consultant Anaesthetist

James Pearson,
Operating Department
Practitioner

'We owe our lives to the technology and this team of specialists. It is a new start for us, a new life.'

In the Autumn of 2006, a 23-year-old science teacher and her younger sister, a university student, were both found to be in the early stages of a life threatening, genetically inherited disease that had claimed the lives of several older family members. The sisters agreed to be participants in a special research programme at Addenbrooke's Hospital in which medical staff were working together to learn how such conditions might be treated and hopefully in time cured. Initially the young women spent time with a local clinical geneticist. They then acquired two specialist consultants backed up by a highly expert research lab team, and two surgeons then joined this problem-solving group. The surgeons' personal assistant was key throughout this stage of the process, organising appointments with the relevant specialists, providing moral support for the young women and ensuring good communication systems within and across the team itself.

   The research carried out by this multi-disciplinary group was to show that the young women were carriers of a previously unknown gene. The research also identified the best mode of intervention for the sisters. Major surgery followed in which the young women were supported by two specialists nurses who had been seconded full-time to the research project. They co-ordinated the complex treatment and operations by means of face-to-face visits, phone calls and e-mails. For a short period other experts had to be briefed in order to inform the work of the core team and to carry out in turn a range of specialist tasks – radiographers, a consultant, an anaesthetist, the operating theatre team and staff in the intermediate dependency area and the hospital ward where the sisters were to convalesce side by side. This work was also impossible without the charge nurse from the acute pain service and a consultant histopathologist and dietician.[93]

(Continued)

(Continued)

A key element of this intense learning experience was that the problem was shared. Participants were intensely committed to the core aims of the work, knowing just enough about one another's expertise to effectively contribute their particular perspective to the overarching problem. Without the collective knowledge and expertise of individuals the problem would not have been solvable.

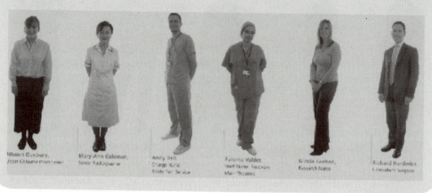

The power of this kind of real life learning being addressed to a pressing problem has been recognised in some teaching settings. From this perspective learners take on a variety of roles and are able to see themselves as making a unique and valued contribution to their learning community, with the opportunity to carry out a range of tasks indispensable to the group as a whole. Such an approach calls for independent as well as group research on a shared project which is ultimately the joint responsibility of all members of the group. The sharing of individual expertise leads to the performance of a 'consequential task' or activity that demands that all students have learnt about aspects of the joint topic. A wide range of resources is seen as integral to this approach, both human (for example, visiting experts, older tutors, support via electronic mail) and artefacts and tools (for example, books, videos, hands–on experiments, periodicals, computers, and so on).

PLACE

We have noted that participatory views of learning depend on the location and agency of learners in their local, overlapping communities. In this sense the location focuses on the quality of social structures that enable the learner to feel central or marginal, active or passive, empowered or disempowered, in the various groups to which they belong. From another perspective the importance of location, in the sense of physical places for learning (places that generate a sense of belonging) is key. *Place* is our sixth theme.

In Maori pedagogy a child's learning is seen as being at the centre of life and culture – a series of multi-faceted dimensions that need to be understood each in relation to the other. As indicated in the visual diagram above the unique life force and creativity of the child (*Tamariki*) are at the centre of the Maori pedagogic model, surrounded by radiating wheels integrating wide ranging local family, educational and cultural practices encompassed by the broader world and the universe (*Te Aorangi*).[94] Maori pedagogy emphasises that learning depends on these interlocking experiences and understandings being in balance – but such experiences must always be outward looking, moving the learner well beyond the familial and local to other experiences and new forms of cultures and expertise. '*The university of ancient Hawaiiki*[95] *is the universe. Education in this context knows no boundaries.*' This concept of learning environments as having limitless physical and intellectual boundaries is common to the practices of many settings described in this book, where learners are encouraged to participate in an ever-broadening trajectory that takes them well beyond the immediate physical classroom, enabling exploration of a wide range of possible worlds, knowledges and identities.

Paradoxically the importance of specific, local, physical places with clear boundaries is as integral to the Maori model of pedagogy as their concept of borderless learning. Specific places for learning include *Kainga* (the place of abode), the homestead where children's early learning in families takes place; *Whenua* (the placenta or land[96]), where children learn about their obligations to care for the environment and pass it on intact; *Hui* (congregate), the communal meeting place; *Turangawaewae*, an ancestral place where the child stands as of right, where her roots are deep; and *Wharekura*,[97] a building or area in which the learned impart knowledge. Teachers working in the *Wharekura* are seen as specialists accountable to the community they serve, always aiming at excellence and perfection. In contemporary New Zealand *Wharekura* is used in the Aoteoroa state system to denote ordinary state schools.[98]

Social theorists in the Western hemisphere have made detailed analyses of the interaction of physical setting and learning. Numerous research studies, especially in the field of architecture, provide illustrations of how the physical elements of settings not only influence but also generate learning.[99] Three planes of analysis were identified in one study of schools:[100] the *official school*, including curriculum teaching materials and methods; the *informal school*, including the interactions in all areas of the school; and the *physical school*. Embodiment and space and their relation to learning have also been demonstrated in research, showing that spatial dimensions shape practices and processes. Learners in one research study were asked to complete the sentence: 'School is like a … '. Some metaphors were recurrent – for example a factory, a prison and an ants' nest. Research found different assumptions about space in gender terms in particular. The physical school was seen as a more spacious place for boys than for girls. For them, the schoolyard was larger, the corridors wider, the classrooms bigger, and the area surrounding their bodies greater. For girls, the schoolyard was smaller, the corridors narrower, the classrooms tighter, and the space surrounding them smaller. Girls used less space when taking their places. The study argues that a confident use of the body and space is important for all learning, impinging on a learner's sense of autonomy and independence.[101]

Reggio Emilia's philosophy of learning pays great attention to the quality of the immediate physical environment that learners experience and this is considered as a 'third teacher'. In any planning of new spaces or the remodelling of old ones, the integration of each classroom with the rest of the school and the school as a whole with the surrounding community is always paramount. Reggio Emilia's preschools are generally filled with indoor plants and vines, and awash with natural light. Classrooms traditionally open to a central piazza, kitchens are in full view, and access to the surrounding community is assured through wall-size windows, courtyards and doors to the outside in each classroom. Entrances capture the attention of both children and adults through the use of mirrors (on the walls, floors, and ceilings), photographs and children's work accompanied by transcriptions of their discussions. These same features characterise classroom interiors, where displays of project work are interspersed with arrays of found objects and classroom materials. In each case, the environment is deliberately constructed to inform and engage learners.

Another supportive element of the environment is ample space for supplies that are frequently rearranged to draw attention to their aesthetic features. In each classroom there are studio spaces in the form of a large, centrally located *atelier* and a smaller mini-*atelier*, and clearly designated spaces for large- and small-group activities. No space is marginal, no corner is unimportant, and each space needs to be alive and open to change.

The term 'osmosis' has been used to describe the relationship of a Reggio Emilia school to the world outside: a school should not be a counter-world but the essence and distillation of the society.[102] Thus the design of these schools must reflect the structure of the community. For instance, their central piazzas reflect city piazzas which are important gathering places; vases, red dishes and tablecloths reflect aspects of the home; images of Power Rangers and Sailor Moon mirror children's popular culture.

As we saw earlier, point of view, the 'learning curriculum' is a 'field of learning resources viewed from the perspective of the learner'. Social perspectives would seem to embrace the key role of the physical design and the organisation of settings and this is supported by a range of research studies.[103] An important question about the learning places we create is 'What does this environment teach'?

NARRATIVE

The role of narrative as a mode of thought and meaning making has been an important strand in the view of learning held by thoughtful literacy teachers and specialists in literary theory, anthropology and history for more than half a century. Such ideas became influential as a result of the work of Barbara Hardy, herself a literary theorist, who published a provocative essay on life and narrative in the early 1960s. This work was an early attempt to approach narrative in cognitive terms: narrative skills were seen 'as a primary act of mind transferred to art from life'.[104] 'What concerns me are the qualities which fictional narrative shares with that inner and outer storytelling', she wrote, 'that play a major role in our sleeping and waking lives. For we dream in narrative, daydream in narrative, remember, anticipate, hope, despair, believe, doubt, plan, revise, criticize, construct, gossip, learn, hate, and love by narrative.'[105]

A couple of decades later, Bruner[106] was to formulate similar ideas in a slightly different way, but also by emphasising the role of narrative in the cognitive process:

> I believe that the ways of telling and the ways of conceptualizing that go with them become so habitual that they finally become recipes for structuring experience itself, for laying down routes into memory; for not only guiding the life narrative up to the present but directing it into the future. I have argued that a life as led is inseparable from a life as told – or more bluntly, a life is not 'how it was' but how it is interpreted and reinterpreted, told and retold.

Western conceptions of narrative implicitly assume forms of linearity, with beginnings and endings (indeed you might say like traditional lesson plans). We believe narrative, however, can be conceived from different perspectives. The anthropologist Mary Douglas[107] has pointed to the way in which non-Western cultures use circularity rather than linearity to provide narrative drive. She says that Western readers' confusion with some Chinese novels or Persian poetry stems from an unfamiliarity with this form of narrative. Writings that baffle and dismay unprepared readers, when read correctly, can turn out to be marvellously controlled and complex compositions. Many epic works in non-Western cultures, she writes, have a distinctive shape: they are constructed in the form of rings. She also points to some Western work (Tristream Shards, for example) where the narrative line can only be understood in terms of circularity.

Here is how the ring works. First there is an introductory section, a prologue that presents the theme and context. The story then proceeds toward its crucial centre: the turning point and climax. Once there, the beginning is invoked again and the tale reverses direction. The second half of the story rigorously echoes the first, using verbal markers – like repetition or changes in style – but still proceeding as a mirror image, as if the writer is walking backwards through the plot. The ending is a return to the beginning. The ring structure also resembles an unrolling thread that is then pulled back onto its spool.

Mary Douglas's ring structure resonates with Bruner ideas of a spiral curriculum and the most creative pedagogic practices, we would suggest, work in these more complex ways.

'Once upon a time'; the telling of the tale, the invitation to listen, the casting of the teller as story teller and the listener as audience – devices that are primal and irresistible

In fact the importance of narrative in learning should come as no surprise. We all read, write and imagine narratives long before and long after formal schooling has taken place. Words spoken as stories, instructions, conversations, remembrances, these all form the basic constituent elements of narrative. Indeed narrative has an astonishing range of other uses – confession, excuses, justification. Certainly, as Bruner has pointed out, we would appear to organise and manage our knowledge of the world and to structure our immediate experience in two broad ways: through logical scientific thinking (an analysis of physical behaviour) and narrative thinking (an analysis of people and their predicaments).[108] No culture is without these approaches, although they clearly privilege them very differently. In our Western culture scientific thinking has become pre-eminent with narrative consigned to those concerned with the arts. Yet 'not knowing' is the condition of the real scientist as much as the student – we live most of our lives in a world constructed according to the rules and devices of narrative. James Stredder, formerly Head of Arts at the University of Wolverhampton, uses narrative as the basis for his highly effective work with young people and adults of various ages in the urban context of Wolverhampton. He argues that it should be harnessed across the disciplines as a pedagogy for encouraging questioning, eliciting competing interpretations, and exploring moral dilemmas, scientific evidence and controversial issues.

James Stredder sees narrative as a key learning mechanism that, he maintains, is effective whatever the object of study.[109] 'The first principle is to take the motive and cue for action from the material itself', he argues. 'This means careful analysis of the structures, conventions and workings of the narrative we are teaching so that we can harness its latent energy. Teaching strategies are derived from that analysis – this applies whether one is teaching Shakespeare, French, history, chemistry ... It also means doing the analysis for oneself and making one's own plans to suit one's situation and way of working.'

In his own field of drama he uses strategies such as concentration exercises that allow individuals to create imagined worlds in their own immediate space, living genealogical diagrams and 'twin pictures'. He identifies three key elements of narrative in his pedagogical approach: its licence of pretence; its structuring of groups; and speech and experience. *Structural* approaches to teaching narrative are the most familiar and easiest to use, he argues. Simple 'tableau' techniques, freeze frames or photographs are disciplined and controlled but enable all the participants to be fully involved. *Dynamic* approaches to narrative develop out of these structured activities: for instance, a group can do a slow motion transition to make a second tableau showing how a narrative transforms the first image to the second. All dynamic approaches focus on the progression and unfolding of the narrative, enactment, doing. *Investigative* approaches, by contrast, lead off with a mental challenge or enigma. The 'hot seating' of a character, for instance, allows them to defend or explain actions that might seem puzzling.

(Continued)

(Continued)

One student describes an exercise in small groups, based on speeches by Horatio and Marcellus in the opening scene of *Hamlet,* in which Stredder asked them to interpret the speech by assigning different lines to each member of the group. 'This exercise encouraged us to think creatively about the different ways in which these speeches could be interpreted on stage and what thought processes an actor might go through when reviewing a speech, allowing us to bounce ideas off one another.' Another exercise in which Hamlet questions Horatio about the details of the ghost's earlier visitation helped 'focus our minds on what was actually being said by Horatio, and how an actor could deliver this. It forced us to consider alternative deliveries of the scene depending upon Hamlet's relationship with his father. How might this scene be different if Hamlet is anxious/frightened/angry/eager at the prospect of a possible meeting with the ghost of his dead father?'

Stredder is clear about the nature of the teacher's role when working with narrative. The teacher is the 'teller', who must 'move over', positioning him/herself within the learning group, involving learners as co-tellers of narrative. In this respect Stredder raises the same tensions inherent in Freire's account of the teacher's role. Teachers' expertise, even their enthusiasm, Stredder argues, can exclude learners from the object of study, yet it is this same expertise that is critical for effective pedagogy. You will recall Freire's argument that the educator has to be an active presence in educational practice. But educators should never allow their active and curious presence to transform the learner's presence into a shadow of the educator's presence. Nor can educators be a shadow of their learners.

In arguing that collaboration and participation are inherent to narrative structure, Stredder sees communication between learners, as well as the expertise of individual members, as being central to the theatrical 'production'. Possibilities are released in the process of collaboration on narrative that allow both for group cohesion and individual absorption and commitment to the subject of study, all essential in his view to the cultural bridging process. He sees pedagogy as being located at the intersection of learners' own knowledge and a critical reading of the narrative, the teachers' own knowledge and objectives, and the teaching relationship.

The *transposability* of narrative is useful in supporting students' literacy development. For example, *Romeo and Juliet* can appear as a play in the theatre, or as a ballet, a cartoon, a musical, or a film – and in all these guises can still maintain a recognisable identity as a story about two feuding families whose respective children fall in love. Narrative, then, is not media specific. It is open to re-interpretation and re-invention across a whole range of communicative modes. In this sense the sequential placement of categories remembered or initialised as narrative propositions might be said to underpin almost every rational thought and action. Narrative is *the* construction we use to make meaning from visual, printed and aural media and a number of narrative schema have been suggested as the basis for a recognition of the form.[110]

If this is the case, why are the kind of pedagogic strategies so powerful in Stredder's work for analysing texts so little used in physics, biology or citizenship? In a recent lecture at the University of Oxford, and we quote from the transcript, Bruner strongly criticised education for neglecting the role of narrative in learning:

> Why are we so intellectually dismissive towards narrative? Why are we inclined to treat it as rather a trashy, if entertaining, way of thinking about and talking about what we do with our minds? Storytelling performs the dual cultural functions of making the strange familiar and ourselves private and distinctive. If pupils are encouraged to think about the different outcomes that could have resulted from a set of circumstances, they are demonstrating usability of knowledge about a subject. Rather than just retaining knowledge and facts, they go beyond them to use their imaginations to think about other outcomes, as they don't need the completion of a logical argument to understand a story. This helps them to think about facing the future, and it stimulates the teacher too.

AFFIRMATION

The theme of narrative introduces the importance of past, present and future possibilities as being integral to the learning process. A process that enables learners to dream forward, as well as to recognise their place in history. Our next theme, *affirmation*, also addresses this important notion of learning as an ongoing process across time, a process that involves significant changes in individuals and their communities as opposed to a process of discrete, unconnected activities. The notion of affirmation, we hope to show, emphasises the importance of a positive approach to the process of assessing learning, while underlining the role of public endorsement of such an assessment.

A range of contemporary and innovative professional development programmes has been developed in post-apartheid South Africa and the ideas of leading Xhosa[111] educators have been central to the conceptualization of learning and teaching on which these are founded. A key concept within traditional Xhosa culture is *ubuntu,* a concept that encapsulates a view of learning and development as being inherently social and community-centred rather than individualistic. It takes seriously the view that we are social beings and reflects a world-view that might be best summarised as humanness: *a person is a person through other persons.* This notion of *ubuntu* serves as the basis for a morality of co-operation, compassion, community (spiritedness) and concern for the interests of the collective and for the dignity of personhood, all the time emphasising the virtues of that dignity in social relationships and practice. As a result the Xhosa people have a powerful tradition of democratic debate that always impresses newcomers. This notion of *ubuntu* surfaced significantly in our joint work with Xhosa educators particularly with regard to issues of assessment for learning. In the course of working together on a range of professional development programmes,[112] this led us to understand the importance of the notion of *affirmation* of learning.

Within the development of the Digital Education Enhancement Project (DEEP) teacher professional development programme, participants were certain that it was not simply the individual teacher who was learning, it was also her learners and their communities. In this sense, while contemporary Western notions of individual competences, assessment frameworks and certification were recognised as useful tools within the new programme, these had to be embedded in a broader cycle in which the community played a key role. The community had to publicly endorse the learning that their teachers achieved and such learning was, in turn, seen to be communally owned. This is also a key feature of Maori pedagogy.

'It is not simply the teacher who is learning, it is also her learners and their communities.' Affirmation ceremony at a rural school in the Eastern Cape, South Africa

For teachers to enrol on a DEEP professional programme, for instance, schools must commit to an action agenda that has been approved, supported and formally signed by members of the community, including the principal teacher, a parent, a governor and a community leader. Ongoing feedback from the teachers on their progress and learning is required and an affirmation ceremony is the culmination of this learning cycle. In such ceremonies, the community physically comes together, both as witnesses to 'culminating performances' by teachers and their learners and also as validators of this learning. These are often inspirational, celebratory and very noisy events!

Such public 'performance assessments' are less well acknowledged in approaches to learning in the West. However, over the last decade the idea of performance assessment has come to represent an important expression of unease with traditional forms of assessment of learning, as well as an expression of hopefulness for the future of education. Performance assessment demands that learners exhibit what they know and what they can do with what they know in a real time dimension. At its best it is also an important opportunity to validate, affirm and celebrate learning. To teach for performance is to believe in the capacity of learners to create and construct knowledge and to assign meaning and praise for what they have learnt and experienced. This approach to assessment for learning has also been called 'teaching for understanding'. The importance of the approach lies in its potential to enhance students' abilities for problem solving, critical analysis, higher-order thinking, or flexible understanding of academic subject matter. Howard Gardner and his colleagues, who have developed the Teaching For Understanding (TFU) Research Project at Harvard, offer the following definitions:

> When a student knows something, the student can bring it forth upon demand – tell us the knowledge or demonstrate the skill. Understanding is a subtler matter, which goes beyond knowing. Understanding is a matter of being able to do a variety of thought-demanding things with a topic – like explaining, finding evidence and examples, generalizing, applying, analogizing, and representing a topic in a new way … In summary, understanding is being able to carry out a variety of *performances* that show one's understanding of a topic and, at the same time, advance it.[113]
>
> I consider an individual to have understood when he or she can take knowledge, concepts, skills and facts and apply them in new situations where they are appropriate. If students simply parrot back what they have been told or what they have read in a textbook, then we do not really know whether they understand.[114]

The TFU Project has created a four-part framework that provides a language for teachers as they plan understanding-oriented classrooms. Four key concepts include: Generative Topics,[115] Understanding Goals,[116] Understanding Performances,[117] and Ongoing Assessment.[118] This framework, in reflecting constructivist beliefs about learning, assumes that teachers have a deep knowledge of their subject as well as pedagogical knowledge. It also assumes a knowledge of the learner and presumes new strategies of classroom interaction. Caswell, for instance, uses a variety of student 'performances' which allow learners to demonstrate their understanding: explanation, interpretation and relating in 'expert groups'; jottings in lab books; questions and theories placed in the knowledge forum; written experiments and hypotheses.

A similar approach is that of authentic assessment. Authentic student work requires the sort of mastery demonstrated by successful adults:

> Persons in diverse fields face the primary challenge of producing, rather than reproducing, knowledge. To progress on this journey, students should set their sights on authentic expressions of knowledge and should hone their skills through guided practice in discourse, in manipulating objects, and in preparing for artistic and musical performances. The conventional curriculum asks students only to identify discourse, things, and performances that others have produced … The production of knowledge must be based upon understanding of prior knowledge, but the mere production of that knowledge does not constitute authentic academic achievement.[119]

Authentic student work possesses three qualities. First, it involves the production of knowledge in the form of discourse (conversation or writing), the production of things (objects), or performance (as in music, dance, athletics, or other public demonstrations of competence). Second, authentic work relies on disciplined inquiry, namely the use of a prior knowledge base, in-depth understanding, and the integration and use of information in new ways. Finally, authentic student work has value beyond evaluation as it possesses aesthetic, utilitarian, or personal value for the student.[120] The ultimate value of authentic student work and assessment is that it enhances student engagement and motivation, tends to sustain hard work, and should cultivate high order thinking and problem solving. The notion of affirmation, we would argue, binds these processes together, providing the glue of encouragement and an emotional context for progress.

As part of the Harvard research, Stone Wiske[121] worked alongside teachers to develop and evaluate a range of pedagogic approaches to Teaching For Understanding in the classroom. Wiske underlines that the TFU framework is neither a set of predetermined scenarios or a recipe for successful practice, nor can it be transmitted and implemented in a direct linear way. As a project, however, it is illustrative of teachers involved in the process of change – cast in the role of learners and starting from some of the key questions about pedagogy we have been exploring thus far. She articulates some of the dilemmas involved in developing any such curriculum framework. The need for clear learning goals, for example, became apparent when teachers attempted to assess students' performances but it was not always easy to extrapolate these. Some of the dilemmas included: distinguishing different kinds of goals, depending on the knowledge being assessed; the competing demands of interest groups such as the students themselves, parents, administrators, politicians; the vague conception of subject matter held by some teachers; being explicit about implicit views of learning. For Wiske and her colleagues the key question for teachers in the programme is what do you want your students to understand by the end of the term or year in your class? Several ways of articulating goals are used to support teachers in the programme, for example throughlines,[122] concept maps and sentence stems.[123] 'Performances of understanding' involve seeing understanding as being both developed and demonstrated by a variety of performances throughout the year. Wiske distinguishes three levels of performances: messing about, guided inquiry, and culminating performances. Examples of methods used include journals, drawing and demonstrations, presentations, visual maps, and experiments.

Fenway High School strongly advocates assessing their students' performance in a variety of ways: classroom-based diagnostics; portfolios; exhibitions; standardised tests; work internships; integrated projects; junior reviews and college acceptances (for seniors). Students are expected to work independently, to demonstrate a mastery of competencies, to learn in the workplace and to exhibit good citizenship through community service. As will be seen from the following letter to senior students, a panel made up of members of the community, governors and parents will be called as to listen to and affirm students' public exhibitions.

'Dear Fenway Seniors,

You now have in your hands the Senior Humanities Portfolio[124] requirements for the class of 2006. To help you to pace your work, your position paper and your Annotated Bibliography are both due before the completed portfolio.

A successful Senior Humanities Portfolio will contain pieces that demonstrate your competence in these areas: creative writing, expository writing, historical research, reading, listening, and artistic expression/appreciation. You will notice that the Senior Portfolio looks a lot like a regular term portfolio in Humanities. It is just like a regular portfolio but all the pieces in your Senior Portfolio will centre around one important person or event of your own choosing. Further, your Senior Portfolio must achieve a very high level of competence and polish. It will not pass with weak research, the wrong format, unstructured paragraphs, or incomplete editing. Please be very careful to follow the directions for each piece and to put real energy and time into your work.

The Senior Portfolio Exhibitions will happen in front of panels from other Humanities classes during the first two weeks of January. You must bring four copies of your research paper to your Exhibition, one for each of your panelists. Your panel will not evaluate your paper but they will need to read it in order to get 'into' your topic. In general terms, you will show to your panel that you can use the Habits of Mind to present and discuss your historical event or person. You will be assessed on whether or not you can offer a fresh perspective on your person/event, give concrete evidence from your thinking and your research to support your ideas, show connections to other people or events, offer suppositions based on your research, and make judgments about the relevance of your study.

Use the Habits of Mind grid that is attached to your portfolio to help you structure your exhibitions. Your portfolio will pass with the Humanities Team only if it is very well done. We wouldn't want you to graduate without showing us that you can think, talk, read, and write well. We know you wouldn't want anything less than that either. Talk to me early and often about your work, your joys, and your trials. I'm available most days before and after school and during D-block. Make an appointment to work with me so we will not be interrupted. Mr____ and Ms____ will also be available for help and encouragement.

(Continued)

(Continued)

Work hard. Have faith. Use your mind well.

Sincerely yours',

The graduate requirements for students who attend Fenway are multiple and demanding.[125] It is worth remembering that Fenway students will have slipped through the cracks of other schools and most are from severely disadvantaged backgrounds. These performances of assessment are not easy, but Fenway expects a good deal of its students – and is rarely disappointed. It is also noteworthy that the students are addressed as equals, with the language of assessment made fully transparent.

Affirmation of learning engages the whole person and sees progress as a process of becoming a new kind of person in the community. A range of strategies is being researched to support the notion of cumulative learning histories. At Deptford Green School in South London, where a new approach to the teaching of citizenship is being piloted, students are using Hyperstudio[126] to build up an electronic history of their achievements including their 'performances of understanding'. This portfolio stores fieldwork, notes and photography, as well as multimedia presentations that students have given to members of the local community about what changes they would like to see locally, how they think this can be achieved and who they will work with to achieve these changes. London's Centre for Literacy in Primary Education, in association with the CfBT Education Trust, is currently carrying out a research project to develop an assessment framework that fully reflects students' achievements in learning through their engagement in a creative curriculum. It is researching existing frameworks that already provide positive models in order to develop a new assessment framework for communication and learning in creative contexts. In particular, it is exploring tools that will recognise, support and affirm progression in learning and teaching. These include a portfolio that will document both collaborative and individual performances of understanding (see the illustration below) for a range of audiences.

The Assessment for Learning research project in the UK[127] has also been concerned with learning mechanisms that encourage student understanding within a supportive, affirmative climate. It has focused particularly on micro strategies that teachers can develop in relation to three specific areas of activity: questioning in the classroom, feedback through marking and peer and self-assessment. This research shows *first* that where teachers allow a longer 'wait time' during whole-class discussions, students soon realise their learning depends less on their capacity to spot the 'right' answers and more on their readiness to express and discuss their own understandings. In this sense teachers shift their role from being presenters of content to leaders of exploration

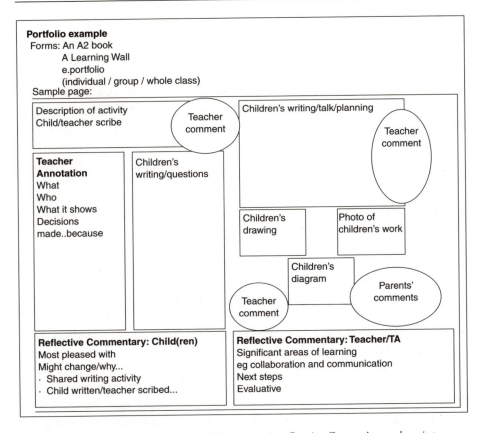

Portfolio example
Forms: An A2 book
         A Learning Wall
         e.portfolio
         (individual / group / whole class)
Sample page:

Portfolio Example: 'Assessing Learning and Communication Creative Contexts' research project, London Centre for Literacy in Primary Education

and the development of ideas. Put simply, 'the only point of asking questions is to raise issues about which teachers need information or about which the students need to think': all students can be actively involved and their learning affirmed. As the Harvard research found, such work demands that teachers and students share clear learning goals. Teachers are also required to develop the 'big questions' that are worth asking and that explore those issues that are critical to students developing understanding.

A *second* focus of this research is the role of quality feedback on students' oral and written work, as distinct from the awarding of grades. The research indicates that when teachers abandon marks, students begin to engage more productively in improving their work in response to detailed, focused, comments. Three key pedagogic strategies are encouraged here: the building up of a shared construct of quality between teachers and students; opportunities for follow up that are explicitly built on shared learning goals developed over time; forms of feedback that overtly develop students' thinking and understanding.

Third, this research has also investigated the role of peer and self-assessment. Students will only achieve understanding, it is argued, when they become experts in self-assessing. Once they have developed an overview of their work and a set of learning goals, they are then empowered to work at a metacognitive level. Peer assessment is an important supplement to this process: 'It is uniquely valuable because students accept criticisms of their work from one another, which they would not take seriously if made by their teacher. Peer work is also valuable because the interchange is in a language that students themselves naturally use, and because students learn by taking the roles of teachers and examiners of others.'[128] None of these public performances of understanding, however, can be dissociated from a positive climate of affirmation in which achievements against personal goals (be they past, present or future ones) rather than failures and competitive comparisons are the key focus of activity.

TRANSFORMATION

So far we have considered eight key themes for learning (expectations, constructivism, intersubjectivity, participation, distributed learning, place, narrative and affirmation). Our final theme is *transformation*. While social theories of learning will provide rich insights for pedagogy, in common with cognitive theories these fail to adequately account for developments of the new, the radical, or indeed for the kind of creativity that inspires new movements across the arts, sciences and humanities. Over the last decade, Yves Engestrom[129] has reinterpreted a theory of learning that combines cognitive and social views of learning[130] to develop his theory of 'learning by expanding'. This work is important, because unlike other learning theorists Engestrom is chiefly preoccupied with ways in which completely new forms of learning, change and innovation occur, especially in the workplace. It introduces this final theme of transformation.

Taking a social perspective, human activity (Engestrom agrees) always takes place within communities. Such communities are governed by particular divisions of labour dictating the differing activities and roles that participants take and by certain rules. Inherent in this process is always a contradictory unity of production and reproduction, invention and conservation.[131] Thinking as a mental process likes (so to speak) to go on in closed systems, he argues. This 'thinking as usual' gives it a wide apparent range and rids it, as completely as possible, of all ultimate uncertainty. But the thinker is more than a thinking machine. So in practice tremendous struggles grow up between those forces that try to reduce all forms of human knowledge to the closed-system variety and those forces that lie behind the human zest for adventure and are continually revolting against and breaking out of the closed system.[132]

In the kinds of learning identified by the constructivists, learners need to be faced with a problem and then to try to solve that problem. This is the case, for example, in May and Caswell's classrooms – and also in the Addenbrooke Hospital case study. In the more expansive, developed modes of learning proposed by Engestrom, the problem or the task itself must be created: problems do not present themselves as givens. They must be constructed from the materials of problematic situations that are puzzling, troubling, and uncertain.[133] In such a process, Engestrom argues, learners become conscious and gain an imaginative and thus potentially practical mastery of whole systems of activity, not simply in terms of immediate issues but in terms of the past, the present and the future. Manifestations of this kind of learning, says Engestrom, are often referred to as 'crises', 'breaking away', 'turning points', or 'moments of revelation'. Bateson, one originator of Engestrom's ideas, has named this process the 'double bind'. Engestrom stresses that where people learn to do things they have not done before, Vygotsky's zones of proximal development are more properly interpreted as a collective rather than individual phenomena. The new is a collective invention in the face of felt dilemmas and contradictions that impede ongoing activity and impel movement and change.[134] An essential feature of this view of learning is the notion that developmental processes do not coincide with learning processes. Rather, the developmental process lags behind the learning, as was Vygotsky's thesis. This view of learning has also much in common with Freire's view of conscientisation, in which 'problem posing' rather than problem solving education demands that the dialogue and the relationship between educator and learner become a critical co-investigation into real-world dilemmas.

We have used Engestrom's model in our study of how colleagues in Albania faced the hugely challenging process of educational reform with which we opened this chapter. This case study, we would argue, is relevant generally to the process of innovation in professional development whatever the setting.

Our research indicated an initial phase in this process of change, which we call **the context of criticism.** It was generated by teachers' experience of a 'double-bind', a dilemma that generates 'stuckness' and prevents progression. '*I dashior mesues*' (*Dear Teachers*) writes one of the key educators, '*Recent years have seen many changes. We have both a need and a desire to change things in our profession. But it has been hard to respond to the many questions such as What is change? Why change? How do we change?... Our society is changing in many different directions. There are new requirements ahead of us. We cannot meet these demands with old concepts and practices.*' This initial phase of activity necessitated educators breaking their encapsulation and moving out of the 'thinking as usual' of traditional practice. They needed to be involved in a critical examination of everyday, familiar ways of working that had been made routine by the Hoxha regime. Tacit practices – the hidden curriculum – as well as the more explicit forms of oppression within classrooms and schools had to be collectively analysed and made explicit. This was a powerful and often fraught and painful process for teachers. Key processes of resisting, questioning, contradicting and debating were engaged in

(Continued)

(Continued)

for the first time ever by teachers countrywide. The Kualida professional development programme facilitated this process, enabling teachers country wide to come together in joint forums to discuss and critique current practices.

In a second overlapping phase, which we have called **the context of discovery**, Albanian educators needed time and space to design a way out of the practice under criticism and to find new models for pedagogic activity. They were provided with time for joint professional development so they could begin to learn something that was not yet there; they acquired their future activity while creating it.[135] In this phase they began processes of experimenting, modelling, symbolising and generalising new forms of teaching activity, supported by critical friends and colleagues facing similar challenges in adjacent countries (such as Hungary).

Finally, many of the teachers were able to move into a third and final phase, **the context of practical social application,** in which they implemented these new, expanded objects of their learning into their own classroom settings. 'It is the opening of a window that breaks the framework of the ex-regime. It is legitimatising a new system in a new educational setting – it is a programme for the future' (School Inspector, Gjirokastra). Here the process of guided experience within communities of practice took centre stage. This transformation of learning into new and challenging areas also demanded the formation of professional networks of support that went well beyond local institutional boundaries.[136]

This transformational view of learning raises key questions for pedagogy about the teacher's role as learner and the nature of structures for professional support. It highlights the importance of collaboration within and across learning settings and collective forums for professional learning.

In the course of this chapter we have identified nine themes around learning. We suggest that each one can provide a set of conceptual tools with which we can explore and interrogate views of learning. They can enable us to revisit and compare approaches to the notion of learner agency, how learners view themselves, the nature and purpose of learning activities, the varied roles and relationships of both teachers and learners and how we construct learning environments. They can also encourage movement between micro issues relating to the quality of discrete learning mechanisms[137] and the big picture of how learners construct their identities and developing life histories.[138]

5

Knowledge

At the heart of the pedagogic process is the space in which the planned, enacted and experienced come together.

Knowledge profoundly influences pedagogy. And pedagogy can transform knowledge in myriad ways. This symbiotic relationship is central to any understanding of pedagogic processes and ambitions. Knowledge is intrinsically linked to the way our minds make sense of the world. The dispositions we elaborated on in the previous chapter are manifest in knowledge contexts. We have, for example, argued the importance of seeing learning as a social process, something that does not happen just 'inside the head' but through interaction with the world around us. And that involves not just the physical world but the knowledge we have of what others know. Our minds have very sophisticated ways of thinking through such contexts. Henri Bergson points this up in an essay entitled 'Laughter: An Essay on the Meanings of the Comic'[1] where he asks us to imagine our minds working contrary to the sophisticated ways we take for granted:

> Suppose, then, we imagine a mind always thinking of what it has just done and never of what it is doing, like a song which lags behind its accompaniment. Let us try to picture to ourselves a certain inborn lack of elasticity, of both senses and intelligence, which brings it to pass that we continue to see what is no longer visible, to hear what is no longer audible, to say what is no longer to the point: in short, to adapt ourselves to a past and therefore imagining situation, when we ought to be shaping our conduct in accordance with the reality which is present. (page 6)

It takes a fair degree of intellectual elasticity to get our 'heads round that'. We use this vernacular phrase purposefully because popular imagination does see the exercise of each of our minds as being in the head rather than in the social knowledge communities through which our learning takes place.

Bergson's imaging is, of course, impossible in the real world (although our capacity to imagine and 'know' unreal world situations is one of the defining characteristics of our creativity). Our intellectual curiosity is always wandering ahead. It is because we have minds and engage in a wide variety of mental activities that are inextricably social in nature that we have a concept of education. Some see education as the development of the mind. Our concept of the mind, however, is much wider than this would imply. As we saw in the previous chapter the mind is an elusive concept, a rather mysterious entity – distinct from the body but acting upon it, with a form of life peculiarly its own. A form of life that is better expressed through adjectives than nouns. Imaginative, creative, persevering, for example, are ways of expressing aspects of the mind, even potentialities, that transcend and belie any fixed notion of mental capacity.[2]

In this way pedagogic understanding has to embrace a wide interpretation of what we have come to mean by knowledge. Too narrow a conception of knowledge leaves large parts of our mental life untouched. Knowledge can too easily become a commodity, almost literally information for delivery to the empty head. A wider and more generous interpretation of knowledge allows a special relationship between the education of children, or others, and the growth of knowledge. To know more and better does not seem to be one among several kinds of mental activity. It has a privileged place.

The knowledge dimension of pedagogy is manifest in many ways. What types of knowledge, for example, can be introduced or encouraged in a pedagogic setting? A common reference point in responding to this question is the distinction between propositional (knowing that) and procedural (knowing how) knowledge.[3] There have been strong arguments that curriculum planning and teaching focus excessively on the former, particularly in formal school contexts. And the distinction has provoked considerable philosophical controversy. Paul Hurst, for example, has argued that all knowledge is of the 'knowing that' variety and that the distinction cannot be made. 'Knowing how' knowledge, he argued, is essentially 'knowing that'[4] plus experience. Freire accepted this distinction:

> In the first moment, that of the experience of and in daily living, my conscious self is exposing itself to facts, to deeds, without, nevertheless, asking itself about them, without looking for their 'reason for being'. I repeat that the knowing 'because' there is also 'knowing' that results from these involvements is that made from pure experience. In the second moment, in which our minds work epistemologically, the methodological rigor with which we come closer to the object, having 'distanced ourselves' from it, that is, having objectified it, offers us another kind of knowing, a knowing whose exactitude gives to the investigator or the thinking subject a margin of security that does not exist in the first kind of knowing, that of common sense.[5]

To us there seems value for the teacher in reflecting on the different categories of types of knowledge that can be constructed. In the CSILE project in Ontario, the ideas of Carl Bereiter and Marlene Scardamalia have been influential and central to thinking about the forms of pedagogic settings.[6] They suggest a five-fold distinction:

- formal knowledge;

- procedural knowledge;

- informal knowledge;

- impressionistic knowledge;

- self-regulatory knowledge.

The first two categories repeat the 'knowing that'/'knowing how' distinction. Informal knowledge is somewhere between the two. It represents knowledge we use in problem solving but somehow cannot formulate in words. Others have referred to this as tacit knowledge. A very experienced teacher may know how to act in a variety of settings but may not always have the words to communicate this to novices. In all sorts of organisations tacit knowledge is increasingly recognised as being crucial to achieving goals. Hence the importance now being given to the informed guesses and hunches of creative organisations.[7] It is this type of knowledge with its hesitations and uncertainties (what Freire called 'epistemological inquietude') that can cause much misgiving, perhaps to the point of being shut out in formal learning and teaching situations.

Impressionistic knowledge is even more difficult to define. It refers to that background knowledge which can, in an amorphous way, exert a strong influence on the positions we take up. We both have strong recollections of 'discovering Shakespeare' (one of us through *Macbeth*, the other through *Much Ado About Nothing*) and the impression that left with us.

Self-regulatory knowledge, which may include elements of the other four, refers to a personal understanding of strengths and weaknesses – those ways in which we personally come to have ideas about what works for us.

Others have taken the ways of our type of knowing approach to explore key situations.

The Women's Ways of Knowing Project focused specifically on the ways women think. Culminating in a book entitled *Women's Ways of Knowing: The Development of Self, Voice and Mind*, Mary Field Belenky, Blythe McVicker Clinchy, Nancy Rule Goldberger and Jill Mattuck Tarule analysed and coded 135 in-depth interviews that asked women about their gender, their relationships, their ways of knowing and their moral dilemmas.

From their research, they formulated a theory consisting of **fives types of knowing** by which women perceive themselves and approach the world. They saw that the ways that women think about education and learning also affect their self-perception.

The first of these ways of knowing is **silence**, that by blindly following authority and sticking with stereotypes provides a very hard time in defining oneself.

(Continued)

(Continued)

Next is **received knowledge**, where one listens to the voices of others, followed by **subjective** knowledge, where one listens to oneself and severs the sense of obligation to follow other views.

The next category is **procedural** knowledge, consisting of connected knowing and separate knowing. Connected knowers believe that truth is personal, particular, and grounded in firsthand experience. They attempt to find truth through listening, empathising, and taking impersonal stances to information, whereas separate knowers completely exclude their feelings from making meaning rely and strictly on reason.

The last way of knowing that Belenky *et al.* define is **constructed knowledge**, where one integrates one's own opinions and sense of self with reason and the outside world.

It is this sort of analysis that prompted the CSILE project to look at the limitations of existing pedagogical settings, particularly the didactic emphasis of 'telling about' without recourse to the wider range of strategies which utilise and build other types of knowledge. The pedagogic settings of CSILE formulated a wider conception of knowing, one that reflected different principles of knowledge building.

Twelve principles of knowledge building

1 **Real ideas and authentic problems**   In the classroom as a knowledge building community, learners are concerned with understanding based on their real problems in real world.

2 **Improvable ideas**   Students' ideas are regarded as improvable objects.

3 **Idea diversity**   In the classroom, the diversity of ideas raised by students is necessary.

4 **Rise above**   Through a sustained improvement of ideas and understanding, students create higher level concepts.

5 **Epistemic agency**   Students themselves find their way in order to advance.

6 **Community knowledge, collective responsibility**   Students' contribution to improving their collective knowledge in the classroom is the primary purpose of the knowledge building classroom.

7 **Democratising knowledge**   Every individual is invited to contribute to knowledge advancement in the classroom.

8 **Symmetric knowledge advancement**. A goal for knowledge building communities is to have individuals and organisations actively working to provide a reciprocal advance of their knowledge.

9   **Pervasive knowledge building** Students contribute to collective knowledge building.

10 **Constructive uses of authoritative sources** All members, including the teacher, sustain inquiry as a natural approach to sustaining their understanding.

11 **Knowledge building discourse** Students are engaged in discourse to share with one another, and to improve knowledge advancement in the classroom.

12 **Concurrent, embedded and transformative assessment** Students take a global view of their understanding and then decide how to approach their assessments. They create and engage in assessments in a variety of ways.[8]

We have found a number of examples of knowledge building that adopt such a social participatory approach.

The University of Manchester's BSc course in biology has used mentoring and fieldwork to produce a highly innovative approach. We asked one of the students to describe the experience:

The scheme was initially constructed to help students with more difficult subjects or modules, with the teachers drawing up worksheets that the students would go over together. The scheme had evolved by the time I became involved into something that the students had a lot more control over. The lecturers would be involved in sessions with the student mentors to go over what was being found difficult, what input they might be able to give, etc. Activities were gradually becoming more creative; I remember a mind map that I constructed with the students I was mentoring in which I laid out the skeleton of a map and the students worked together using textbooks and their own resources to pack it out, the aim was to get them to think in categories. The crossword was more a factual test but also to get them thinking more abstractly about the information they were being given in lectures. The scheme aimed to get students working in a sharing way, providing routes to answers but not answers themselves; there was a strong message that student mentors were not able to give answers out. The group, led in the latter part of my third year, and developed strong friendships and trust in a group that they could feel comfortable asking questions in. I felt this was especially important in an environment where large numbers were attending lectures, and occasionally unapproachable lecturers tended to deter younger, more timid students from asking the questions that often many of their peers were thinking too.

The field trip dimension to the programme was amazing; I went to Greece to study freshwater biology, and to Ecuador to study tropical

(Continued)

(Continued)

biology. On both trips I had a strong feeling that the university had made an effort to be involved with and help local education where possible. In Greece our base was a local wildlife learning centre used by schools (primary and secondary) in the area to learn about their environment. The presentations we created on the local lake and river were passed on and used afterwards with the schools. In Ecuador, Spanish students were encouraged to give English lessons to the Payamino we stayed with; we had local guides and were encouraged to be aware of their culture and traditions with respect to their environment as well as in general. We were staying in a really rural part of the Amazon, two hours canoe from the nearest town with any kind of healthcare. I helped rig up the solar panels that powered the few lights we had and the laptops when it came to writing up our reports. There was a great debate raging as to whether or not we should be using laptops; there was a sense that given the situation we were in it would perhaps be more practical to use pen and paper but maybe that was a little romantic? Writing up the reports electronically was of benefit to both lecturers and students. Those who were collecting massive amounts of data were able to electronically compute in moments statistics and data that were vital for making any real deductions about their experiments. Lessons in Ecuador consisted of nature walks in the jungle, both at night and during the day. We learnt to recognise common species of both flora and fauna which was then tested in a *University Challenge*-style quiz. We were also taught how to survey the plants and trees of an area in the traditional way used by explorers since the beginning, including how to identify the species by using complicated dichotomous keys …

It is rare to find such examples of experimentation in higher education. However, as this phase of education expands there is increasing concern about the quality of teaching supplied and some highly innovative work of this sort can increasingly be found.

Here we can see that an analysis of different types of knowledge has profoundly influenced the way a pedagogic setting is conceived and conceptualised. The ideas here, we suggest, could be transposed to many classrooms or learning situations irrespective of their geographical context.

In the categories of types of knowledge, formal propositional knowledge has an important place. But as with the typological, forms of knowledge have been the subject of much debate. The way knowledge has come to be organised represents a socially constructed and situated process. The intellectual lineage of subjects such as science or history may be a long one but it had to be created as such and some interesting studies in the history of subjects have shown just how contested that could be. Such controversies surface with some regularity in political and public debate. Should Shakespeare be compulsory in the teaching of English? How should biology address the question of evolution? Some teachers have identities that are inseparable from a subject.

When we remember our maths or language teacher we will simultaneously think about mathematics or French, and with history too we will tend to remember specific knowledge terms, just as the daughter and mother discussed the subject in Elio Vi Horinsi's novel *Conversations in Sicily*.

> Don't you remember anything from your school days?
> She [mother]: 'I only went up to third year.'
> And I [daughter]: 'You must have studied a little history.'
> She: 'Mazzini and Garibaldi.'
> I: 'And Caesar, Musius Scaevola, Cincinnatus, Coriolanus. Don't you remember anything about the History of Rome?'
> She: 'I remember what Cornelia, the mother of Gracchi, said.'
> I: 'Good! What did Cornelia say?'
> She: 'She said that her children were her jewels.'
> I: 'See? Cornelia was proud of her children.'
> Now my mother smiled. 'How silly!', she exclaimed.

History then is remembered in terms of Garibaldi or Cornelia rather than the weighing of evidence or the methodologies of historical investigation.

Here knowledge is conceived of in terms of the content or subject content. The selection of such content raises important questions.[9] Is the evidence being presented correct? Has a particular interpretation of evidence stood the test of time? Propping up such questions, however, are deeper structures in the organisation of knowledge. Let us take three examples here[10] – the stratification of knowledge, the growth of knowledge, and the way different fields of knowledge interconnect.

The way some kinds of knowledge come to be more valued than others is not a matter of chance, but rather the playing out of power relations in any group. This can work in a formal political way, such as which subjects are to be included in a national curriculum, or in more informed subtle ways, such as the way senior academic members of a university research group might work to exclude certain ideas and approaches. The choices research councils make about which areas of research to fund illustrate another power dimension. There need not be anything sinister or dysfunctional about this[11] because the exercise of such power relations is part and parcel of the human condition, but this does mean a stratification of knowledge which needs to be seen and understood. This can happen as much within as between subjects. Gary Spruce,[12] for example, looking at the teaching of music, has shown for just how long the guardians of the music curriculum held out against popular and world music displacing the nineteenth century canon of great composers. And in the same way, just how long it took to allow children to make music before learning the basics of musical notation.

A recent example of the way in which power can be exercised in relation to knowledge and curriculum was the formulation of the National Curriculum for England and Wales in the late 1980s. The then Conservative

1904	1935	1988
English language	English language	English*
English literature	English literature	A modern language
One language	One language	Geography
Geography	Geography	History
History	History	Mathematics*
Mathematics	Mathematics	Science*
Science	Science	Art
Drawing	Drawing	Physical education
Due provision for manual work and physical exercises (Housewifery in girls' schools)	Physical exercise and organised games	Music
	Singing	Technology
	Manual instruction for boys, dramatic subjects for girls	

* = core foundation subjects
National Curriculum in England and Wales 1904–1988

government of Margaret Thatcher was determined, as they perceived it, to impose a 'traditional' curriculum based on established subjects. They saw no merit in interdisciplinary approaches to the curriculum, or even at school level the sort of prevocational and vocational approaches adopted in their own recent technical and vocational initiatives.[13] The consequence of this was a National Curriculum that had few differences in character to that laid down for the first state run secondary schools at the beginning of the twentieth century (see the table above).[14]

The build up of each of the subject areas of the National Curriculum then became socially and politically contested, with some subjects such as history and English provoking ongoing controversy.

Alongside this stratification of knowledge comes the question of specialisation and the ongoing ways in which knowledge comes to be construed through an increasingly differentiated perspective. This is perhaps most evident in medicine where, at the consultant level, status and respect have become associated with increasingly specialised knowledge. Our medical friends tell us that at the end of the twentieth century a gynaecologist would have been expected to have a knowledge of cancers. Just a few years on, however, specialists have emerged focusing on gynaecology and cancers. Michael Young[15] has referred to this as the 'property' aspect of the stratification of knowledge, or the way in which access to knowledge in modern societies is controlled by professionals and other experts. Such power structures can serve to make for relatively open or relatively closed relations between knowledge areas. In our experience at the secondary school and university level establishing links between knowledge areas is difficult. It is noticeable, for example, that research councils across the world have had to introduce interdisciplinary areas of research into issues such as global warming or ethnic conflict as a way of overcoming the barriers between knowledge areas.

Today knowledge is constantly in a state of tumult. In every field new ideas and new discoveries are profoundly challenging accepted wisdoms and even questioning the disciplinary boundaries that seem so monolithically to define the school curriculum. Analyses of the exponential growth of knowledge are numerous. There is some fairly robust evidence to suggest, for example, that technical knowledge is doubling every two years. Anyone starting on a three year degree course can now find in Year 3 that the knowledge from Year 1 is simply out of date. We know that 3000 books are published daily and these are in traditional hard copy format. The web expands publishing even more.

It is a fair certainty that the epistemological debate that surrounds the curriculum, particularly in the formal institutions of education, schools and universities, will continue and become even more vexed. Perhaps one of the major challenges of the twenty-first century is the way in which teachers and then formal institutions adapt to the changing and expanding knowledge base of society. Pedagogy needs, therefore, to be understood in terms of historical and contemporary contestations about knowledge. Subjects or content are not handed down but made.

The forms and structures of knowledge are also important for learners. The maps of knowledge constructed by a teacher are not necessarily self-evident to the learner. A young child has no innate understanding of the National Curriculum, although at an early age they might begin to pick up some general understanding about the way the world handles knowledge (early years dictionaries, even encyclopaedias, are now commonplace).[16] As Jerome Bruner has said, children, like adults, are seen as constructing a model of the world to aid them in construing their experience.[17] Pedagogy then becomes the process to help them understand better, more powerfully, less one sidedly.

This is an important point. With Bruner we strongly believe that the initiation of learners into the currently understood structure of knowledge is a key aspect of the pedagogic endeavour. And we view with some scepticism any attempt to build a model of pedagogy that sees the child, as opposed to the curriculum, as the starting point for learning and teaching. Each represents a starting point.[18]

Acquiring and building content knowledge is, therefore, an important part of teachers' initial and ongoing professional development. Teaching, we would agree with Lee Shulman, is essentially a learned profession.[19] Teachers are members of a scholarly community. They must understand the structure of subject matter, the principles of conceptual organisation and the principle of inquiry that help answer two kinds of question. What are the important ideas and skills in this domain? How are new ideas added and deficient areas dropped by those who are recognised to be the experts in this domain?[20]

Pedagogy, as Brian Simon has strongly articulated,[21] begins with a formulation of what has to be known, namely the process of defining the objectives of teaching, and from this pedagogical means can be defined and established.

This approach, as we have indicated, is the opposite of basing the educational process solely on learners, and their immediate interests and spontaneous activity, with the futile search for a total differentiation of the learning process on an individual basis.

Pedagogy is a social, collective process. It requires an engagement with groups as well as individuals, and learning expectations that go beyond the personal. In some societies an orientation to the group rather than the individual is taken for granted. We remember, for example, sitting in on a Japanese teacher's termly meeting with parents when the parents en masse were being chastised for the slow progress of the class. An individualistic approach to learning and teaching does derive from philosophical traditions that, while strong in Northern Europe and North America, are less significant in other parts of the world. We believe that the wholesale individualisation of learning and teaching is highly undesirable. Children (and adults) learn best when they learn with one another, with common goals and common forms of evaluation assessing progress towards, and the achievement of, such goals. Individualisation can often be associated with another perspective which can be misunderstood, even abused: namely the notion of readiness to learn. In Chapter 3 we were critical of deterministic ideas about ability and potential. We are similarly concerned that naïve ideas about maturation can curtail pedagogic ambition. In particular, overzealous and mechanical interpretations of Piaget's developmental psychology had a distorting influence on the pedagogic models and the ideas of many teachers, particularly in the early primary years. One of the strongest critics of this organic view of development, Lev Vygotsky, argued that the approach led to a pedagogical pessimism.[22] In Vygotsky's view, if a child showed an incapacity to deal with or insufficient understanding of a certain field, one should concentrate every effort on this deficiency and compensate for it through pedagogic means.

It was this idea that so influenced Jerome Bruner. His seminal text published in 1960, entitled *The Process of Education*, argued that schools waste a great deal of people's time by postponing the teaching of important areas because they are deemed 'too difficult'. Bruner began with the hypothesis:

> that any subject can be taught effectively in some intellectually honest form to any child at any stage of development.

And from this Bruner derived two important ideas. The first was the importance of making structures in learning central to the pedagogic process:

> the learning and teaching of structure, rather than simply the mastering of facts and techniques, is at the centre of the classic problem of transfer … If earlier learning is to render later learning explicit, it must do so by providing a general picture in terms of which the relations between things encountered earlier and later are made as clear as possible. (page 12)

The second was the concept of the 'spiral curriculum', whereby a curriculum as it develops should repeatedly revisit the basic ideas that make up the general picture, building upon them until the student has grasped the full formal apparatus that goes with them. It was this approach that led to the controversial MACOS project we discussed in Chapter 2. For Bruner, therefore, pedagogy involved a process of curriculum creation. The building and constructing of knowledge as a social process, becomes, literally, one of the teacher's most important tasks. We believe that the process of identifying the big ideas and working pedagogic strategies around these is important. It might be seen as self-evident, but much curriculum design (including many formal regulatory syllabuses) is often about coverage rather than structure, and coverage is often the enemy of understanding.

By making the organisation of the curriculum central to the pedagogic process, we have to reflect on the structure of knowledge. For many teachers, as we have already noted, their very identity is linked to a certain subject, and subjects, disciplines or domains can have a very strong hold on the forms of knowledge that schools especially are given the responsibility to teach.

Disciplines, however, are not equal in their structure, power and status. Some will appear to have strong boundaries (mathematics), while others are more fluid in the forms they take (social studies).[23] Some disciplines have a direct titular link to the high status knowledge of universities (science), while other parts of the curriculum can have a more temporal, even political, form (citizenship, as taught in England, is one example that comes to mind)[24] that would not be accorded the descriptor of 'discipline'. Some disciplines also appear to have a more overt, linear, sequential structure (French) than others (art), although how pronounced this sort of juxtaposition really is remains a matter of some dispute.

Over the years the importance of the disciplines of knowledge, as they have been created over the centuries, has been the source of much disputation. The hegemony of the traditional disciplines, for example, legitimised by traditional and established forms of authority has been frequently challenged. They do, however, provide important points of reference that seep into all the corners of our pedagogic endeavours. Here we return to Bruner,[25] who in a more recent expansion of his ideas has stressed the importance of knowledge that has been accumulated in the past. This is how he puts it:

> Now to pedagogy. Early on, children encounter the hoary distinction between what is known by 'us' (friends, parents, teachers and so on) and what in some larger sense is simply 'known'. In these post positivist, perhaps 'post modern' times we recognise all too well that the 'known' is neither God-given truths nor, as it were, written irrevocably in the Book of Nature. Knowledge in this dispensation is always putatively revisable. But revisability is not to be confused with free-for-all relativism ... teaching should help children grasp the distinction between personal knowledge, on the one side, and 'what is taken to be known' by the culture, on the other. But they must not only grasp this distinction, but also understand its basis, as it were in the history of knowledge. How can we incorporate such a perspective in our pedagogy? Stated another way,

what have children gained when they begin to distinguish what is known canonically from what they know personally and idiosyncratically? (page 61)

The disciplines, therefore, become more than a framing reference for pedagogy, rather they nurture and feed the forms of pedagogy that evolve to serve the sorts of interests Bruner outlines. This is the very knowledge base of teaching – the intersection of content and pedagogy. The main task of teachers then becomes to transpose the context knowledge they possess into forms that are pedagogically powerful.[26]

We use the word 'transpose' to some purpose. In creating pedagogically appropriate formulations of knowledge the teacher's task is to transpose and not to transform. Such a process, we believe, requires much thought and ingenuity and represents a dimension to pedagogy that needs practice and strengthening.

We derive the notion of transposition from the European tradition in the study of didactics. This has received little attention in the Anglo-American research world despite a well developed and extensive literature.[27] We want to explore this perspective through the work of Yves Chevellard and André Verret.[28] In different knowledge domains they have developed the concept of didactic transposition, a process by which subject knowledge is transformed into school knowledge and an analytical category in its own right, permitting us both to understand and question the process by which disciplinary transformations take place. The range of historical examples in Verret's work also provides for the social and ideological dimensions of the construction of knowledge. *La transposition didactique* is defined as a process of change, alteration and restructuring which the subject matter must undergo if it is to become teachable and accessible to novices or children. As this work is less known and less accessible to English-speaking discourse, we will give a little more space to an explanation here. Verret's original thesis was that school knowledge, in the way it grows out of any general body of knowledge, is inevitably codified, partial, formalised and ritualised. Learning in this context is assumed to be programmable and defined in the form of a text, syllabus or national curriculum, with a conception of learning that implies a beginning and an end, an initial state and a final state. Verret argued that knowledge in general cannot be sequenced in the same way as school knowledge and that generally learning is far from being linear. Such a model, he suggested, lacks cognitive validity as it does not take into account the schemes, constructed representations and personal constructs of the learner.

Verret's thesis is illustrated by a range of historical examples. He describes, for instance, the transformation of literature and divinatory magic into the scholastic forms of Confucian schooling and of Christian metaphysics into school and university philosophy. He looks in detail at the version of Latin that was constructed for the French schools of the seventeenth century and the way that this evolved didactically in the centuries that followed.

For Chevellard, as with Verret, 'didactic objects', (which could be termed school knowledge), are under constant interpretation and reinterpretation, a process which operates at a number of different levels. The didactic transformation of knowledge, therefore, becomes a progressive selection of relevant knowledge, a sequential transmission involving a past and a future, and a routine memory of evolutionary models of knowledge.

These ideas go with the grain of Bruner's proposition that the learning and teaching of structure, rather than simply the mastering of facts and techniques, are at the core of the pedagogic process. We return to this in Chapter 6 where we explore a model for understanding teachers' professional knowledge.

In this tentative exploration of the knowledge dimension of pedagogy we have described a number of interrelated perspectives. First, that our understanding of the ways in which knowledge can be typified offers important creative possibilities for transforming pedagogy. A stronger analysis of the types of knowledge we use ourselves, and that we encounter in learners, offers significant possibilities for extending the repertoire of strategies we bring to our modelling and practice of pedagogic activity.

Second, that knowledge creation is a social process with knowledge domains constantly in a process of flux and expansion, often into increasingly specialised sub-groupings. In an important sense this can be seen as illustrative of the power of pedagogy. Those on the front line of research in any field have to try to communicate (teach) not only the commonly known but also the new, and perhaps contested, insights and understandings. The process of transposition works from the most basic to the most advanced of institutional pedagogic settings.

Third, in creating a curriculum we have to be aware of the way the relations of power influence our designs. This perspective also works at many levels, including that ever-present human propensity to establish barriers and frontiers of a form and strength that transcend any practical purpose. We both remember, for example, in the range of secondary schools we have worked in the strident debates about the organisation of the science curriculum. Should the curriculum be organised around topics like global warming or environmental problems rather than physics, chemistry or biology or earth sciences? And if it were the latter, what curriculum weight should be given to each? In England this debate has led to constant changes in the organisation of the science curriculum, with more than one 'Royal Society' representing the traditional sciences weighing in to protect their subject. Such power relations work in other types of knowledge domains. There are ongoing arguments in vocational subjects about the relative weight that can be given to generic skills and understandings (communication skills, numeracy) as opposed to the practical realisation of those skills and understandings in specific vocational domains (plumbing, electrical work, information technology).

The fourth perspective that we have outlined is that the initiation of learners into an understanding of the deeper structures that have come to frame knowledge areas is an essential part of the building of meaning. This has led some to argue that the classroom should try to replicate the authentic settings that scientists or mathematicians inhabit.[29] And in this, as we have learnt from

Vygotsky and Bruner, the pedagogic process rather than trying to develop individual understanding independent of others (too often the implicit, even explicit, *modus vivendi* of many classrooms) more appropriately gives due attention to individuals 'as they become fully effective, functioning members of communities'. In other words you do not acquire 'the knowledge'. Rather knowledge building is a social process which may precede the appropriation[30] of certain skills and understandings into a personal repertoire.

In this way knowledge and learning became inseparable. Different forms of knowledge may presuppose certain forms of pedagogic activity (contrast the work of the science or art teacher). But in general terms knowledge building is a social process. At the heart of the pedagogic process is the space in which the planned, enacted and experienced come together.[31] It presupposes a view that cognition, activity and the world mutually constitute each other.

6

Toolkits

Culture shapes the mind ... it provides us with the toolkit by which we construct not only our worlds but our very conception of our selves and our powers. Without these tools, whether symbolic or material, we are not a 'naked ape' but an empty abstraction.

During the summer I (Jenny Leach) made the steep climb from a small, verdant valley in Perigord to the entrance of a rocky, natural auditorium, its hollowed out and bulging flanks worn by water and time. Through a narrow, upright gash in the rock near the top of the cliff I entered a deep cave known as Font-de-Gaume, its high but narrow main gallery and numerous side passages going far into the mountainside. I was tremendously excited. The little I knew about prehistoric painted caves came from photographs in books and magazines. Now, some of these paintings were right in front of me in all their magnificence! There were rotund bison drawn in gentle curving lines, with deep, expressive eyes and tiny legs drawn in perfect perspective. Mammoths with long, curved tusks standing placidly beside a woolly rhinoceros. Horses outlined in black, now partially obscured by natural excretions, leaping across the cave wall. Most impressive of all were two large reindeer facing each other. The one on the right, a female, was on her knees. The male on left, whose antlers formed a long magnificent arc, had

(Continued)

(Continued)

gently lowered his head toward her and had begun licking the top of her brow. The grandeur of the male and the delicacy of the female in this quiet moment, so intimate and tender, made the painting irresistible and touching. I was astonished by the way the Magdalenian artists, working some 17,000 years ago, had used the contours of the cave wall to enhance their art, something even a quality photograph cannot convey. The powerful shoulders of one animal, for instance, had been painted over a bulge of rock, making the muscles swell realistically. In this sense the animal was as much suggested by the natural rock as imposed by the artist onto the surface. A frieze of bison curved around the wall of the cave, appearing in three-dimensional movement in the flickering lamplight. Their legs in perfect perspective, this added to the strong illusion that they were charging down the cave's narrow corridor.

These startling paintings demonstrated high levels of artistry, with many punctuated with indecipherable symbols – possibly an elaborate code – with each variation having a specific meaning (a number or clan or time of year?). The signs seemed to identify the paintings in some way, classifying or ordering them. It gave me a start to realise that, for the artists at least, the paintings by themselves were not enough. As they worked by the light of simple stone lamps, using reindeer shoulder-blades as palettes to hold their pigments of red and yellow ochre, haematite, manganese oxide and charcoal, these painters were giving their work a gloss, an elaboration.

Humankind is not depicted, but the few representations found elsewhere of the Magdalenian people are somewhat startling – wearing shoes, trousers, coats, and even hats, with the men clean-shaven. Sewn clothes, tailored with collars and sleeves, as well as bracelets and necklaces and the remains of numerous bone needles (with tiny eyes) have been found together with obsidian 'razors'. The Magdalenians are best known for their elaborately worked bone, antler and ivory items. Examples of their mobile art include figurines and intricately engraved projectile points, as well as items for personal adornment including sea shells and perforated carnivore teeth (presumably as necklaces) plus fossils together with musical instruments – even bone calendars carved with symbolic notations.[1]

We are unlikely to know the true meaning of these paintings, created as they were some 17,000 years ago. Font-de-Gaume is deeply imbued with purposes we can't decipher. The potency is palpable, but we are culturally blind to its meaning. In one sense we know a lot about the traditions and selections of artefacts that make Magdalenian culture quite distinct from that, say, of the San Peoples, who were also executing exquisite cave paintings of bushbuck and antelopes in South Africa's Drakensburg Mountains around the same period. We can make informed guesses about these people's everyday lives and activity. Yet we know nothing of the values, beliefs, world views, human roles and relationships that both shaped and were shaped by these marvellously rich artefacts, tools and activities – because we are unable to penetrate the totality of the cultural 'toolkit'. Culture becomes central here, meaning both 'a whole way of life' and 'ordinary'.[2] In seeking to understand our ancient origins, I came away from Font-de-Gaume with a deep conviction of connectedness and humility at the power of human communities. Yet I also had a new understanding of how the inseparable material and symbolic aspects of our cultural 'toolkits' shape and facilitate human activity, learning and development.[3]

In this chapter we want to develop further this concept of a 'toolkit': the multifaceted, shared, repertoire of values, concepts and dispositions, stories of practice, rituals and protocols, together with physical tools and artefacts, from which individuals and groups make differing selections in order to construct lines of activity and forms of life.[4] We believe the metaphor is at once simple and profound in relation to pedagogy. First, because it brings together many of the ideas about the mind, identity, learning, knowledge and community that have been developed in previous chapters. Second, because it reconciles the seemingly competing views about the mind and learning (acquisition/symbol processing and participative/social) discussed in Chapter 4. Third, because it enables us to foreground the rich complexity of material and symbolic arte-facts, tools and technologies that we rely on daily. They are critical for advances in human understanding across the centuries and therefore fundamental to our activities, identities and meaning making as educators, yet they are so often overlooked, we will argue, in contemporary discussions of pedagogy.

In Chapter 4 we noted the importance within pedagogy of *symbolic* tools of the mind,[5] particularly language and the notion of learning mechanisms such as heuristics and other conceptual tools. In this chapter we will look at the interrelationship between *symbolic* and *material* tools and artefacts in more depth and the key and sometimes transforming roles they play in the devel-opment of learning and knowledge building. As Bruner has emphasised, how our *mind* works is itself dependent on the physical tools at its disposal. How the *hand* works, for example, cannot be fully appreciated unless one also takes into account whether it is equipped with a screwdriver, a pair of scissors, or a laser gun. Physical tools and artefacts are the instruments that define and shape our work and thinking even before we complete them – the spirit-level begets the horizontal measurer, and the rebus was used for building the pyramids long before there was a theory of mechanics.[6]

To this extent physical tools and artefacts are integral to and also shape dif-ferent ways of knowing and thinking about the world. The material evidence, documents and artefacts of the past, for example, help to inform and shape the systematic historian's 'mind', which 'works' in many respects rather differently from the mind of the classic 'teller of tales' (we might substitute here *teacher of history* and *teacher of literature*) with her stock of combinable myth-like mod-ules. Similarly, a myriad physical technologies and artefacts help shape the nature and development of contemporary scientific thinking. Yet scientific knowledge is not something that exists objectively 'out there', as discussed in our previous chapter. It is a tool in the mind of the knower, whether as sci-entist, science teacher or novice student.[7]

It is these insights that have led some commentators to develop the notion that individuals and groups draw on a multidimensional *cultural toolkit* when par-ticipating in the activities that comprise their multiple identities – be it a bas-ketball game, a family reunion or a day at the office. Such toolkits can be defined as identifiable repertoires that bind together shared customs and knowledge, activities, rituals and events, and symbolic tools, as well as a range of material technologies and artefacts. In this sense scientific toolkits lead to radically different ways of perceiving and acting on the world from those adopted by historians, philosophers, engineers, plumbers, or artists. By the same token the tools and artefacts that support and shape such diverse practices are themselves radically diverse, be they test tubes/scanners/hammers/ancient records/archaeological implements/sports equipment/musical instruments/paints and canvas, though some (such as pens/books/computers/data bases) may be common. From this perspective, cultural practices are not unified systems that push action in a consistent direction, rather culture can be thought of as a provisional toolkit or conceptual map from which individuals and groups select differing elements for constructing activity. Toolkits in this sense help us to shape, and are in turn shaped by, our worldviews – our mindsets, purposes, passions and responsibilities – thus enabling us to act within the practices of our choice.[8]

Consider for a moment the remarkably different toolkits for teaching at the disposal of history teacher Wanda May, drama teacher James Stredder, and primary science specialist Beverley Caswell.

As a drama specialist, Stredder stresses the value of physical activity to explore dramatic texts such as those of Shakespeare. His toolkit encompasses 'living genealogical diagrams', freeze frames, twin pictures, photo images and, of course, stories. He regularly deploys physical artefacts such as sticky labels, chairs, cards on string necklaces, and character cards, using them as scaffolds to develop conceptual thinking. As adult learners laughingly rearrange their freeze frame, argue, and move around to interpret a portion of text, or a character or a theme, this pedagogy (he argues) generates an intensity of textual analysis that becomes, in part, the focus of the learning. Physical activities and artefacts are thus used to facilitate an investigative, problem-solving approach, in which Stredder seeks to create the 'mental challenge of enigma'. In this sense he also formalises within his toolkit of practice a range of key symbolic tools – *structural* approaches (using still images to focus analysis), *dynamic* approaches (using scenarios to focus on progression and unfolding), and *investigative* approaches (using the enigma to focus on exploration and intrigue).

May's approach to history teaching – focusing on metaphor, visual representation and dialogue – is also based on practical activities, including the manipulation of physical objects. She painstakingly assembles a wide range of physical artefacts and resources in her toolkit of practice to support classroom activity: 'It became clearer to me that knowledge is not always revealed, nor acquired through textbooks and didactic pedagogy. I gravitate towards the visual and visceral to understand the past and present: art, photographs, scrapbooks, and film; music; products and forms of persuasion; people; and texts which do not always contain scholarly footnotes (diaries, oral histories and old school books). Such 'goods' are cultural artefacts, imbued with a chain of attributes that imply desirable values such as power, status and freedom – a hidden ideology of meaning.'[9] Thus she provides students with a wide-ranging toolkit of media artefacts, as well as historical references, articles and excerpts, time frames and communication structures such as seminars within which to operate. Most importantly, however, May's classroom toolkit incorporates artefacts, biographies and experiences contributed by the students themselves, as they are encouraged to build three- dimensional *visual* models to represent a chosen pattern or theme in curriculum history. Additional support structures are created by the students themselves (for example, via home study groups or by including family members in their learning). This pedagogical approach puts May in the role of risk taker. By allowing her classroom toolkit to be provisional, open to change and incorporating a wide range of unplanned components, she deliberately creates uncertainty for her students and herself. Learners are encouraged to see the everyday experiences and artefacts of their home communities (physical as well as intellectual) as being integral to the pedagogic setting – a connection to their own and others' history. Such an approach demands that they problematise historical interpretation and understand how history is constructed and contested. A learning community is then built which continues a conversation 'begun long ago by others'.

Both Stredder and May place a high value on narrative as a key element in their toolkits of practice: 'Once upon a time', the telling of the tale, the invitation to listen, the casting of the teller as story teller and the listener as audience. Such devices are 'primal and irresistible'.[10] For as we saw in Chapter 4, narrative is what is needed to create the mode of feeling and thinking that helps learners create a version of the world in which they can envisage a place for themselves.[11] In this way both these teachers show their concern to make certain that the toolkits of their practice will 'draw students into the field of study'. They are keen to ensure that the process of 'cultural bridging' – linking students' own worldviews and personal repertoires with the world of the classroom – will be achieved.[12] These concerns are driven by their views of pedagogy – not least that active ownership (what Bruner calls 'agency' and Freire terms 'critical consciousness') should be at the heart of learning. This frame of reference is carefully reflected in each and every aspect of their carefully chosen repertoires.

Caswell's toolkit is radically different. In helping young students to develop the habits of mind of research scientists, she provides them with the opportunity to use a new toolkit of practice comprising hands–on investigations, concepts of adaptation and evolution, research teams, lab notebooks and journals, equipment for implementing research experiments, discussions with scientific experts and visits to the zoo lab. It is as true of the sciences as of messy daily life that the construction of meaning is not from some Apollonian 'view from nowhere'.[13] Caswell encouraged her learners to create a 'roach ballad' and to try out wildly imaginative hypotheses and experiments. In so doing she is recognising that even when engaged in understanding the world of nature, she cannot stereotype them as 'little scientists' unless they are participating in the quirkiness of daily life as described by James Watson in the double helix or by Pais in his study of Einstein. If you make science classrooms more like the unpredictable world of working scientists – full of the humour of wild hypothesis and the exhilaration of unconventional procedures – the dividends are quickly evident in better performance.[14]

Learning to be an historian, scientist or storyteller is not the same as learning science/history/drama: instead, it is learning a culture with all the attendant non-rational activity and meaning making that is facilitated by imaginative toolkits of practice. Understanding the indissoluble connection between conceptual and material tools in the process of learning and development for different groups and communities enriches pedagogy. It is central to the socially-situated theories of learning explored in Chapter 4. From this perspective learning is not limited to what happens to individuals, but rather is understood as jointly focused work, distributed between or 'stretched over' individuals, colleagues and their activities while mediated by physical artefacts, tools and semiotic resources. Learning, as we also saw in Chapter 4, demands mutual engagement and joint enterprise, but it also depends on a shared repertoire that includes physical and material dimensions. The illustration below shows Wenger's conceptualisation of the interaction between mutual engagement, joint enterprise and a shared repertoire. From this perspective shared repertoires bind together routines, words, tools, and events. Ways of doing things, stories, gestures, symbols, genres, documents, protocols, concepts that the community has produced or adopted in the course of its existence, and which have become integral to practice.[15] The elements of such shared repertoires can be very heterogeneous, as Wenger has argued.[16] They gain coherence not in and of themselves as discrete activities, symbols, or tools, but from the fact that taken together they uniquely belong to the mutual practice of a particular group or community pursuing a quite specific joint enterprise.

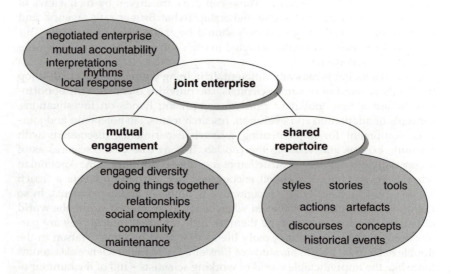

Dimensions of practice as the property of a community
Source: Wenger, E. (1998) *Communities of Practice* (Cambridge: Cambridge University Press)

One of the questions raised by May's graduate history teachers concerning the building of visual models was 'I wonder if you could do something like this in math, or has it to be history or social studies?' Similar questions should wend their way through this exploration of toolkits. How provisional are the toolkits with which we work as teachers? How open are we to change and innovation?

By identifying elements of our personal toolkits – be they to support our multiple identities as teachers, family members and perhaps as sports fanatics, musicians, churchgoers, political activists or whatever – we can begin to look below the surface of custom and practice to the accumulated knowledge and skills each framework draws on. Consider for a moment just the material elements of your personal repertoire, the physical tools and artefacts you have used in the last 24 hours. These are likely to be numerous, their origins complex. For me the list seemed infinite. It included a mobile phone, cooker, calculator, credit card machine, bicycle, piano, lawnmower and garden spade, car, pencil, kettle, fountain pen, washing machine, tin opener, TV and radio, computer, novels, thesaurus, journals, newspapers, reference volumes and so on and so on.

Whatever our setting, we make selections each day from a huge variety of ever-increasing, available technologies. Whether it be the stick in the sand or contemporary forms of artificial intelligence, combined with 'soft tools' (language, shared symbols, special vocabularies, notational systems and the like), such technologies have always offered a range of affordances for making people smart (though none of them guarantees it).[17] And a good deal of our everyday social interactions, and thus our relationships with one another, are mediated by the uses we make of communication technologies, be they phone conversations, letters, blogs, faxes, posters, text messages, memos or e-mails. In all of these ways, tools characteristically play a double role: as means to act upon the world and as cognitive scaffolds that facilitate such action.[18] Indeed human epochs and leaps of intellectual achievements are often defined by the dominant material tool of the time – the Stone Age, the Iron Age, the Steam Age, the Industrial Age, the Computer/Information Age and so on. The complex binaries linking the inside-outside/physical-mental/individual-social combination of the material and symbolic are also reflected in everyday language. Specific technologies are imperceptibly woven into everyday idioms about human processes. We get steamed or wound up. We hit the nail on the head or hammer our point home. We wonder what makes people tick or why traffic grinds to a halt. Politicians spearhead campaigns and cut their opponents down in debates. We call humans 'resources' and so on.[19]

Tools and technologies, we would therefore argue, are critical to pedagogy. They facilitate knowledge and understanding. Some assist us in interpreting everyday experiences, in solving problems, and making ideas concrete. They enable us to define and participate in the daily activities, products and achievements of the educational groups to which we belong. Freire argued that tools and technologies are the material evidence of human agency and creativity. Let it be clear that technological development must be one of the concerns of the revolutionary project he argued, for critically viewed, technology is a natural phase of the creative process which engaged humans from the moment they forged their first tools and began to transform the world for its humanisation.[20]

The role of tools and symbol systems as both reflecting and affecting human thought and development has long been recognised. But it is mainly due to the Russian socio-cultural tradition of thinkers such as Vygotsky, Luria and Leont'ev, together with their Western interpreters (particularly Wertsch and Bruner),[21] that scholarly attention began to be focused on material tools as social mediators of learning. Vygotsky argued that material and symbolic tools play an equal role in the process of human development. However, it was to be his research on the role of symbolic tools in thought, and language in particular, that was to dominate the thinking and imagination of Western educators working in a predominantly cognitive paradigm. Indeed, recognition of the key role played by material tools in the learning process has only really begun to gain significance among educators as a result of the dramatic developments in information and communications technologies over the last decade. Contemporary interpreters of these Russian thinkers, often known as activity theorists, have now begun to explicitly highlight the role of tools and artefacts in their work. Engestrom, for instance, analyses learning as we have seen (see Chapter 4) on a cultural activity system. His visual model of 'expansive activity'[22], now frequently used and adapted by learning theorists, emphasises the way that tools, artefacts and signs mediate all human activity:

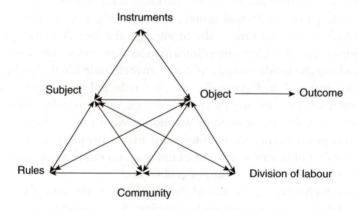

Vygotsky used the term 'higher functioning' when referring to thought processes that are supported by material and symbolic tools in combination. While pole-vaulter and pole together enable individual athletes to achieve great physical leaps, shared languages and numerical signs – the tools of thinking – enable whole communities to hypothesise, conjecture, theorise, and guess.[23] Researchers across a range of disciplines can take unique and creative cognitive leaps when using statistical tools in combination with a socially-shared symbol system. In mathematical practices, for example, history shows that increasingly sophisticated activity has been afforded by the gradual adoption of new instruments – from mental arithmetic, to paper and writing implements, abacus, slide rule, mechanical calculator, electronic calculator, computer software. These material tools are said to 'wrap up some of the mathematical ontology of the environment and form part of the web of ideas and actions embedded in it'.[24] And it is commonplace that any maths student in a modern university can do more mathematics than, say, Leibniz, who 'invented' the calculus. We stand on the shoulders of the giants who preceded us.[25] In this way the development of both physical and symbolic tools in combination has moved forward our knowledge and understanding across the millennia.[26]

Whatever selections we make from the myriad tools available to us, each physical artefact or technology also carries its own history, as well as cultural capital as May's pedagogy emphasises. Roger Saljo calls the codex, books, videos, libraries, and data bases that tacitly embody shared cultural understandings and enable communities to build on centuries of prior knowledge and understanding 'Public Storage Systems'.[27] In this sense, he argues, we enter into an intellectual partnership with – or at least can be greatly helped by – cultural artefacts in the form of shared information sources. Human knowledge is thus advanced by a wide range of representational or 'computational' tools at one and the same time: physical tools manipulated by the body (for example books, maps, computers) and symbolic tools manipulated by the mind (for example literary ideas, geographical signs, software programs).

From a socio-cultural point of view material tools and artefacts serve as social mediators of learning in other important ways. Since tools and artefacts are themselves historically and culturally situated, they also carry the wisdom and hidden assumptions that went into their original design. They reorganise action, and determine what can be carried out when, where, in what form, and for what purpose.[28] None of the mathematical instruments mentioned above, for instance, exists independently of the culture and context in which it was created. A mathematical tool such as an abacus or calculator only becomes a useful instrument when someone appropriates it for herself and integrates and directs it towards some relevant purpose. Such appropriation is never simply an individual process. In the maths classroom, for instance, calculators only take on a social meaning when both the teacher's and the students' responsibilities are engaged.

Development of the map as both physical artefact and mental tool provides a particularly vivid example of the intersection between cognitive, historical

Psalter Map, The British Library

and social processes – a physical, symbolic and cultural tool in combination. In medieval times maps created by scholars in the western hemisphere, such as the Psalter Map shown below, generally showed Jerusalem securely at the centre of the world in accordance with the dominant worldview of the time.[29]

When we google 'Multimap'[30] today in order to find out how to travel from A to B, or when students use a map more or less as a photograph in geography lessons, we are generally oblivious to the centuries of discussion, debate and conflict that went into their development.[31]

Yet tell a Palestinian geography teacher that the map of her homeland is stable, objective, factual, uncontentious. Or tell it to the geography teachers we worked with in Albania in the early 1990s. As we saw in Chapter 4, children there were only just beginning to learn how to read maps, since world maps of any kind had been banned country-wide since the 1970s by the Hoxha regime. In making sure that a map of Europe was on every classroom wall in Tirana, Albanian teachers not only saw themselves developing children's knowledge and understanding of the world they inhabited, they were also asserting a new found identity and freedom of thought.

Research also points to the transformations of understanding triggered by certain tools and physical artefacts and two quite different effects on learning. One is learning effects *with* a particular tool. This recognises the changed functioning and expanded capability that take place as we use and get used to a particular technology or artefact. In this sense, impact occurs through the redistribution of a task's cognitive load *between* the user and the device, including symbol-handling devices (for example, a spell checker) or *across* users, mediated by devices and symbol systems in combination (for example, telephones, fax machines/written, spoken language). Besides effects *with,* there are effects *of* the tool. These relate to the more lasting ripple effects of using a particular tool beyond actual occasions of use – the long-term impact on shared toolkits, our arsenal of skills, perspectives, and ways of representing the world.[32] For example, research has shown that the writing/planning cues discussed in Chapter 4 have a lasting effect on the quality of students' approaches to writing. The visual models created by May's students enabled them to comprehend on a permanent basis the provisional, constructed nature of historical enquiry. Research shows that students who read texts with a computer 'Reading Partner' often became better readers of novel, print-based texts and also better essay writers, apparently as a result of having learned to be more self-regulating by following the tool's original model. To take a quite different example, medical robots used to assist surgeons in carrying out operations now make such procedures safer. The Da Vinci system has three arms (and a fourth can be added) with 3D stereo imagery available during surgery. This system has a motion scaling concept, which can be scaled down to five-to-one, so a surgeon can be much more precise than when using her own hand, while feeling very similar in sensation as if she was working with her real hand. Such robots extend the practitioner's skills during surgery – *with* the tool she is able to perform better, improving both control and precision. There is also a longer-term effect *of* the tool, enabling surgeons generally to become aware of the difference between expert and novice hand and eye movements. This impacts on the quality of surgical procedures more broadly, especially for the training of new surgeons.[33]

This distinction between *with* and *of* the tool in some senses parallels the contrasting cognitive/acquisition-oriented and social/participatory views of learning. The acquisition metaphor emphasises how tools can affect cognition both in immediate and relatively lasting and generalisable ways, even when people are functioning without the tool. Scribner and Cole, for example, studied the cognitive effects of literacy without schooling in the Vai people of Africa.[34] By contrast Olson, Torrance and Hildyard argue that it is misleading to think of literacy solely in terms of cognitive consequences. What matters is the participatory aspect of learning – what people do with literacy, not what literacy does to people.[35] While master surgeon Professor Ara Dazi of the Faculty of Medicine, Imperial College, London (and currently Junior Minister for Health in the UK government) is researching the difference between expert and novice surgeons' eye movements when using the Da Vinci robot, what really matters to him in the longer term is the future expertise and surgical training that such knowledge will facilitate for medical teams internationally.

In all these ways we can see how the invention or use of a new physical tool, or the modification of an existing one, can transform cultures' toolkits and the repertoires for problem solving and development available to us, opening up new possibilities for action, learning and development.

There can also be significant transformations in the social organisation of groups when they adapt to using a new tool, in particular in the ways in which members of groups relate to one another. Early clay tablets found in Syria dating back to 4000BCE, for instance, are said to carry the legend 'ten goats here', 'ten sheep there'.[36] We can only speculate on what these tablets represented to the farming community that used them in the fertile valley of Tel Brac (was it a personal record or shared data base?). Historians[37] suggest, however, that these rudimentary technologies began to afford new ways of recording economic data and as a result led to the emergence of quite new socio-political structures deriving from new agricultural and urban settlements and the rise of an elite.[38]

A very different contemporary example would be the Internet, which enables professional discussion between educators who are physically far distant from one another – an entirely new and highly sophisticated mode of communication and knowledge sharing that was unthinkable even ten years ago that has facilitated new modes of educational activity, relationships and educational structures (see the illustration below).

Transformations such as these that have been facilitated by new tools may have initially involved quite small steps in both communities. And they were not always positively evaluated by all users! Nevertheless, it is small changes that successively and cumulatively contribute to the construction of the developmental trajectories of individuals, groups and, in time, of whole cultures and practices.[39] Understanding these complex aspects of human development and learning provides a new recognition of the significance of each and every activity we engage in, of the transformative potential of the manner in which we participate, but most especially the ways in which we use and reshape

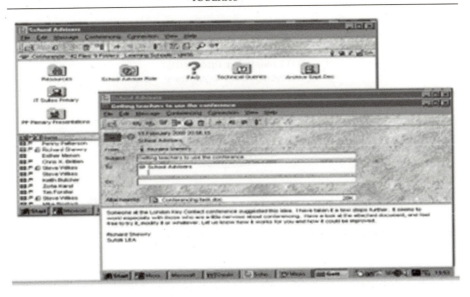

material and symbolic tools and construct new toolkits within our chosen communities.

Although we have been focusing specifically on material tools and technologies, we can nonetheless interpret the 'toolkit' in the widest possible way. We suggest that the concept should indicate wide ranging symbolic and physical repertoires encompassing concepts, activities, shared dispositions and stories, rituals and events (examples of which we have discussed in previous chapters), mediated by many and varied tools and artefacts. For Bruner the shared understanding and use of such toolkits within any learning community are hugely significant:

> One of the most radical proposals to have emerged from the cultural–psychological approach to education is that the classroom be reconceived as … a sub community of mutual learners, with the teacher orchestrating the proceedings. Note that, contrary to traditional critics, such sub-communities do not reduce the teacher's role or his or her authority. Rather the teacher takes on the additional function of encouraging others to share it.[40]

Our own point is that if we as teachers are to understand the importance of toolkits for developing authentic pedagogy and extending the understandings of our learners, we need to understand explicitly the role they play in our own learning and practice. In the next section we explore the role that toolkits appear to play in teacher development and the implementation of pedagogy.

Any institutional setting is a 'constellation' of very diverse practices or sub-communities that are likely to have members in common, as well as share artefacts and technologies, geographical relations, overlapping styles and discourse, and compete for the same resources.[41] At this level of practice senior managers, office staff, various cross-functional teams such as year teams and subject faculties in schools – and most importantly, classroom communities – can be said

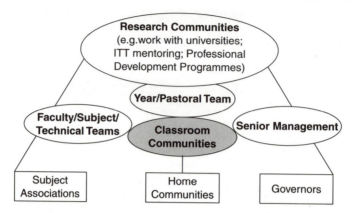

An example of a constellation of practices in a secondary school

to be sub-communities, each with their own specific membership, roles, allegiances, purposes and goals (as illustrated in the figure above as a constellation of practices).

Each of these groups over time, we would argue, develops a distinctive toolkit in order to enact and support its core values, practices and identity in ways that are relevant to its unique interpretation of the educational enterprise. This notion of sub-communities can be exemplified by looking back at the case study of Lucy.

Lucy was required to introduce an A-level English group to Chaucer's *General Prologue* (a set examination text) as part of her final, school-based, teacher training. In the process of planning and teaching this sequence of activities she moved between activities in and across several sub-communities, including her classroom community of A-level students, the school's English faculty and – more marginally – the local community, with the latter encompassing students' parents as well as the national subject association for English teachers (NATE). We are told little about the communities she interacts with outside the work context, although clearly these also impinge on her thinking (for example, her view of subject English). As Lucy participates in these different groups, she knits together elements of a pre-existing toolkit, developed over time, for the practice of (English) teaching. This toolkit comprises national schema, exam requirements and exemplar practices of English teaching built up by a UK-wide body of experts, together with the local wisdom and values of her placement school's innovative English faculty. To this she adds prior subject expertise developed within a university's English department.

Though her academic study has given Lucy a grasp of the traditional discourse and conventions relating to Chaucer, she adds a standard 'Study Guide' (a 'short cut' to key literary ideas, well known to university students and teachers) to her toolkit to refresh her knowledge, along with an audiotape from the English faculty's resource bank that will help with reading Middle English aloud. In transferring the notion of a pilgrimage into a modern 'protest' she selects a standard strategy or heuristic from the repertoire of English teachers – analogy. Curricular-related artefacts prepared by departmental members for previous year groups (a map of Canterbury and pictures of pilgrims) also support her planning and the department encourages her to establish what relevant materials are available in the school library, on web sites and on CD-ROM.

In addition to these important material and symbolic tools and artefacts, Lucy participates in a range of ritual activities integral to the development of her overall repertoire and hence her framing of the task of being an English teacher: parents' evenings, mentor sessions, faculty meetings and INSET sessions, as well as informal chats (including the inevitable daily stories of what transpired in the classroom and how problems were resolved). These create important points of focus in the whirl of school activity.[42] This mutuality and connectedness help her to unfold the meaning of practice, much of which has been permanently reified[43] in the form of departmental documents, minutes of meetings, lesson notes, shared planning templates, class lists, assessment protocols, posters on classroom walls, notices on the English faculty's pin board, and so forth.

In this sense we see Lucy drawing on – and adding to – an existing toolkit, or framework of established practice, or way of thinking about 'being an English teacher', by integrating:

- the **vision and values** of the English faculty (including the belief that all children can achieve highly, the key role of language in learning, the importance of working as a team);

- **joint activities and points of focus** (shared departmental and local authority INSET/mentor sessions/team planning/parents' evenings/informal peer meetings/friendships);

- the **discourse and concepts** of the school subject 'English' (Chaucer/A-level English, including historical and cultural background/setting/authorial voice/theme/tone/textual evidence); faculty discourse of 'achievement'/'equality'/collaboration;

- **stories of practice** (observation and talk with mentor/department members/other staff/conversations at parents-evenings);

- **pedagogic strategies** (group work/expert groups/use of research/analogy of pilgrimage);

- **material technologies** stored in or available to the English department (computer-CD-ROM/data projector/audio recorder and audio tape/flip charts/pens);

- **symbolic tools and data bases** such as textbooks/study guides/reference texts/websites/map of Canterbury;

- **shared artefacts, documents and protocols** e.g., minutes of meetings, lesson notes, class lists, assessment protocols, blank lesson planners/schemes of work/mentor records, posters on classroom walls, notices on the faculty pin board.

(Continued)

(Continued)

By giving Lucy explicit access to the many and varied elements of this shared toolkit, both material and symbolic, her mentor allows her development within the English faculty's practice to be both transparent and meaningful. The explanatory burden for learning is placed on the broad cultural practices in which Lucy is encouraged to participate. Lucy is also encouraged to contribute to and extend the faculty's existing repertoire, by sharing new ideas. In this way the faculty's toolkit develops and moves forward rather than becoming an ossified and stultifying framework.

Such processes may seem obvious. However, in reality many schools fail to be explicit about the elements of their toolkit of practice, and neither do they encourage newcomers to really participate in practice – either because they are unaware of its importance, or through a desire to maintain distance and status. In addition, many schools perpetuate habits of mind that are constraining rather than mind opening, the result of an inflexible, static toolkit that merely endorses prevailing pedagogical styles and personal theories[44] at the expense of new thinking. In this sense a community's toolkit can be thin, threadbare, resource poor. The mindset can be limiting, narrow, stultifying. We have seen A-level English trainees, for example, being encouraged simply to use a set text and printed notes in their teaching – the former to read aloud to students, the latter for students to copy verbatim. Many school communities rely on long-standing customs and outdated practices, avoiding the evaluation of contemporary learning mechanisms, innovative technologies and artefacts, as well as the power of peer networking and informal activities. We need to take seriously the fact that our intellectual development depends on materials, tools and how we understand things in context. As John Seeley Brown and his colleagues put it, we should be explicit about the toolkits of those reckoning devices, heuristics and accessible friends that we call upon. Our micro cultures of praxis encompass the reference books we use, the kind of notes we habitually take, the computer programs and data bases we rely on and perhaps most importantly of all, the networks of friends, colleagues and mentors on whom we lean for feedback, help and advice, and even just for company.[45]

This concept of a toolkit for teaching (see the following illustration) – whether it is the shared repertoires for mathematics, English or history faculties, senior managers, or Year 6 primary specialists – is not, therefore, simply descriptive. It can offer an analytical mechanism through which the quality of a community's design for learning and its views of pedagogy can be explored and evaluated.

Tim Brighouse has paid considerable attention within his urban pedagogy to the importance of teachers explicitly moving beyond traditional repertoires. In tandem with the big ideas of his radical project (see Chapter 2) he has conceptualised a range of discrete points of focus that might enable

A TEACHING TOOLKIT

"If pedagogy is to empower human beings then it must transmit the toolkit the culture has developed for doing so." Bruner (1996op cit)

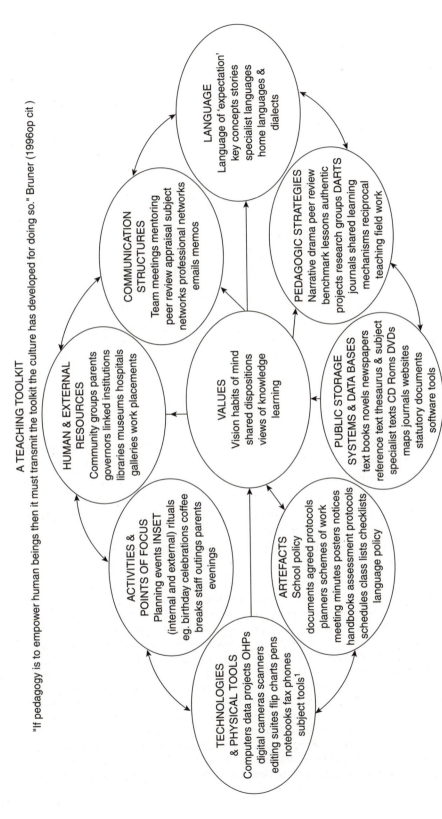

1 these will be numerous eg. science lab; test tubes; scientific equipment/maps; compasses; field work kits/sports centres equipment/musical instruments etc

learning communities to develop and extend that which may have become routine, rather than meaningful rituals within their collective toolkits of practice. He calls these points of focus 'butterflies'[46] – seemingly small activities, fresh rituals or the adoption of a new artefact (such as a journal article or new class reader) which, while not requiring a major re-organisation, expenditure or resource, could have a major impact on the mindset of a particular team[47] or group of educators.

For example, weekly faculty meetings (or staff meetings in primary schools) are traditionally used to inform, to consolidate roles and relationships, and to confirm shared routines, processes and the allocation of resources. So often these become inflexible rituals in the teacher's toolkit of daily practice. Brighouse suggests teams abandon traditional agendas and venues for a period of time and physically relocate meetings to teachers' classrooms, rotating to a different classroom each week. Take time to critique the physical setting itself. Is the space conducive to learning? Is it a stimulating, resource-rich environment? Make the main point of focus of each meeting the progress of three or four students selected by the host teacher. Analyse these students' work and evaluate the feedback they are being given on their learning. Discuss points of failure and their achievements. In this way new approaches and insights will emerge that will extend existing repertoires. These can include the introduction of innovative teaching strategies, a selection of new tools to support specific learners, the use of a new technology or the introduction of a new class reader or more appropriate resource.[48]

Explicitly acknowledging and sharing existing repertoires with newcomers is a vital prelude to understanding a community's prevailing pedagogy as we saw in the previous case study of Lucy. However, it can often be difficult to identify aspects of taken-for-granted, habitual practice. One teaching Primary Care Trust (PCT) in inner London has developed a shared protocol to help it pay attention to both explicit and implicit aspects of its collective toolkit of practice when designing learning programmes for newcomers.

Seven GP practices in north London are collaborating in an Assistant Practitioners in Primary Care Project, designed to enable refugee doctors from Albania, Kosovo, Sudan and Afghanistan to gain experience within the London healthcare system, prior to possible long-term retraining. This project requires a delicate appreciation of the significance of cultural differences and expectations, since UK practices differ in so many ways from the health systems that the refugees have been used to in their home countries – for example, in terms of mission, acceptable protocols, language, roles, and standards to be achieved, as well as the range of physical resources available. The team facilitating this learning experience considered what they thought were the key elements of a health practice repertoire, and used these to devise a checklist that members of participating practices could discuss prior to the arrival of the newcomers. The refugee doctors (known as Assistant Practitioners) and their mentors also use a version of the checklist as a point of focus in support and progress meetings.

This checklist (below) includes references to the practice's shared values and protocols, to formal and informal ritual activity (for example, practice meetings/coffee breaks), to the development and use of resources and technologies, to the assignment of roles and relationships and to the use of physical space. There is an acknowledgement of informal as well as formal structures of communication. Importantly, the checklist also requires members of the practice to consider how they can value and build on the prior experiences and expertise that the Assistant Practitioners themselves bring. This helps APs to find their niche in the practice and in turn to contribute to the team's development, extending and enriching its existing repertoire. As we noted in Chapter 4, it is critical that newcomers can 'legitimately participate'[49] in different aspects of practice if they are to get under the skin of activity and meanings in an unfamiliar culture. The organisers of the project hope that this shared protocol – which has itself become part of the health workers' toolkit – will begin to encourage transparency and awareness among all participants, of both formal and informal dimensions of their daily practice.[50]

Assistant Practitioners in Primary Care Project Practice Checklist

The purpose of this checklist is to provide sponsoring practices with help in supporting refugee doctors as new Assistant Practitioners (APs) so that APs and practices can both make the most of the opportunities that this exciting scheme has to offer. The checklist is intended for use by practice-based mentors and APs, and by other practice staff.

Checklist	Yes	No	Notes
First things			
• Has the proposal to appoint an AP been discussed at a team meeting? Is the practice clear about how the AP will help it achieve its priorities in 2007–8?			
• Are practice staff aware of the particular skills and experience of their named AP?			
• Has the AP been given an opportunity to introduce themselves and their experience and expertise to the team?			
• Has the link between the AP's day-to-day tasks and the vision and priorities for the practice generally been discussed with the AP?			

(Continued)

(Continued)

Checklist	Yes	No	Notes
Spaces & places			
• Has the AP been given a tour of the premises with an explanation of where she will be based and can go/not go?			
• What opportunities have been arranged for her to visit significant places with or without members of the team (home visits, hospital visits ...)			
Resources			
• What physical resources in the practice are being made available to the AP (equipment, books, computer, on-line resources ... other)?			
• How does the AP know what is available?			
• How does the AP access written protocols or guidance?			
• Is time allowed for the AP to observe members of the practice team carrying out their roles and using specific protocols?			
• Have essential forms and practice documentation been shared and explained?			
• Has the AP had an opportunity to see how essential documentation is collected and used by an experienced professional?			
• Are there opportunities for the AP to ask questions, understand terminology and any other special language used by members of the practice?			
Informal relationships			
• What opportunity does the AP have for informal meetings with other members of the practice?			
• What opportunities are provided for the AP to meet other relevant professionals outside the practice?			
• Is time being allowed for meeting peers via the project's peer support group?			

Checklist	Yes	No	Notes
Team meetings			
• Is time allowed early on for observation of practice meetings?			
• Is the AP given the opportunities and space to raise questions,			
• including questions about the use of terminology, jargon, procedures, etc?			
• Is the team aware of the particular language, cultural and professional skills that the AP will contribute to the group?			
• What opportunities will there be for the AP to contribute to the actions of the team by using her particular skills and experience?			
Standards & accountability			
• What are the essential standards of the practice and how are these communicated to the AP?			
• What opportunities exist for joint reviews of performance connected with these standards? Can the AP be involved?			
• How will the practice support the AP in carrying out self-reviews?			
• How will practice assessments of the AP's performance be communicated to the AP?			
Communication			
• How is new information communicated within the practice?			
• What are the day-to-day communication channels?			
• Does the AP know about these channels and how to access them?			

Most of the GP practices involved have assigned a network computer to their AP as part of their induction programme. A key aspect of induction is introducing them to the Primary Health Care Trust's website that supports a range of practices across the north London boroughs, giving them vital access to evidence-based research in diverse areas of health care. In the next section we look specifically at the important role new information and communication technologies can play in contemporary toolkits and pedagogy.

CL is 16 and has recently moved schools from an inner city comprehensive to the local sixth-form college. As part of a research project she was asked to represent the way she thought about Information and Communications Technologies (ICT).[51] The image above shows her response. The text on the right, emanating from this self-portrait, articulates the words and ideas that came to mind as she considered the task. Her mobile phone (represented as an aerial behind her left ear) triggered the word 'RELATE'. Though switched off during college hours (a rule), she uses it several times a day to text-message close friends. She also has two e-mail accounts, one provided by college, though text messaging and the use of Facebook have largely replaced her use of these. A Nintendo (represented by two function buttons on her neck, together with the words 'FUN' and 'PLAY') she bought jointly with her brother several Christmases ago. She uses it for playing adventure games, mostly with friends. The TV (reflected through her left eye – 'TRANSMISSION'; 'WATCH') she watches for a few hours each day, including one or two DVDs, usually as a background when chatting in friends' homes. Unlike most of her peers she has no TV in her bedroom, but music (on her lips – 'LISTEN', 'MUSIC', 'WAVES') is constantly playing on her i-pod. The family PC, appearing from her right as binary code, is used for homework. During the week in which she drew this image she had created a spreadsheet for maths, had used the Internet to research the risks of smoking for her biology coursework, and had downloaded images of Giacometti sculptures and Salvador Dali paintings from an on-line art gallery as part of an art assignment ('LEARN', 'KNOWLEDGE'). In this surreal image, influenced she says by her study of Dali in art class, technologies represent elements of her self – her identity ('BE', 'YOU', 'ME').

Through ICT she expresses personal preferences and feelings, learns new concepts and ideas, relates to the people she loves, cements her membership in differing groupings, and delineates both the geographical and imaginary borders of her world. CL's personal repertoire of ICT, encapsulated through this striking image, is integral both to the individual she is and to the multiple communities to which she belongs. Through them she reflects on fresh ideas, new people, and envisions a wider world, as, for example, she accesses medical web sites and an on-line community of painters. She is able to imagine herself in relation to what are, at present at any rate, unfamiliar adult practices, as well as participating confidently in the varied yet very familiar groups to which she belongs. She is already keenly aware that ICT provides her with essential tools for the present, but also new contexts and future possibilities.

As a young school student, CL is integrating a wide range of new technologies into her personal toolkit with each one to differing degrees framing new ways of knowing and thinking about the world, her modes of participation for acting on the world, as well as her overall sense of self. It is sometimes difficult to appreciate the immense changes in new communication technologies that have occurred in this young person's lifetime, transforming so much of the world she will experience when she leaves school, both for leisure and working practice.

In workplaces of all kinds across the developed world, the nature of practice has been subtly but significantly transformed as new knowledge and skills are created through computer and telecommunication networks.[52] The rapid development of highly sophisticated data bases and other more powerful computational tools has led, for instance, to greater efficiency and the extension of working practices. Large chemical engineering companies, for example, now expect their researchers to employ computers to carry out sophisticated simulations of chemical processes that would be impossible by other means. Lawyers meanwhile will use new technologies to check the progress of a client's case or point of law, or use e-mail to contact solicitors. Drawing boards, so resonant of architectural and design practices, have been replaced by computers that facilitate innovative design processes, while occupations such as accountancy, stock broking and marketing have been significantly changed by the introduction of data bases that identify patterns and problems in current practice, as well as in the quantitative aspects of future developments. Health services are beginning to see the various networks of people involved in patient care being connected to one another to deliver medicine no matter where patients may be. Online doctors, for instance, already provide medical advice based on standardised symptoms. Increasingly, however, remote diagnosis (telemedicine) is based on real physiological data from the actual patient. Off-the-shelf personal data assistants, such as a Palm Pilot mobile phone, allow a patient's vital signs to be transmitted by telephones portable enough to be carried in a personal first aid kit. Some medical technology groups are already looking to apply telemedicine to rural care, while others are investigating the use of telemedicine as a tool for disaster response and especially after an earthquake. In many fields then the trend is towards global access to data and expertise through distributed human intelligence.

Despite this rapidly changing context schools frequently fail to build on students' existing skills and knowledge of ICT, or the kind of understandings about ICT that will be demanded in their adult lives. Research confirms that teachers' perceptions of technology use can be strongly constrained by habits of mind that are dependent on the kind of inflexible toolkits we referred to earlier, which limit new thinking and the consideration of new practices. In addition, much statutory 'school' ICT in the UK, as in many countries worldwide, fails to take account of the many innovative uses of ICT in the real world outside the classroom.[53]

Our research into innovative, outward looking pedagogies indicates that the use of tools and authentic technologies of their time has always been critical to extending learners' understandings of the world. Consider Loris Malaguzzi's now celebrated account of a Reggio Emilia project, for instance, involving pre-school children – an amusement park for birds – which as a matter of course encouraged learners to integrate both school and home technology use into school investigations.

'Suggestions were made [in class assembly] for houses and nests in the trees, swings for chicks to play on, elevators for the elderly birds. Ferris-wheels and rides with music. And then – everyone laughs – water skiing for the birds, providing them with tiny slats of wood for skis. Then came the fountains, which had to be big and real, and spray the water up really high … As part of this project Andrea has drawn an elevator for tired birds. After doing this he goes to the computer corner to build an animated version … Andrea is unable to complete the animation by himself; he takes his project home where his elder sister helps him to finish it. The next day Andrea goes to the school workshop area and adds to the animation a picture of a real bird taken with a digital camera, and records birds singing. Once Andrea has completed his work on the computer he shows it to the class. […] Now there is a new project. The children go out to observe actual elevators and take pictures of them. Then they discuss and draw how they think an elevator works. With the help of Giovanni, Andrea and Alice made an elevator using Lego motors and a sensor attached to a "programmable brick". The elevator is to be placed in the amusement park for birds.'[54]

Beverley Caswell also integrated sophisticated new technologies into the scientist's toolkit that her young students were trying out for size. Beverley taught them to use the powerful computational tool, Knowledge Forum, a computer software program that creates a multimedia community knowledge space.[55] In the form of 'Notes', participants can contribute theories, working models, plans, evidence, reference material, and so forth, to a shared space. The software provides knowledge building 'Supports' both in the creation of these notes and in the ways they are displayed, linked, and made objects of further work. Revisions, elaborations, and reorganisations over time provide a record of group advances, just as the accumulation of research advances in a scholarly discipline.[56] Beverley used this tool to make her students' activity explicit and reflective, to support collaborative thinking, and to enable their thinking, to move in new and unpredictable directions.

The CSILE technology was not introduced discretely, but on a need-to-know basis, Beverley explained. Initially students used it as a graphics tool simply to draw the roaches, but gradually they were encouraged to enter questions onto the shared data base, so that the Knowledge Forum could support and scaffold their scientific thinking. As their activity developed, students gradually entered one or two pressing questions into the data base. Questions ranged from, 'What kind of food do they prefer?' to 'What did roaches evolve from?' And because these questions were stored in a data base, each child's question could be 'heard' and resources gathered to support each child's pursuit of knowledge in a particular interest area. The students found it exciting to be adding notes to build up the data base. In the course of one week alone, 100 new notes were entered.

The data base showed questions falling into specific categories that helped to inform the creation of the small research groups, variously studying perception, learning, communication, evolution and anatomy. It also documented the progress and development of students' thinking. For example, as a result of one student's curiosity after reading a book about the Ice Age, the evolution group decided to investigate *How did the Madagascan roaches survive in the Ice Age?* This problem was entered into the data base and the group planned and carried out a real experiment concluding 'Roaches don't like hot areas, they like room temperature'. As a follow-up Caswell invited a graduate student to give a lesson on the Ice Age followed by new entries into the Forum.

Caswell and her co-researcher were explicit about their intention to create a scientific community by providing students with sophisticated tools that enabled them to reflect on ideas and to hypothesise, and that also allowed for multiple ways of developing understanding. The Knowledge Forum software was in a sense pivotal to the whole project, supplying students with a cumulative data base as well as a means of recording information and ideas. It acted as a tool for making thinking explicit and encouraging creative thinking – the making of inspired hypotheses, the articulation of probing questions, the blending of others' findings with one's own, and intensive attempts to solve authentic problems.

'My theory is that you are right, that roaches can learn', Danel B commented after one experiment. 'And I think you have a very good experiment. But how can your experiment proof tha (sic) roaches learn?'

The use of new technologies for providing a means of communication and joint problem solving between learners is far from a new idea. *Il Paese Spagliato*,[57] written by the Italian educator Mario Lodi in 1970, is a country teacher's diary, peppered with examples of student projects, dialogues, writings and special pedagogic projects over a five-year period at an elementary school in the village of Vho, in southern Italy. In his school, and that of his friend and colleague Bruno Ciari in the distant village of Certaldo, students were given access to the state-of the art technology of the 1950s and '60s! Typewriters and printing machinery enabled them to have direct control over every aspect of the publishing process, enabling them to write and edit *il giornalino* or newsletters (*Il Mondo* and *Insieme*) for fellow students, parents and (eventually) subscribers in ten countries.[58] This process served as a catalyst for students' emerging literacy skills and 'in effect transformed their classrooms into literacy learning laboratories'.[59] Later Lodi and Ciari used audio tape recorders to encourage students to exchange *les letteres parlate*, or spoken letters (audiotapes), through which they conducted local oral history projects in collaboration with their distant correspondents.

> It was through recording that students first noticed the marked difference in dialect between the two villages, leading both partner classes to launch a sophisticated linguistic investigation into Italian dialects. They jointly developed a common system for writing their dialects and then tested their new scheme by investigating, recording and transcribing lullabies from each village's communal traditions. Thus, both partner classes served as catalysts in the creation of new knowledge with their distant correspondents.[60]

This work, reflecting 'immense respect for the intricacies of children's learning', established Lodi and Ciari as two of the most influential European educational reformers of recent times. Ciari, as we saw earlier, went on to help found the Reggio Emilia schools, while Lodi's pedagogy is widely read and available in translation in Spain, France and Germany, although it remains unavailable in English.

Contemporary communicative tools provide still greater flexibility for creative collaborative work. Across schools in Chile for example, young students in the Enlaces Project[61] created the first ever dictionaries in native dialects by collaborating via electronic mail. The Internet provides a medium that allows students to move in unpredictable directions and to extend the range of tools currently available within a particular 'subject' discipline, as well as enabling collaborative products.

The Virtual Identities Digital Arts Project[62] involved post-16 art and design students from two Liverpool schools and two Kent schools in the UK in the early days of the Internet. As in Lodi's work this project unlocked new ideas and ways of working by encouraging collaboration between students from different geographical areas, cultures, experiences, and perceptions. Each student was assigned a partner, with whom they exchanged a digital postcard representing one aspect of their personal identity. Every e-mail image received had to be responded to, modified and interpreted, while retaining 20 per cent of the original in order to provide a sense of sequence.

The stimulus for these images and artistic statements was open-ended, largely chosen by the students themselves. In addition to using images and texts that represented their individual identities, students were encouraged to think about their own values and concerns, collecting newspaper cuttings reflecting local, national or global issues such as ecology or peace studies. One student scanned images of her hand, which she then digitally manipulated and modified.

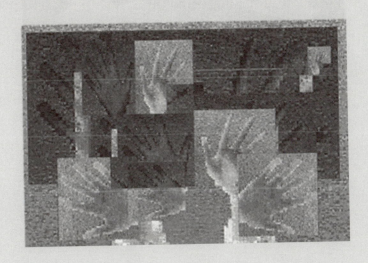

Her teacher commented, 'This was intended to reflect her identity in a subtle way. As with fingerprints, the truth was there, but only if the code could be interpreted. There was a deliberate attempt to be obtuse and enigmatic, to see what it would draw from her collaborator. Her image was then altered and posted to the website. It now contained military elements and references to the war in the Middle East, which was threatening to escalate. The hands, which originally appeared to be welcoming, now looked as if they were surrendering or imploring. By restricting the colour of the whole image to tones of red, the fingers resembled flames within a sea of fire. She decided to make the conflict with Iraq more explicit in the work. She used the modified image as a background, overlaying images of war and incorporating the flags of the UN and Iraq.' Students became highly focused 'artists', passionate about the project in hand. One teacher commented: 'I was keen to exploit the vast potential of the Internet for art and design. In this sense the collaboration was intentionally creative, indeed this remained the first and key "possibility" of the project i.e. the possibility of moving in exciting and unpredictable directions.'

(Continued)

The use of the Internet enabled students to transform physical objects into digital images. It also provided a medium by which they could explore visual phenomena, experimenting with visual language and thus extending the range of tools traditionally used in art, including image manipulation and layering. The resulting images and web site became a visual record of the development of students' ideas, a joint *oeuvre*, with a potentially international audience.

In common with so many examples of pedagogy in this volume, this work drew on a range of expertise both within and outside the schools, including the work of a talented and experienced teaching team and a visiting artist. By extending their traditional toolkit of practice, art teachers and students were able to interact collaboratively, communicating with different audiences at a local, national, and international scale. This initiative represented a totally new way of working and the development of new habits of mind for both the department and the students involved. As we will see in the next chapter with more recent examples of communications technology use, the ease with which school students can now connect with peers near and far recreates our concept of what a learning community might look like.

Over time, as part of our research, we have identified six ways[63] by which we can consider the differing roles that new technological tools play within the toolkits of practice and pedagogy. These are:

- *Informational tools* supporting the process of knowledge building within student and teacher communities.

- *Communicative tools* creating and sustaining the kind of coherence and ongoing collaboration that support a community of practice. For teaching communities these can be particularly important in overcoming professional isolation and challenging ossified practices.

- *Tools of the discipline* enabling teachers of whatever subject or age group to develop more effective teaching of core disciplinary concepts, extending the range of tools available within the subject and offering a wide range of new opportunities and contexts for learning that is grounded in authentic practices outside the school environment.

- *Productivity tools* allowing students and teacher professionals to carry out everyday tasks more effectively. Many generic software tools (word processors, desk top publishing, presentation software, spreadsheets, and so on) can be used to develop and store the kind of artefacts essential to teachers' practice, such as lesson plan templates, presentations for governors, and parents' newsletters.

- *Pedagogic tools* focusing explicitly on supporting, developing or changing a student's or teacher's understanding of a concept, aiding collaboration and situating a student's or teacher's own practice in a specific context.

- *Research tools* providing teachers and students with access to authentic electronic data as well as to systematic research evidence. These allow hitherto separately bounded research- and school-based communities to connect. Teachers experienced in the key concerns of schools and classrooms can work alongside colleagues experienced in the processes, tools and discourse of research practices.

The case study that follows illustrates the potential of technological tools to support the process of teacher pedagogy itself,[64] particularly the development of teacher understanding and collaboration.

From a large cohort of trainee teachers, over 100 UK-wide have signed up for a two-month seminar on 'Language and Grammar Use in the Classroom' (these are primary and secondary modern foreign language and English specialists). A room has been allocated for this seminar (open 24/7) that houses a resources area for relevant materials (for example books, research papers and examples of model lessons). An introductory lecture by a national expert in the field sets the agenda. Subsequent discussions are facilitated by tutors.

(Continued)

(Continued)

Across the two-month period there are vigorous exchanges of theoretical debate, explorations of lesson models and approaches to teaching, discussions of a range of resources and analyses of classroom observation and practice. The seminar room is always in use, with one or other participant always there to make a contribution. A core group of 19 trainees leads the discussion: some students drop into the seminar daily, others once a week or so. Students can listen and learn as there is no pressure to contribute. There are never any interruptions. Individual contributions can vary in length from one minute to ten. Most of the time the discussion is intense and serious – there are disagreements, but also frequent bursts of humour. Some contributors will be asked to repeat arguments several times for clarification. Participants leave to read/reflect on particular ideas or to compose a response to an argument, sometimes returning several days later to make their point. Some pairs or small groups continue the discussion elsewhere. Across the two-month period the resource area grows, with books, materials, lesson plans and other teaching materials brought in from homes, libraries and schools.

This account was constructed from observations of a two-month professional development seminar carried out via the Internet[65] for trainee teachers. Here is a summary of the electronic data on which the account is based:

- 110 trainee teachers from across the UK regularly participated in the on-line seminar across an eight-week period (May–June).

- A core group of 19 contributors (defined as posting between 3–10+ messages each) developed.

- Individual participants selectively read electronic message 'threads'.

- Some trainees re-read electronic messages on as many as three separate occasions.

- Response times (namely 'time message read to time replied to') varied between one and ten days.

- Participants articulated their intentions to reflect, check information, search for a resource, and compose a reply (actioning of intentions varied from one hour to one week).[66]

- Many and varied resources were both posted and downloaded by trainees and tutors.[67]

- Message postings varied in length from one brief comment of a few words, to 50 lines of closely argued prose.

- Personal e-mail exchanges about the seminar took place between participants.[68]

We are only beginning to find a language to describe and analyse electronic environments or indeed to understand the potential of the structures they offer to support learning. We often struggle to compare them with face-to-face learning environments, but they do not translate neatly into traditional professional development activity, since there are some learning opportunities afforded by such communication that cannot be so interpreted. In our in-depth study of this innovative professional development environment, we were able to elicit eight significant elements particularly facilitated by the electronic medium that seemed to support authentic pedagogy.

Authentic professional task

`How do you teach grammar?' was a real question for all participants, raising important and controversial aspects of learning and teaching in their specialisms. Most were attending job interviews during this period and knowledge about language was a topic much under scrutiny. The launch lecture emphasised a variety of ways of looking at and resolving the question under discussion. It encouraged a climate of critical debate, frank analysis and understanding of the theme that could be engaged in when and wherever students were situated (early morning/late at night/from any location in the UK).

Varied roles and relationships

'Old timers' (the tutor), 'novices' (the trainees), 'aspiring experts' (some of the trainees and recently qualified teachers) and other 'experts' (guest speakers, course tutors) though physically distant were able to work alongside one another on a daily basis.[69] Subject tutors raised key points, new questions and ideas, checked for misunderstandings, and selected and posted relevant electronic resources. A variety of other roles were taken on at various times by student contributors, including facilitator, enthusiast, modeller, friend, critic, opponent, expert.

Distributed knowledge

Participants' resumés revealed a wealth of expertise, illustrating joint learning at its richest. The wide geographical reach of the e-environment meant that it could include native speakers of French, as well as linguists fluent in Spanish, German, Ibo, and Russian. Trainees with specialisms in literature or special needs provided complementary knowledge in discussions. The knowledge of numerous 'others' was woven into such discussions: mentors, other teachers, course texts, tutors, texts about the teaching of grammar, theoretical texts about language, quotes from children's literature and novels. Explicit and implicit references served to illustrate the complexity of the concept of 'distributed' cognition.

Creation of a joint oeuvre

This seminar was of itself a significant oeuvre,[70] a collective work that allowed for explicit sharing and negotiable ways of thinking as a group, as well as supplying a public record of the individual effort involved together with the joint knowledge being developed. 'There were great ideas but it sort of didn't matter who they came from … these were messages … I feel … the fact that somebody

(Continued)

(Continued)

said it before you or said it in a different way … these were important points … it's almost as if anyone could have made them.'[71] Unlike spoken discussion, the permanence of the electronic conference, which could be revisited, made the activity weighty, to be taken seriously.

Sharing the stories of practice

Trainees frequently related anecdotes which were references to school place-ments, stories about mentors, students and their own classrooms, and allusions to their own school day experiences and those of their own children. Cumulatively these stories signalled membership of this community: together they 'acquired' a store of appropriate stories that could be referred back to and, more importantly, knew the appropriate occasions for telling them.[72]

Group reflection

Thinking aloud was characterised by tentative discourse not dissimilar to the best of sensitive face-to-face debate ('It occurs to me that' … ; 'Presumably if' … ; 'I'm finding my feelings to be ambiguous') that frequently led to new angles or further problems to be solved. The physical permanency of the electronic discussion on the Web lent itself to the constant revision and addition of new ideas.

Changing identity

It can be argued that this professional development activity transformed the identity of individual contributors as well as the group as a whole. Over the two-month period trainees showed an increased willingness to formulate and ask questions,[73] a growing acknowledgement of complexity,[74] and increased assurance, confidence and knowledge of the subject at issue.[75] By participating in a carefully designed e-learning environment, individuals developed as sub-ject experts, and as more confident, critical professionals, ready to work within new communities and keen to try out new forms of pedagogy.[76]

Identity has been an underlying leitmotif throughout this chapter. Toolkits, we have argued, are living compasses that support, inform and direct daily prac-tices and ways of knowing. They also have the potential to constrain and limit ways of thinking and pedagogy. Or they can open up new possibilities for action. Material tools, resources and technologies play an important (and fre-quently undervalued) role in these toolkits of practice. Combined with a shared vision of practice and powerful conceptual frameworks, they can be crucial elements of real pedagogy. In our final case study,[77] we look at a teacher development programme that explicitly researched these ideas, demonstrating the key role that new and enriched toolkits play in the process of professional learning, teacher development, identity and self-esteem.

'I did not know how to dream but now I know.' (DEEP learner)

'I could never go back to not using new technologies. I feel in touch with the latest development in education. It enables us to progress into the 21st century by leaps and bounds.' (DEEP educator)

More than 113 million children worldwide go without primary schooling and it is calculated that 18 million teachers are still needed if the Millennium Development Goals of equal access to education for all are to be met.[78] Two thirds of the global poor are currently concentrated in rural areas,[79] so it is therefore unsurprising that 82 per cent of children not in school are located in rural settings. Concurrently, the scarcity of local trained personnel, including teachers, is also greatest in the countryside, especially in Sub-Saharan Africa. Experienced practitioners largely avoid poor rural placements, or relocate to towns and cities as soon as they are able.[80]

The experience of poverty has been described as taking many different forms of 'un-freedom', of which financial poverty is but one.[81] These multiple un-freedoms engender a sense of 'stuckness'[82] that can incapacitate whole communities and those who live and work in them. Teachers in poor communities in developing contexts should be shaping a new future through their work: they are the multipliers, authority figures, and agents of change in schools and the communities they serve.[83] But all too often the 'stuckness' of rural poverty drains teachers' initiative and sense of agency. It is not hard to see why: rural teachers have little by way of support and negligible opportunities for training in new knowledge and skills, yet they are expected to engage daily with huge classes (sometimes of 80 or more students) and to motivate every learner. They are themselves trapped in the poverty of the communities they serve, facing an isolation that is at once physical, social and intellectual. Such experiences therefore limit rural teachers' abilities to engage in those activities required for quality teaching: developing contemporary subject and pedagogic knowledge; planning skills; the ability to make informed choices; motivating learners; developing relevant curricula and being creative. Importantly, they also lack access to a wide range of physical learning resources and informational tools that would enable them to develop and expand both their own and their learners' capabilities. Indeed, they have no routine access to professional artefacts of any kind, let alone the wide-ranging toolkits that many teachers in other parts of the world take for granted (for example, up to date pedagogic ideas; reference materials; well-resourced libraries; planning documents; photocopiers; example lesson approaches; subject-related resources, dictionaries; thesaurus, and so on).

The Digital Education Enhancement Project (DEEP) is working in such settings to investigate whether new information and communication technologies might be used to enhance and extend traditional teaching toolkits – and hence learning and pedagogy. The first phase of the research (2001–2005) was carried

(Continued)

(Continued)

out in primary schools in Egypt and South Africa, with 48 teachers and over 2,000 primary school students, and it focused particularly on the learning and teaching of literacy, numeracy and science[84] with a particular emphasis on student motivation and achievement. Teachers worked in pairs to implement and evaluate a short, curriculum-focused, school-based, professional development programme, facilitated by a 'mobile' toolkit that included laptops, hand-held computers, digital cameras, and a variety of electronic resources, professional activities and support structures.[85]

Four key pedagogic principles were made explicit to project participants:

- *First*, teacher learning and development are social processes.

- *Second*, teachers have the potential to be change agents: proactive and intentionally focused on the purposes of the communities to which they belong.

- *Third*, a social perspective enables us to recognise that the physical boundaries of learning are limitless.

- *Fourth* (and most important for this project), tools and technologies are an essential component of agency. Culture provides the 'toolkit' of technologies, techniques and procedures with which we learn about, respond to, act on and manage our experience of the world. The limits of our mental predispositions can be transcended by using more powerful symbolic systems such as language and notations and also by our uses of human tools, technologies and related artefacts. In this very deep sense, our contemporary knowledge, understanding and forms of meaning making depend on the cultural toolkits we have at our disposal. If pedagogy is to empower human beings then it must transmit the toolkit the culture has developed for doing so.

The research revealed just how exhausting and de-motivating it is for teachers to maintain the intellectually demanding work of teaching day after day without recourse to anything other than the most rudimentary of toolkits. Participants were outspoken about the limitations and restrictions of their customary toolkits, especially as they became used to a much more sophisticated repertoire. They described the daily grind of commuting to work (one and a half hours each way) by train, 'taxi', and thence on foot, to face large classes with only chalk and chalkboard, government curriculum documents, a meagre supply of dated books and no professional development or support: 'Everyday we arrived to write "the lesson for the day" on the board. The next day we rubbed it out and started again. No work could be saved. They (the students) often couldn't read my writing.'

The physical elements of the DEEP contemporary toolkit were designed to facilitate professional learning and new classroom practices, while being easy and flexible to use in a variety of settings, as well as creating minimum physical disruption to school and home environments. A few modest digital devices provided access to an extraordinarily powerful and mobile *'pocket classroom'*, usable in a range of settings. One hand-held computer, for instance, enabled access to e-books, a thesaurus, a dictionary, a notebook, a diary, Xhosa texts, workbooks, curriculum materials, games and puzzles, planners and student resources. The laptop stored a range of additional artefacts designed to enrich

practice: planning tools; captured websites including multi-media case studies of effective subject teaching; model schemes of work; approaches to classroom organisation with large class sizes, and so forth.

Teacher pairings were seen from the outset as an essential aspect of the supporting framework, reflecting the notion of joint knowledge building (a key principle of the conceptual framework set out above). The sharing of study activities and resources was encouraged as was the development of a common portfolio, while a locally relevant environmental theme (Endangered Animals) modelled a range of literacy-, numeracy- and science-focused professional activities. Resources to support these included: a print-based teacher guide and specially devised CD–ROM incorporating a range of related lesson plans; case studies; stories; video clips and websites. Activity cards summarised the professional development activities.

This common toolkit allowed for increasingly demanding classroom activity, as teachers' confidence increased (for example, from simple literacy word processing and Web search activities about local animal species, to the e-mailing of research findings to students in other schools).

Research findings showed that this professional toolkit:

- enhanced teachers professional knowledge and capabilities by extending their subject knowledge, enabling planning and preparation for teaching to be more effective, and by developing the range of teachers' existing pedagogic practices;

- enabled every teacher to introduce a broad range of new activities into planned lessons, with wide ranging evidence of positive outcomes for learning;

(Continued)

(Continued)

- led to students showing high levels of motivation and a range of achievements, including improvements in reading and scientific understanding (as reported by the teachers, parents, school principals and students themselves).[86]

Teachers, together with parents, governors, school principals and community members, gave testimony to the positive impact this expanded toolkit of practice had on learner motivation and the quality of learning. The professional status and self-esteem of teachers were also enhanced within their immediate communities and more broadly in the societies they serve.

Management theory uses the phrase 'helicopter ability' to describe leaders' capacities to rise above the everyday, to look beyond the immediate and distinguish, as it were, the wood from the trees. We term the distancing effect that a new professional toolkit had on DEEP participants as 'the *intambanane* effect' (*intambanane* is Xhosa for a 'dancing kestrel'). For not only did this expanded repertoire of practice allow teachers to rise above the minutiae and the daily, undignified, struggle to teach with minimal resources, training and support networks, but such practice also enabled them to dance, to dip and to dive. Many of the teachers began to think creatively with colleagues about new approaches to pedagogy, and in so doing their own personal and professional identities were significantly transformed.

Teacher development and pedagogy stand as cornerstones for change, but professional work (as many chapters in this book have shown) demands complex professional knowledge. Teacher learning, knowledge and pedagogy, we have proposed, can be significantly enhanced by the analysis and thoughtful development of contemporary professional toolkits.

7

Identities

The child is made of one hundred.
The child has
A hundred languages
A hundred hands
A hundred thoughts
A hundred ways of thinking
... The school and the culture
... tell the child
to discover the world already there
and of the hundred
they steal the ninety-nine.

They tell the child
That work and play
*   Reality and fantasy*
Science and imagination
Sky and earth
Reason and dream are things
That do not belong together
*   And thus they tell the child*
That the hundred is not there.[1]

Education is risky, for it fuels the sense of possibility. But a failure to equip minds with the skills for understanding and acting in the cultural world is not simply scoring a pedagogical zero. It risks creating alienation, defiance and practical incompetence. And all of these undermine the viability of a culture.[2]

To begin always anew, to make, to reconstruct, and to not spoil, to refuse to bureaucratise the mind, to understand and to live life as process – live to become.[3]

The inspiration for our book has been the work of educators who, despite parochial or national pressures, have concerned themselves with advancing knowledge about the processes of learning and teaching. We have been using their work across the chapters to help us to distil a set of new frameworks and conceptual tools, together with an alternative discourse by which pedagogy might be meaningfully discussed and developed, whatever the educational setting and context. In this penultimate chapter we draw on more of their ideas and practices to explore the key concept of identity and its role in pedagogy.

If we believe that learning is essentially a lifelong process, then identity must be at the heart of pedagogy. Thanks to the work of teachers such as those we have exemplified, many young people will never look at themselves, the world, or their fellow learners in the same way again. The pedagogic settings such teachers create enable students to learn empowering ways to use the mind, including how to use technology for extending their powers. They help develop learners' self-esteem and give them the opportunity to play valued and meaningful roles within a range of learning communities. Most importantly, they raise students' awareness of future possibilities. We also know that these learners improve dramatically in conventional performance measures – given such learning opportunities, why would they not? This mix of agentive efficacy and self-esteem combines learners' sense of what they believe themselves to be (or even hope to be) capable of and what they fear is beyond them.[4]

In focusing here on our sixth assertion that pedagogy must build the self-esteem and identity of learners, we want to distinguish five essential attributes of identity that we see as key to the building of such esteem. These attributes, identified through our research with learners and educators, are often neglected in discussions of contemporary pedagogy. We have already discussed aspects of these attributes in earlier chapters, but by highlighting them here, we hope to provide a fresh lens through which identity and its role in pedagogy can be emphasised and further explored. The first of these attributes of identity we call *voice*: this concerns the process by which we take control of our lives, our activities and who we want to be. The second is *relationships*, a key element of identity but so often underestimated in the development of self-image and esteem. The third is *community*, introduced as a theoretical concept in Chapter 4. That subtle combination of people, place and joint enterprise that enables us to define, construct and affirm (or not, as the case may be) who we are. The fourth attribute, also discussed in Chapter 4 in relation to learning, is *language*, the most intimate, personal manifestation of our selves, our communities and our ways of meaning making. The fifth is *imagination*, which allows us to envision what we – and our communities – might in the future become, enabling the gradual modification of mindsets, shared beliefs and activities that can lead to wholly new identities and ways of being. Each of these attributes, we would argue, contributes significantly to learner identity and self-esteem.

First, *voice*. Developing the human potential to be proactive, problem orientated, attentionally focused, constructional, and directed to ends[5] would seem to be a key focus of pedagogy. And as we have suggested in previous chapters decisions, strategies, heuristics and toolkits can all be powerful means of supporting the development of what Bruner calls 'agency', and Freire terms 'critical consciousness'. Students (both pre-school and adult) in the classrooms of Caswell, May and Reggio Emilia, for instance, are encouraged to generate their own questions and hypotheses and they also take on the role of experts and teachers. Fenway High School's young people vocally debated with more than 100 scientists, policy makers and business people the urgent question '*What should be done – in and out of schools to create American scientists*'? In this sense, agency is an unfolding process of knowing, acting and being-in-the-world.

Enabling learners to feel they have a genuine *voice* in the learning process is a key aspect of developing agency and, hence, identity and self-esteem. This is not a new idea. Freire argued, for instance, that one of the first tasks of the adult educator was to break the 'culture of silence' of those who were illiterate, who felt that others knew best about the world and that therefore they should remain silent. He searched for pedagogic practices that would fracture this silence, identifying learners' true potential through new approaches to learning. Such approaches required learners to gradually feel confident enough to move away from an unquestioning acceptance of dominant[6] worldviews, to value their own knowledge and develop their own perspectives and viewpoints.

This notion of 'voice'[7] has a high profile in all the pedagogic settings discussed throughout this collection, including St Saviour's and St Olave's School. Integral to that school's urban pedagogy is a strong focus on the ways in which young people – and members of staff – can have their say on matters that concern them, both in and out of school. This may range from conversations about learning and teaching to inviting evaluative comment on recent developments in the school or classroom policy and practice.

Within the UK, Jean Ruddock's work[8] has been critical in the development of both theoretical and practical understandings of the importance of student voice. However, she became concerned that the much-publicised notion of 'student consultation' arising out of her work and supported by government funding,[9] was concentrating students' thinking on relatively superficial changes (such as their views on school meals, corridor behaviour or school toilets). It remains rare for student consultation to really focus on learning in the way Ruddock advocates. Yet recent research in UK schools[10] on student consultation, carried out by some of her colleagues at the University of Cambridge, has shown that even young learners, across class and gender, are able to express an awareness of how they prefer to learn and what motivates them. In the Cambridge study, activities that *'foster a stronger sense of agency and ownership'* come high on the student agenda. Learners say they value classroom situations in which their teachers engage seriously with their contributions and they also value opportunities to be actively involved in the learning process. One participating teacher in this research study reported a sustained and reciprocated increase in student/teacher confidence as a result of introducing pupil consultation into his classroom practice. His students commented repeatedly on the trust that he had shown in them when in one particular lesson he sent them out in pairs to the school grounds, without a teacher, to carry out a scientific activity. More generally, they made clear how pleased they were at having their ideas taken seriously and by the confidence that their teacher appeared to have in them. This teacher was in turn impressed by how much he had learnt about his students'

attitudes and by the enhancement of his own capacity to reflect on his teaching as a result of the consultation. He was in no doubt about his students'
increased motivation.

In two of the classrooms in the study, teachers' steady and sustained use of
student consultation on the learning process seemed to lead, in just two or
three months, to a higher level of mutual trust and respect between teachers
and pupils, while some six months later these teachers' enthusiasm for pupil
consultation was still evident. Both teachers reported that the experiment had
had a continuing impact on their teaching. One of the teachers said she had
developed new habits of listening informally to what pupils said about their
experiences in her classroom, often to one another; and in addition was
actively planning more formal consultation procedures. The second had
already developed such formal procedures, using questionnaires followed up
by whole-class discussion, and he was planning how to disseminate pupil
consultation across his science department.

The researchers here argued that teachers' motivation to persist in using their
students' ideas stemmed in part from their sense of obligation to do so in solidarity with their students and in part from the growing evidence of its benefits in facilitating more effective teacher-student collaboration. The research
study concluded that students' requests for opportunities to engage more
deeply in their learning, and for more active and independent involvement,
seemed to imply notions of entitlement based on principles of active rights.
Their call was to be trusted by their teachers to act, as opposed to having their
rights fulfilled by the actions of others.[11]

Practices such as these demand intellectual courage, as well as a sense of
autonomy, in teachers themselves. They also demand perseverance, since all
too often the dominant discourse of the statutory curriculum leaves little
space or time for the voice of the learner. Teachers themselves need to feel
autonomous and agentive if they are to enable their own learners to be the
same. The University of Fort Hare's professional development programmes
in South Africa, discussed in Chapters 2 and 6, recognised the importance
of teachers being enabled to see themselves as agents of change and helped
them to develop an authentic voice in their local communities, 'Seeing
myself being able to make a difference in people's lives'. In Chapter 6 we
looked at ways in which new technologies were being used to support
trainee teachers in developing voice and self-confidence in their own
views of practice. Fenway High School uses teacher blogs on its school
website to ensure that the voices of its teachers are heard directly and regularly by parents, partners, policy makers and peers, in a high profile and
multi-media way. The website gives priority to the school's visions, core
values and shared habits of mind, rather than conforming to the traditional
structure of school websites which are so often aimed at informing readers of compliance with statutory requirements, school inspection results
and so forth.

Certainly, if teachers' voices are to be genuinely heard, formal structures of one kind or another are critical. The DEEP programme in Egypt, building on local custom and practice, ensured a highly public sharing of new learning with the local community, parents, educational officials and other key members of the community. Teachers were given a voice to an audience of over 200 people and the ceremony increased teacher confidence, sense of agency and esteem. Such a public and high profile event was also seen to encourage parents and governorate officials to care about and be proud of their teachers, learners and schools and to become more involved in their activity.

A range of newly established teacher networks,[12] supported by new technologies, is providing other means of bringing into the spotlight teachers' struggles to debate and improve the quality of learning and teaching. Such a network in Hertfordshire and Cambridge in the UK, for example, is underpinned by a belief that a real impact in schools cannot occur unless teachers themselves lead change in their classrooms. For too long such leadership has been invisible, members of the network would argue. The network is developing a 'knowledge creation engine' that will enable teachers, advisors and academics to work together to accumulate authentic accounts of teachers' work, especially work that is both strategic and inquiry-based. Such accounts demand that academic researchers play the role of 'story-tellers and secretaries', to enable teachers' voices to be heard.[13] This work demonstrates that, in spite of the unprecedented pressures that teachers face, there is still an enormous desire to actively take on the challenge of change.[14]

There are many other ways in which teacher researchers can express their voices and share with others, such as conducting workshops for other teachers. As we have seen, St Saviour's and St Olave's School supports staff in taking a lead in the professional development of peers. For teachers who want to reach beyond these immediate audiences to the broader field, writing for publication in journals, newspapers or other publications can have a high impact.[15] Teacher research continues to be underrepresented in professional publications, which is understandable given the hectic nature of professional lives that requires such full-time energy. Yet, where teachers such as Caswell, Simpson, Shakespear and May are given time to publish their practice and research in journals,[16] books, official reports[17] and on the web,[18] such work has had tremendous influence on teaching communities, some transforming the profession in important ways.[19] Because teachers are the principal partners in the creation of new pedagogies, as we have argued, their writing benefits the fields of learning and teaching. We need more voices from teachers in the public domain and more accounts of how complicated and exciting learning can be when teachers look closely and aren't afraid to write about what they are seeing.[20]

The second attribute of identity that we want to point to flows naturally from the first, that is *relationships*. One of us remembers going to give a talk to teacher trainers in a very large East Midlands university. Over 300 students had assembled for the weekly invited lecture. A few minutes into the session a large, apparently student-designed banner on the back wall of the lecture theatre became apparent.

Children don't learn from people they don't like

it read. It formed an excellent way into the lecture. There are many manifestations of the relationships attribute that require trust, dependability, respect, consistency and warmth. A teacher who regularly marks our work, returns it on time, and gives constructive feedback is a teacher we will come to depend on and trust. Teachers who are approachable, who create these little moments of time to listen, are also likely to gain our trust. We have all had the experience of working in a group or team that seemed to have just the right balance of mutual respect and trust (and perhaps too often we have had the contrary experience).

How are relationships created and sustained in institutions like schools, colleges or teaching hospitals? Leadership plays a role, but often at the outset when establishing personal commitment as well as supportive protocols and procedures. Thereafter, within a shared and open framework, trust can be built. It's a good feeling. There is nothing accidental, however, about its origins and in formal institutions developing quality relationships a sense of trust has to be worked at. Providing a 'voice' for learners, as discussed in the previous section, is important. It implies empathy and understanding and a recognition of the affective and emotional dimensions of human learning and development.[21]

Reggio Emilia's pedagogy sets great store by this, seeing the interrelatedness of the affective and cognitive processes as being key to young children's development. We have already emphasised the importance of the teacher's role as mentor to students in the vignette of St Saviour's and St Olave's School and the role played by the Advisory at Fenway High School based on the thinking of Theodore Sizer ('If even one person in a school knows him/her well enough to care, a student's chances of success go up dramatically'). Fenway's teachers and their Advisory students become friends and allies, interested in one another's lives − effectively forming a support group.

Paulo Freire also appealed in his pedagogic writings for humility on the part of all educators in light of a huge need for mutual respect between teacher and learner. He believed there were six essentials for successful educational dialogue: love, humility, faith, mutual trust, hope, and critical thinking. His notion of a pedagogy of love demanded that the teacher must always begin with a deep respect for all students, and for what they could bring to dialogue that would make it richer for everyone. Such love cannot exist in a relation of domination, he argues, it is an act of courage not of fear, a commitment to others. By talking simultaneously about reason and knowledge, and about love and hope, Freire brought together the interrelatedness of cognitive understanding and sensitivity (see Chapter 3).

Over the last few decades there have been many attempts to establish schools with a distinctly different pattern of teacher pupil relationships. One of the best known and most written about was A. S. Neil's Summerhill in England.[22] Here pupils worked out their own curriculum, using teachers to support their enquiries, and few if any checks were put on their general behaviour including the ways in which they addressed and worked with teachers. Summerhill, however, is a private, independent school. Attempts to do this in state-funded schooling have attracted fair degrees of hostility. One example of a school that set out to create new forms of relationships and has prospered over time is Stantonbury Campus, a secondary school in the new city of Milton Keynes in England, 50 minutes north of London. The campus was opened in 1974 under a charismatic and influential head, Geoffrey Cooksey. He set out a manifesto for the new school which focused on three Rs: roles, relationships and resources. Working with the first group of teachers (almost disciples, you could say) he sought to establish a new role for teachers, a role that emphasised greater respect, even humility, in working with adolescent learners. To symbolise this new form of relationship pupils and teachers used first-name terms at all times. This caused considerable local and national controversy at the time. But the school also put enormous effort into developing resource-based learning, focusing strongly on multiple modes of pedagogy and establishing binding commitments from pupils (and their parents) about the curriculum objectives they were trying to achieve.

The story of this school is an interesting one (and over the more than 30 years of its existence the story is more complex than this vignette can show). But it does represent one attempt to fuse a powerful, affective dimension on relationships with a tough (if negotiated) approach to both the curriculum and learning. Over 30 years on, the school flourishes while maintaining this interesting balance. The local community and parents approve, examination results are some of the best in the local authoriy, and even the notoriously difficult-to-please English national inspectorate has commended the school's style.

The building of relationships may seem such an obvious feature of any pedagogic setting. And yet we know that down through the ages the school room setting has been parodied and maligned: from Charles Dickens's 'Gradgrind' to Alan Bennett's *The History Boys*, images of teachers, classrooms and pedagogic settings have been presented that too often resonate with the popular imagination in the way they negatively caricature the role of the teacher. It is as if the teacher was apart from the class or group without any shared sense of community, an attribute to which we now turn.

There is a profound connection between identity, self-esteem and our third attribute, *community*. We often think of identity as being about developing a sense of self. But identity is essentially also a social process, for who we are, as we have seen throughout this book, lies in the way we live day to day and the people we care about, interact with (or don't), and the 'projects' we share. This experience of identity within a community is a way of being in the world and for any given individual there will be a plurality of overlapping identities – a plurality that can frequently be a source of stress and a contradiction in both our self-representation and social action. We may for instance, as discussed in previous chapters, have a role to play in a range of groups and communities (for example school staff, governing body, family, neighbourhood group, sports group, national orchestra, religious organisation, union), as well as in sub-communities within our educational community (for example as class teacher, year team member, governor, parent). Agonising as a parent between attending a key meeting at work or going to see our child in the school play is one trivial example of competing demands. This is no different for our students, as the case study of CL's differing loyalties illustrated. The groups they belong to – particularly peer groups – present competing and powerful allegiances and demands. A community's relative weight in influencing our identity depends on the strong or weak relationship we have with a particular group.

Currently the notion of a community pursuing 'shared goals' has only limited validity as an account of what goes on in most school year groups or classes. Indeed one of the central problems of schooling is the lack of a shared agenda among pupils and between teachers and pupils. Students' accounts of their school experiences, collected by colleagues at the University of Cambridge for the research on pupil voice mentioned earlier, are highly consistent with this idea that schools' learning agendas are rarely high on the agendas of many pupils. More importantly students, especially those who are being seen to 'fail', do not feel themselves to be members of the same community as their teachers and more highly attaining peers, as we saw in our case study of British born Asian youths in Chapter 4.[23]

Penelope Eckert, who has researched the implications of community for a school's practice, argues that schools need to articulate with learners' other, more influential, communities rather than setting up conflicts of identities. In documenting a school reform experiment drawing on the concept of 'community', she proposes that classrooms should become places where students take charge of their learning for life – where they become eager constructors of knowledge and view the entire world around them as a rich and welcome resource. Engaged learners of high school age collect and trade baseball cards, stamps, or music; become a Deadhead; play double dutch, Dungeons and Dragons, video games, high performance Monopoly; join a garage band. If such students are to have opportunities for full participation in school, schools need to offer communities with the same drawing power as students' other communities, the same potential for participation that is offered in families, neighbourhoods, communities, workplaces, clubs, and so on. And the communities that students form in school cannot be isolated from the many other communities in which they participate. The school is only a viable community for students to the extent that it supports their participation in other communities as well.[24]

May understands this well in her construction of a learning community for history undergraduates (see Chapters 2 and 6). As we have seen, her concern is to bring potentially competing identities (students' commitment to peer communities and their own families) into the classroom, both as source of knowledge to be taken seriously and studied in the classroom and as a source of support for learners. Caswell, by contrast, explicitly constructs a new and self-contained learning community with her young pupils, ensuring they are motivated by a shared purpose. Students in this developing community are clear about their respective roles, motivated by their responsibilities, and carefully supported in carrying these out.

The influential US educator Ann Brown has argued that even primary school classrooms should construct participation frameworks in which individual learners can regularly carry out tasks and roles that are unique to them and at the same time indispensable to the class community as a whole. Although we believe it to be somewhat romantic to think of young children entering the community of practice of adult disciplines, she comments, awareness of the deep principles of academic disciplines should enable us to design intellectual practices for the young that are stepping stones to mature understanding, or at least not glaringly inconsistent with the end goal. Such an approach requires the development of independent expertise on some topic of 'inquiry mastery' which, while ultimately the responsibility of all members of the class, demands that each student has uniquely contributed (this can be as varied as a test, or a quiz, or designing a biopark to protect an endangered species). The metaphor of a jigsaw illustrates this view of a young community: one piece missing, an individual learner missing, a vital piece of understanding for the whole group missing.

New technologies (Chapter 6) offer some interesting new dimensions to this important concept of community and belonging. The Deptford Mudlarking research project,[25] for instance, has been researching students' use of hand-held computers for exploring and interacting with their local environment and community. The project was designed to enable young people aged 11–14 to actively engage with local places of historic, educational and personal interest in Deptford Creek, South London, by using state-of-the-art mobile technology. Students created multimedia 'enhanced landscapes' of their local environment, which were combined to create a tour of special places in their community through text, drawings, images (still and video) and audio.

Future visitors to the Creek could then access this tour, adding in their own reflections. The outcome was a rich and fluid journey companion illustrating the many new possibilities for extending learning outside the conventional classroom environment into the local community by using affordable and accessible mobile technologies. Although students were divided into groups and pairs, there was a lot of interaction and collaboration at the key nodes along Deptford Creek. Students shared 'hidden stories' from the places that were important to them, fully involved in the learning context and local community by creating their own personal and permanent responses to their live environment.

In preparing trainee teachers for working at Fenway School, Eileen Shakespear is alive to the importance of ensuring that they recognise the important role of community in students' identities and hence learning.

Despite good intentions, many teachers who work with students of racial and cultural backgrounds different from their own have limited experience in teaching them and become frustrated and angry at the conditions in which they must work, argues Eileen.[26] Findings from a major US survey[27] confirmed her view, revealing that feelings of alienation from school were prevalent among students, parents, and teachers at the secondary level; four in ten (39 per cent) secondary school students only trust their teachers a little or not at all.[28] To help face this challenge, Eileen stresses the importance of educators having critical information about their students as well as their families and communities: the knowledge, experiences, perceptions, and expectations of their students; the expectations, perceptions, and desires of their families; and the history and culture of their communities.[29] Building this knowledge and competency takes time. It is important, Eileen argues, to instill in interns and beginning teachers an interested, open posture towards students and their families, one that will become a 'way of life' for them throughout their careers.

Several activities can help to bridge these gaps, she suggests; home visits or conversations with parents about their expectations for their child's schooling; observations of students in and out of school; conversations with students and knowledgeable community members; attendance at community gatherings; volunteering in community-based organisations; and learning and sharing what writers and thinkers of different cultures have to say about themselves and their culture.[30]

In association with Tufts University Eileen has developed a programme for all new interns: *Uncovering Communities: A Community Curriculum for Interns and New Teachers*, which is also published for others to use.[31] The Uncovering Communities[32] curriculum has been refined and developed year on year since 2003. It aims to build community understanding among interns by means of seven half-day seminars conducted in the community or at the school in the first term of the year. Goals include: cultivating in interns a deeper understanding and appreciation of students' cultures, histories, and home communities; reflecting on their assumptions about urban areas; understanding the impact of race, ethnicity, and culture in their lives and their classrooms; providing an opportunity to develop and maintain collegial relationships with other teachers. Activities include formal interviews with community activists and expert people, informal conversations with residents in various neighbourhoods, and half-day tours led by school students showing what children and teens do in their communities – where they play, where they hang out, where they go to church. The guides convey the history of the neighbourhood, point out important landmarks and community buildings, and make interns feel 'invited' into their neighbourhoods.

Seminar 6, 'Bringing It All Back Home', towards the close of the programme, aims to get interns to capture their own neighbourhood in images, to compare it with where their students live, and to see the disjunction and similarities between students' and interns' experiences of place. Armed with cameras, the interns explore their neighbourhoods and capture ten photographs of places of significance. These images are posted for everyone to see during one of the seminar sessions and a discussion is facilitated whereby they can extrapolate themes from their neighbourhoods' images.[33]

Interns' evaluations of their year of study show their growing awareness of their own and their students' identities in broad terms of 'growth' and esteem rather than in conventional, one-off, summative academic outcomes:

> I can't judge the success of my teaching. I know I am definitely doing a lot of good things, but I think the success will come when I see my kids off to college. I want them to be competitive in the world outside of school.

> We got the Math Connections kids to complete electronic portfolios, which live on the school's hard drive. The students' finished products were amazing. They could see their growth over the course of the year.

> I don't know how I'm going to judge my successes. It's not going to be what the teachers next year say about me or my students. It's not from tests or quizzes. It may come from the students choosing a piece of writing that they did during the year that they feel really proud of.

Two of most important questions for interns at the end of the semester, Eileen Shakespear argues, are: how does this work affect how we see our students and does it make us more able to see and to serve them better? Questions such as these are the drivers of pedagogies concerned with the development of identity.

A fourth attribute of identity is *language*. If there is anything so automatic in our lives that it is difficult to achieve real consciousness about, then it is the inseparability of language and identity. We live in language and, like fish who (according to the proverb) will be the last to discover water, have difficulty grasping what it is like to 'swim' in language.

Not that we lack competence in language, far from it. We are if anything too expert. Four to five thousand languages are thought to be in current use worldwide. This figure is almost certainly on the low side. And it seems

reasonable to assert that the human species developed and made use of at least
twice the number we can record today. The language catalogue begins with
Aba, an Altaic idiom spoken by the Tartars, and ends with Zyriene, a Finno-
Ugaritic speech in use between the Urals and the Arctic shore. By comparison, the classification of different types of stars, planets and asteroids runs to a
mere handful.[34] Whatever our home language, it is a symbolic tool: a system
of sounds, meaning and structures with which we make sense of the world. It
also functions, as we have seen in previous chapters, as a tool of thought, as a
means of social organisation, as the repository and means of transmitting
knowledge, and as the raw material of literature. It is the creator, sustainer, and
destroyer of human relationships. And so because language is a fundamental
feature of any community, it is a central aspect of a person's sense of social
identity.[35]

Some children in our classrooms have two or three mother tongues and for
a minority this will not include English. Acquisition of fluency in one or more
will be determined by a combination of its status in the home, community,
and society more broadly.[36]

In addition to the home languages students bring with them to the classroom, there are other complex discourses that we all share. Bakhtin has argued
that the taking on of different voices and their attitudes is part of the 'ideological becoming of a human being'. We daily have to encounter, he argues, social
dialects, characteristic group behaviours, professional jargons, languages of generations and age–groups, tendentious languages, languages of authorities, of various circles and of passing fashion, languages that serve the socio–political
purpose of the day, even of the hour (each day has its own slogan, its own
vocabulary, its own emphasis).[37] In this sense it is more appropriate to refer to
discourses or the forms of language generated by the practices of people with
shared interests and purposes.[38] Such discourses include ways of using language
which are not merely a matter of 'technical' terminology but are also distinctive ways of presenting information, including telling stories, arguing cases (for
example, the genres of scientific reports, business letters, 'Eng Lit'), and producing historical evidence. All represent the conventions practised by a particular discourse community that are integral to our toolkits of practice. Cobb
and colleagues have argued that 'subject' discourse can exclude learners from a
classroom community just as surely as ignoring learners' home languages and
dialects.[39]

Imagination is our fifth attribute of identity, of our understanding of the
world and our place in it. It can not only make a big difference to our experience of identity, but also in how we view our own and others' potential for
learning and development. Drita's schooling in our Albania case study fiercely
sought to extinguish this attribute. The habits of mind engendered by the
Hoxha regime replaced imagination with fearfulness. By literally outlawing
processes such as questioning, making hypotheses, reading works of fiction
and poetry or encountering and producing works of art and music, the

communist regime ensured conformity to its controlling status quo that entailed an inability to dream forward or hope for the future.

Imagination enables us to expand ourselves out of the limits of time and space so we can create new images of the world and our place in it. Sixteen-year-old CL engages in this work of imagination when she envisions herself as a doctor or artist, trying out aspects of those worlds for size. It is interesting to note that one of the most frequent metaphors participants used in reporting on their experiences in both the DEEP and Kualida professional development projects was that of 'opening', as in 'new possibilities' and 'opening a new window on the world'. Or as one learner commented 'I did not know how to dream, but now I know'.

The development of the imagination as we use the term is not an individual process. The creative character of imagination is anchored in social interaction and communal experiences. It exists in the forging and exchanging of new knowledge or innovative products and is essential to the worlds of music, science, business, the arts, technology, industry, politics and education. Imagination exists in the collaborative processes of blending and re-configuring existing ideas, hypothesising, and working with others on common concerns from different standpoints. Creative possibilities are pervasive in the affairs of everyday life, its purposes and problems, and they can be expressed in teamwork, in organisations, in communities and in governments.[40]

So often schooling fails to promote or value the work of imagination, driven instead by a concern for individuals to acquire the past and present knowledge required by statutory national curricula. How often when we ask friends 'How are your children?' do we receive an answer summarising achievement scores, SATs, or examination results? Learning involves the whole person and also implies becoming a different person. Despite this, national mindsets focus us on discrete aspects of achievement that freeze learners in past and present comparisons with their peers, rather than exploring the broader aspects of their identity – passion, purpose, key relationships, future plans and dreams. Research shows that where the work of imagination is an aspect of knowledge that is valued and where imaginative processes become the subject of learning, teachers and learners collectively share and develop a sense of individual and collective possibilities.

Two years ago, students and teachers at St Saviour's and St Olave's School established an ongoing link with students and staff at Butterworth High School in South Africa's Eastern Cape. An urban pocket in a largely rural landscape, Butterworth, formerly at the heart of South Africa's black homelands, has inherited ongoing problems of homelessness and unemployment. Rural-urban migration has contributed to the growth of shanty towns and the school's intake reflects all the area's socio-cultural problems. The link is largely

(Continued)

(Continued)

facilitated by electronic communication in the form of e-mail and sms messaging together with regular video conferencing. However, the head teacher and several members of staff have spent time in the linked school, working out how they can support one another professionally in a long-term way by using new technologies.

The videoconferences began as spontaneous, relatively unplanned chats between a few selected students, but are now carefully planned by staff to support mutual curriculum development. Students have exchanged stories, letters, and photographs, listened to music together and discussed cultural events, customs and language issues. In a recent series of links twelve year olds worked out what ten items they would put into a respective time capsule to represent their lives in the twenty-first century – one to be buried in London, the other in Butterworth. In the final meeting they then endeavoured to jointly agree ten items that would go into a capsule that would represent their common experience as young people straddling two very different cultures.

The young people concerned are constantly surprised by the differences in experience that are revealed. Early on, for example, the London students were challenged by the South Africans' highly thought-through views on politics and issues such as globalisation. 'What do you think about globalisation?' asked one of the students from Butterworth. 'I think it would take away some individualities', was the response from another UK student. 'If all the world worked together it might take away some individual feelings you have about your own country.' A Butterworth student voiced his disagreement: 'Globalisation would help us to know more about people in England. We're not taking away your individuality; we just want to know more about you. It's like making a friend – you're not taking away his or her qualities – you just want to know the person more. We have 11 official languages here in South Africa. But we live together and we still speak our own languages and have our own cultures. It all comes back to what you think of yourself and how much you respect your culture and your traditions.'

One telling moment was when safety issues travelling outside the home were discussed. The South African students were surprised that their friends in South London were fearful to go out in the streets alone, particularly after dark. 'It's quite safe for us to walk around here at any time of the day or night', they replied, 'but where some of us are afraid is in our homes, of abuse from uncles or other relatives.'

Thus students in both cultures were invited to put themselves in the perspective of the other, and examine their own cultural practices based upon this new perspective. What would it be like to live in a place where it was not unusual to come upon a boy wielding a knife or gun? On the other hand, what would it be like to live in a culture where person-on-person crime within the home was commonplace?

Regular contact has extended the horizons of both sets of students and their teachers and has regularly brought surprise, delight, laughter, and a great deal of new learning. Wenger has suggested nine processes that support the work of imagination, many of which are illustrated by this and other case studies in this book:

- recognising our experiences in others, and standing in someone else's shoes;

- defining a trajectory that connects what we are doing to an extended identity, thus seeing ourselves in new ways;

- locating our engagement in broader systems of time and space;

- sharing stories, explanations, descriptions;

- opening access to distant practices through excursions, visiting, talking, observing;

- assuming the meaning of foreign artefacts and actions;

- creating models and representational artefacts;

- documenting historical development, events and transitions, and reinterpreting histories in new terms;

- generating scenarios, and exploring other possible worlds and identities.

Linear theories of learning and development seem to retain as much hold on the practice of teacher education as on the pedagogy of schools and classrooms. These theories suggest there is a single, correct course or sequence of professional development, leading to a fixed end point of mature fulfilment that is measurable in terms of discrete competences. Throughout previous chapters we have discussed wide-ranging research that shows that individual and societal intellectual development never follows such a linear route. Human development and change can only be understood by tracing innovations, disruptions and changes (both historical and contemporary) in relation to collective as well as individual learning histories and identities.

Since the mid-1980s there has been a growing body of research into the complex relationship between teacher professional knowledge and development – and pedagogy. To help us in our own practice as teacher educators, we have developed a model of teacher knowledge and development that takes account of the central importance of teacher identity. This model has been subject to development and change from 1995, when we first began to fashion it, to the present. The very diverse work of Lee Shulman, Howard Gardner and Jean Lave was important in our initial creation of the model.

Lee Shulman's influential work in the field of teacher professional knowledge arose from the pertinent question *how does the successful college student transform*

*his or her expertise into the subject matter form that high school students can compre-
hend?*[41] Shulman's conceptual framework of teacher professional knowledge
and development was based on the now well known distinction between
subject content knowledge, curricular knowledge and the category of *pedagogic content knowledge.* This analysis spawned a plethora of research.[42] While our
own exploration of professional knowledge and teacher development took
Shulman's analysis as an important starting point, it seemed to offer only partial insight into the complex nature of knowledge for teaching. Shulman's
emphasis on professional knowledge as a static body of content somehow
lodged in the mind of the teacher seemed to go against the grain of contemporary ideas about learning (see Chapter 4). His work, we felt, was
informed by an objectivist epistemology, underpinned by an implicit view
that academic scholars search for ultimate truths while teachers 'merely seek
to make that privileged representation accessible to ordinary mortals'.[43] In
this sense his theorising leaned on a view of knowledge as a contained, fixed,
and objective body of information and on a teacher-centred pedagogy. Both
focused primarily on the discrete skills and knowledge that a teacher might
acquire, rather than on the process of learning itself, including teachers' prior
knowledge and experiences and their complex participation in a range of
learning settings.

> The key to distinguishing the knowledge base of teaching lies at the intersec-
> tion of content and pedagogy, in the capacity of *a teacher to transform the content
> knowledge he/she possesses* into forms that are pedagogically powerful and yet
> adaptive to the variations in ability and background presented by the students.[44]

It was essentially a banking model of pedagogy.

Gardner's work (see Chapter 3) provided us with a different perspective on
professional knowledge, one rooted in a re-conceptualisation of knowledge
and intelligence. His theory of multiple intelligences seemed to us to encourage a new perspective on pedagogy that prioritised student understanding.
Gardner's theory helped us widen our preoccupation with teacher knowledge
to embrace learner understanding, from technique and content to purposes
and processes. The five entry points which Gardner originally proposed for
approaching any key concept (narrational, logical–quantitative, foundational,
experiential and aesthetic) did not simply represent a rich and varied way of
mediating a subject. Rather they seemed to us to emphasise the process of
pedagogy and a practice that sought to promote the highest level of understanding possible in learners.[45] At the same time, Gardner's work placed discipline and domain at the core of pedagogy and this was of interest to us.
Drawing extensively from Dewey, he had argued that understanding through
disciplinary knowledge was indispensable. And in response to widespread criticism that this simply offered progressive programmes to achieve traditionalist
aims[46] Gardner quoted extensively from Dewey to back up his claim for the

pre-eminence of understanding through disciplinary knowledge in the reform of teaching and schooling:

> Organised subject matter represents the ripe fruitage of experiences ... it does not represent perfection or infallible vision; but it is the best at command to further new experiences which may, in some respects at least, surpass the achievements embodied in existing knowledge and works of art.[47]

Gardner's espousal of disciplines combined with an exploration of curricula which were rooted in, but moved beyond, disciplines into 'generative themes', was important in helping us to conceptualise the distinction we came to make between 'subject' and 'school' knowledge.

But it was to be the work of Jean Lave that was to really capture our imagination in the mid-1990s and influence our emerging model of teacher development. We began to recognise that any conceptualisation of professional knowledge needed to be rooted in a social theory of learning. Lave's research underlined the way in which cognitive change was an attribute of situated pedagogical relationships in particular settings and contexts.[48] As discussed in Chapter 4, her research with adult learners engaged in new learning situations emphasised the social situation or participation framework in which learning takes place, a process of involvement in communities of practice. We realised that any representation of teacher knowledge and development must acknowledge teachers' overlapping identities. First and foremost within the sub-communities of complex school settings, but also more broadly in terms of the complementary and competing allegiances and roles in other groups and communities that teachers held which shaped personal passions and motivations, as well as their views of their subject specialisms, of learners and knowledge.

The figure below represents in diagrammatic form our synthesis of professional knowledge based on what we observed of teachers' overlapping identities. In school: as 'subject' experts (subject knowledge), subject specialist teachers (school knowledge), and classroom experts (pedagogic knowledge). And in and beyond school: as individuals with key commitments to a range of other groups and communities (personal knowledge).[49]

We have used this model in a range of international settings to argue that the development of professional knowledge is a dynamic process. It depends on the interaction of the elements we identify, but is brought into existence by the learning context itself – learners, setting, activity and communication, as well as context in its broadest sense.

Most importantly we emphasised that the personal construct – the identity – of the teacher lay at the heart of this process: a complex amalgam of past knowledge, experiences of learning in a range of communities, a personal view of what constitutes 'good' teaching and a belief in the purposes of the subject. This model holds good for any teacher, novice or expert. A student teacher needs to question his or her personal beliefs as they work out a rationale

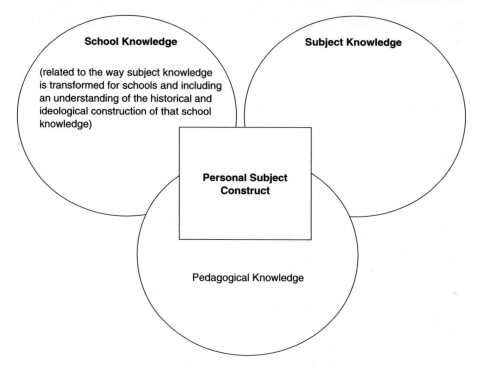

School Knowledge

(related to the way subject knowledge
is transformed for schools and including
an understanding of the historical and
ideological construction of that school
knowledge)

Subject Knowledge

Personal Subject
Construct

Pedagogical Knowledge

Teachers' professional knowledge[50]

for their classroom practice. But so must those teachers who, although more expert, have experienced profound changes in what constitutes subject or pedagogic knowledge during their career.

It is important to note that in 2004 Lee Shulman (LSS) was to publish with Judith Shulman (JHS) a significantly modified version of his original model of teacher knowledge to incorporate a more situated view of teacher learning. 'In our earlier studies of teacher learning', he writes, 'one of us (LSS) employed constructs that were strictly cognitive and individual ... The other member of the team (JHS) employed theoretical models that described how teachers learned via disciplined critical reflection on their own practice. But neither of these conceptions seemed comprehensive enough to account for what we were encountering [in teacher learning] ... We recognized the need to frame a more comprehensive conception of teacher learning and development within communities and contexts.'[51]

The figure below illustrates the way in which our own model was exemplified by a group of English teachers. They recognised a clear distinction between 'English' as practised, for example, in their university and college communities ('subject' knowledge) and school communities ('school' knowledge). Most school departments, for example, required that members know about authors, themes and styles (mostly texts written for children or teenagers, or deemed suitable for the younger reader) that were distinctively different from the literature they had

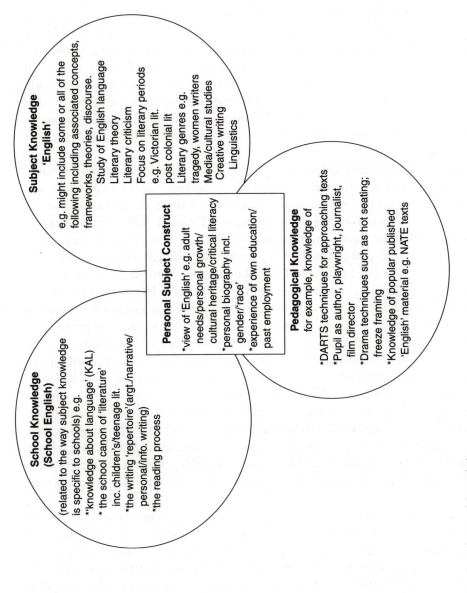

Subject Knowledge 'English'

e.g. might include some or all of the following including associated concepts, frameworks, theories, discourse.

Study of English language
Literary theory
Literary criticism
Focus on literary periods
e.g. Victorian lit.
post colonial lit
Literary genres e.g.
tragedy, women writers
Media/cultural studies
Creative writing
Linguistics

School Knowledge (School English)

(related to the way subject knowledge is specific to schools) e.g.

*'knowledge about language' (KAL)
* the school canon of 'literature' inc. children's/teenage lit.
*the writing 'repertoire'(argt./narrative/ personal/info. writing)
*the reading process

Personal Subject Construct

*view of 'English' e.g. adult needs/personal growth/ cultural heritage/critical literacy
*personal biography incl. gender/'race'
*experience of own education/ past employment

Pedagogical Knowledge

for example, knowledge of

*DARTS techniques for approaching texts
*Pupil as author, playwright, journalist, film director
*Drama techniques such as hot seating; freeze framing
*Knowledge of popular published 'English' material e.g. NATE texts

English teachers' professional knowledge

studied in university and college seminars. Few degree-level communities incorporated knowledge about the reading process in their curriculum, but this was a statutory part of school 'English' in the UK.

Lucy and her mentor (see Chapter 4 and Chapter 7) explored the earliest version of our model together as a way of sharing their views about the different elements of English practice, noting where there was overlap and possible misunderstanding. Lucy's mentor annotated her model (see the figure below) with comments ('English − language and literature is endlessly fascinating'; 'Mentoring is so challenging and satisfying because it requires you to draw from all three circles and present the material to the student in digestible form!'), and it is noticeable that within the category 'pedagogic knowledge' she includes: 'child as thinker/communicator/performer/reader' and 'praise/confidence/attempt to improve' − the kind of positive discourse identified as integral to the toolkit of the community into which she was inducting Lucy.

Within the category 'personal construct', Lucy's mentor indicates the communities of practice that forged her personal identity, values and expertise as a teacher: 'grew up in a non-conformist chapel in Wales, so frequent exposure to exposition of text [Bible] and preaching. No TV until sixth form so reading encouraged. Since then … written and produced plays, organised day and week holidays for 4–12 year olds and drama groups'. Very different passions and experiences are brought to the model by Lucy, who worked as an unqualified teacher in Nigeria before her four children were born. Her personal construct of English teaching is centrally informed by the fact that English is her second language: 'I think … English to me would … mean a mode of expression … expressing oneself. It's communication … the language of … speech … er … business … er … instruction … A language! It's a mode that takes you out of isolation into a kind of community where you can communicate with other people. That's as far as I think it is. Because to me … English is … because English is not my first language … I probably look at English from a different point of view from an English person, because I speak other languages as well. So English to me is just another way of communicating with people in a language they understand … and … um … English is not much different from what you're doing in other classes … you're concentrating on the language itself as a science … '

We would argue that teacher education bears a major responsibility for formulating theoretical frameworks that will encourage an understanding and evaluation of pedagogical practices. Teacher education must provide ongoing challenges to the educational bureaucracies that seek rather to define teachers primarily as technicians and pedagogical clerks, incapable of making important policy or curriculum decisions.[52] Our experience with the use of this model with teachers in many parts of the world, including New Zealand, South Africa and Hungary, gives us optimism that it is a useful and meaningful model to assist in the articulation of teachers'

English-language and literature is endlessly fascinating

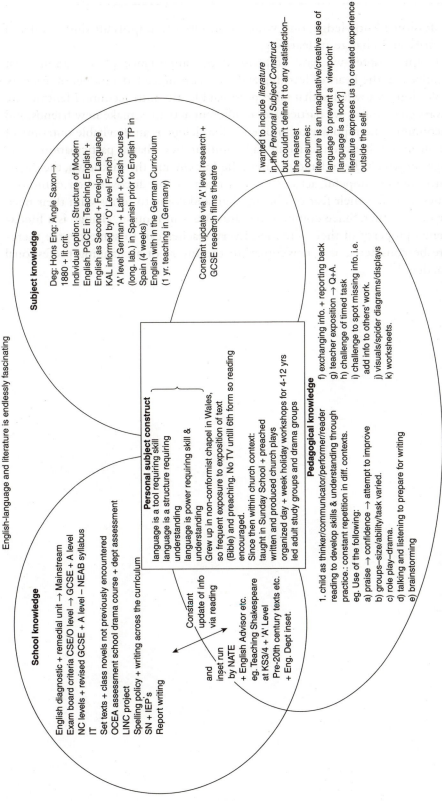

School knowledge

English diagnostic + remedial unit → Mainstream
Exam board criteria CSE/O level → GCSE + A level
NC levels + revised GCSE + A level – NEAB syllabus
IT
Set texts + class novels not previously encountered
OCEA assessment school drama course + dept assessment
LINC project
Spelling policy + writing across the curriculum
SN + IEP's
Report writing

Constant
update of info
via reading

and
inset run
by NATE
+ English Advisor etc.
eg. Teaching Shakespeare
at KS3/4 + 'A' Level
Pre-20th century texts etc.
+ Eng. Dept inset.

Subject knowledge

Deg: Hons Eng: Angle Saxon →
1880 + lit crit.
Individual option: Structure of Modern
English. PGCE in Teaching English +
English as Second + Foreign Language
KAL informed by 'O' Level French
'A' level German + Latin + Crash course
(long. lab.) in Spanish prior to English TP in
Spain (4 weeks)
English with in the German Curriculum
(1 yr. teaching in Germany)

Constant update via 'A' level research +
GCSE research films theatre

Personal subject construct

language is a tool requiring skill
language is a structure requiring
understanding
language is power requiring skill &
understanding
Grew up in non-conformist chapel in Wales,
so frequent exposure to exposition of text
(Bible) and preaching. No TV untill 6th form so reading
encouraged.
Since then within church context:
taught in Sunday School + preached
written and produced church plays
organized day + week holiday workshops for 4-12 yrs
led adult study groups and drama groups

I wanted to include *literature*
in the *Personal Subject Construct*
but couldn't define it to any satisfaction–
the nearest
I consumes:
literature is an imaginative/creative use of
language to prevent a viewpoint
[language is a look?]
literature expresses us to created experience
outside the self.

Pedagogical knowledge

1. child as thinker/communicator/performer/reader
reading to develop skills & understanding through
practice.: constant repetition in diff. contexts.
eg. Use of the following:
a) praise → confidence → attempt to improve
b) groups–size/ability/task varied.
c) role play–drama.
d) talking and listening to prepare for writing
e) brainstorming

f) exchanging info. + reporting back
g) teacher exposition → Q+A.
h) challenge of timed task
i) challenge to spot missing info. i.e.
add info to others' work.
j) visuals/spider diagrams/displays
k) worksheets.

Mentoring is so challenging and satisfying because it requires the mentor to draw from all three circles and present the materials to the
student in a digestible form!

Lucy's mentor's version of the teacher knowledge models

professional knowledge, one which honours the important dimensions of identity and change in learning.

In this chapter we have emphasised the importance of recognising that identity is at the heart of learning and have also suggested a model of teachers' professional knowledge that takes personal identity into account. Identities are always changing as we participate in different activities, make new friends, and encounter contemporary technologies, for change is an inevitable outcome of the deep link between learning and communities. Shared participation is the stage on which the old and the new, the known and the unknown, the established and the hopeful, act out their differences and discover their commonalities, manifest their fear of one another, and come to terms with their need for one another. Since communities are always in motion, change is a fundamental property of their activities. Every teacher can to some degree therefore be considered as a 'newcomer' to the future of a changing professional practice.[53]

8

Pedagogies

Pedagogy can change people's lives, it has a power to transform.

Pedagogy, we believe, is going to take centre stage in social and economic debates in the twenty-first century. Creating the conditions and means for successful and relevant learning we see as a prerequisite of freedom and democracy. In this book we have illustrated this in a number of ways. There are the big picture ideas of people like Paulo Freire, who linked pedagogy and oppression, particularly in the developing world. But we also have the smaller picture stories around individual teachers in the post-totalitarian world of Albania in the 1990s, or the Eastern Cape teachers in post-apartheid South Africa. The picture below was taken in a primary school just outside Lesotho a few years into the present century. This chart was in the very small and cramped teachers' room. Lesotho abolished primary school fees at the turn of the century and primary enrolment doubled. The teachers in grades 1 and 2, who were teaching these classes, had no extra resources and no extra classrooms, but hundreds of children had a new opportunity and hundreds of their parents had new expectations.

NAME OF TEACHER	CLASS	ROLL
Mrs Mokoteli	1	
Mrs Ramokejane		210
Mrs Molotsi	2	
Mrs Mpalami		205
Mrs Thamae	3	
Mrs Liketso		98
Miss Molaoa	4	

There is an inexorable demand, thrust even, for education at all levels of the system. The expansion of primary schooling in Sub-Saharan Africa has created, in many countries, a new crisis around the provision of secondary places. The expansion of secondary education in most parts of the world has led to the expansion of higher education. In the UK, when we went to university, less than 10 per cent of our peer cohort had the same chance. Now nearly one in two do and the ratio in other parts of the world has even greater numbers grasping the opportunity for further study. The trajectory of educational expansion is firmly upwards.

Such expansion is uneven across the world. In the older industrialised countries the foundations for provision of primary schooling were laid in the nineteenth century, secondary schooling in the twentieth, and higher education in the present century. In middle income countries like Brazil, China and India the process is running behind, but it is clear that catch-up times will be much foreshortened. In the poorer parts of the world, considerable national and international commitment is being made to simultaneously expand all levels of education. There are social reasons for this. Child survival and mortality have been convincingly shown to relate to the literacy and education levels of mothers. The experience of economic growth in Asia also points to the importance of good basic education.[1]

In making these observations we want to locate pedagogy in a global perspective. As we perceive it, the more educated the population, the more concern there is around pedagogy.

The traditional attitude of parents towards teachers has largely been one of deference and a large element of this exists today. But new and successive generations of better educated parents are coming to question the quality of the education their children receive. In the USA, in his period as governor of Arkansas, Bill Clinton[2] exploited three worries in making education and the quality of teaching one of his key topics in his campaign for President. Tony Blair, in part modelling his approach on Clinton's strategy, did the same in winning and retaining power in Britain from 1997 onwards.[3] His election campaign refrain, 'Education, education, education', included to the surprise of many teachers an implicitly tough line on the nature and quality of pedagogy in British schools.[4]

We think that, rather than politicians creating unrest about schooling (as some would argue) these moves recognised and tapped into a public disquiet. Disquiet that could, in a better educated world, be articulated more clearly had been possible before. We see these phenomena in other parts of the world. A report, for example, published by the Nelson Mandela Foundation in South Africa,[5] talked of a deep growing rift between teachers and parents. Criticism of teachers, the report said, encompassed a complex set of issues relating to their lack of qualifications, subject knowledge, commitment and sense of vocation. Here is a transcript of part of an interview with a parent that the Foundation researchers thought exemplified the problem.

Some teachers are not well-qualified and they are a problem to learners who are willing to learn. Due to the lack of knowledge on the part of teachers, learners are forced to study what they don't like or want and in which they are not interested. Again what I have discovered is that if one is doing a job one doesn't like, one does not commit wholeheartedly to it. For example, we have teachers who hate teaching but they are teaching, the reason being that they will be earning at the end of the month.

Nelson Mandela took up this theme in a speech in 2007:

> To create a just world we should not underestimate the power of education. It is an area in which I believe we have not done nearly enough. Too many children of Africa are denied schooling. When they do attend school, it is often at schools that do not stimulate them and bring out their full potential … There can be no contentment for any of us when there are children, millions of children, who do not receive an education that provides them with dignity and honour and allows them to live their lives to the full.
>
> It is not beyond our power to create a world in which all children have access to a good education. (press release)

The attention, therefore, has shifted, or is in the process of shifting, from 'we need schools' to 'we need good teachers', and at the heart of this is a desire for learning and teaching of the highest quality. 'Pedagogy' may not be the term parents use, but the area of activity that might arise has been seen as a professional preserve that is more open to public scrutiny than ever before.

Parents and others in communities are intuitively aware that social and economic wellbeing in today's and tomorrow's world requires not only good levels of education but also good skills and a knowledge of educating and re-educating that are becoming increasingly central to new forms of the knowledge economy. The 'education for life' that preoccupied our parents is being transformed into 'education throughout life' for the present generation, not as some rather vague aspiration but as a social and economic necessity. And this new social movement, identifiable in different ways in all parts of the globe, is being fuelled by the radically different forms of information and communication technologies now becoming available to us. These, we have argued, are fuelling change but also creating the means of responding to these changes, and forms of pedagogy are central to this process, and this presents important and fascinating opportunities.

Like a storyteller we have tried to deploy a number of narrative devices to set out our analysis of the power of pedagogy. Our choice of chapter titles makes an important statement about the journey taken. We are aware, as discussed in the chapter on knowledge, that the academic world around learning and teaching has become increasingly specialised. Many aspects of the analyses we have been suggesting appeal to well established fields in their own right (learning theory, for example, in Chapter 4). Yet we have been keen to emphasise from the outset that this book is not primarily seeking to provide an introduction to such fields of enquiry. Rather we are attempting to propose a framework for understanding and developing pedagogy that, in its own terms, makes a statement about new ways of thinking about learning and teaching. The building blocks of such a framework – the essential dimensions that have to be taken account of – are, we believe, essential to teacher development.

In suggesting such a framework we are not recommending particular forms or models that prescribe learning and teaching, hence our use of the term 'pedagogies' to title this final chapter. Neither are we concluding with some grand design or diagrammatic representation of what a pedagogic model might look like. The book only contains one model (see Chapter 7) and this is because it is one we have successfully used for many years to facilitate debate around different aspects of teachers' professional knowledge. The model is just one small facet of what could be termed our 'pedagogic framework'. Any further diagrammatic representations would, we believe, stultify the sort of fluidity and flexibility of use and interpretation that we have argued throughout the book lie at the heart of any pedagogic endeavour.

Although our own values, as we have emphasised from the outset, infuse this analysis, we have also tried by appealing to a range of historical and contemporary references to offer a range of evidence-based ways of critically exploring pedagogy. In Chapter 1 we made seven assertions, in order to be explicit about the personal views underpinning this book:

- Any understanding or theory of pedagogy needs to encompass all the complex factors that influence the process of learning and teaching.

- The mind must be viewed as complex and multifaceted: a broad understanding of the human mind and cognitive science is a crucial aspect of teacher knowledge.

- Learning is a social process. This view of learning takes a broad view of learners' trajectories through the world – their sense of self, where they are coming from, where they think they are going, what sort of person they want to be.

- The development of knowledge is inseparable from the process of participating in a culture of practice – the space in which the planned, enacted and experienced come together is at the heart of the science of pedagogy.

- Pedagogy needs to imaginatively consider the wide range of tools and technologies, both material and symbolic, that humankind has developed to make sense of and shape the world in which we live.

- Pedagogy must build the self-esteem and identity of learners, developing their sense of what they believe or indeed hope themselves to be capable of.

- Pedagogic settings should create the conditions for reflection and dialogue and productive cognitive conflict. Developing habits of mind that are questioning and critical is central to pedagogy.

But we have also drawn deeply on research in order to formulate some characteristics of authentic pedagogy (Chapter 2), the notion of dispositions as integral to the teaching task (Chapter 3), a range of perspectives on learning (Chapter 4) and five key attributes of identity (Chapter 7). Research has similarly informed the conceptualisation of a 'toolkit' for teaching as is presented in Chapter 6 and a model of teacher knowledge as is discussed in Chapter 7. The development and use of these heuristic devices, taken alongside a range of case studies, images, poems and accounts of pedagogic debates, have together served as guides in this critical analysis.

In the course of this enquiry we have also explored the capacity of the human mind to move seamlessly between past, present and future in non-linear and sometimes episodic ways. We are not, therefore, intending to impose order on this analysis. Instead we are seeking to explore and debate the conditions for the development of critical habits of mind towards pedagogy.

In constructing this framework for understanding and analysing pedagogy, we have argued that the overarching unit of analysis must always be the *pedagogic setting* taken as a whole – be it at the micro level of classrooms or institutional praxis or the macro level of national practice. To understand learning and pedagogy, we have argued, we need to consider the interactions of all participants in a setting. Settings at micro level are inextricably influenced by wider institutional and social norms, though not inevitably dictated by them as we have seen. This interrelationship of levels can be illustrated as a set of nested boxes (below).

A pedagogic setting we have defined as the practice that we as teachers, together with a specific group of learners, create, enact and experience over time. The vignettes we have used throughout the book in order to illustrate different pedagogic settings (a Canadian primary classroom, an American high school, a consortium of GP practices in the UK, for instance) provide only brief glimpses, snapshots of longer-term interactions between specific participants across time in specific contexts. We have sought to emphasise through this concept that pedagogy is never simply the accumulation of teaching strategies: arranging a classroom, formulating questions, developing schemes of work. Pedagogy is an ongoing process shared by teachers and learners, crucially informed by views of learning, with the nature and forms of knowledge seen as critical for the learning process – and above all by views of educational purposes and outcomes.

Important too to the understanding of this concept is the notion that pedagogic settings are always socio-historically and culturally situated. In this sense the interplay of theory and practice across a wide range of learning and teaching settings inevitably gives rise to a multiplicity of pedagogies, as we have illustrated. Pedagogic settings we have also argued do not have fixed physical boundaries. One example would be the virtual seminar between students and teachers described in Chapter 6. Another would be the inclusion of museums, galleries, heritage sites and the activities of local communities as

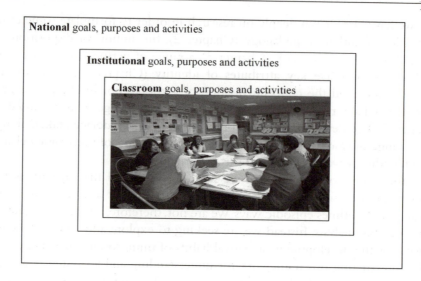

National goals, purposes and activities

Institutional goals, purposes and activities

Classroom goals, purposes and activities

integral to the curriculum, as evidenced in the work of Caswell and May. In this sense the boundaries of pedagogic settings are always determined by participants.

In addition pedagogic settings as we have defined them always have a past, present and future. Learning goals, activities and discourse are informed by expectations and interactions beyond any single moment in time. It is the interdependence of all its parts over time that makes a particular setting a single entity. Participants create, enact and experience (together and separately) purposes, values and expectations; knowledge and ways of knowing; rules of discourse; roles and relationships; resources; artefacts; and the physical arrangement and boundaries of the setting. All of these together and none of these alone.

In all these senses, the term 'pedagogic setting' emphasises the notion of learning and teaching as an ongoing, sometimes daunting, risky, but hopefully adventurous process. In our role as teachers we may plan, dream and initiate the process, but its nature is only defined and sustained across time through the unfolding and shared interactions, dispositions, beliefs, practices, activities and interconnected learning trajectories of ourselves and our learners.

Having emphasised the contextual, political and socio-cultural nature of pedagogy through the concept of the pedagogic setting, we have also progressively presented across the course of the book a number of enduring, interrelated dimensions that define any setting, regardless of context. These dimensions emerge and re-emerge relentlessly and have enabled us to develop a shared pedagogic framework across the particularities of culture and context. The pedagogic dimensions endure across these particularities, enabling comparative analyses of goals and purposes for learning; views of learning, mind and knowledge; learning and assessment activities; roles and relationships (between teachers and learners); discourse tools and artefacts (see the illustrations below).

The first of these dimensions is

- *Goals and purposes*, the key ideas that inform (often implicitly rather than explicitly) all pedagogic settings and how they are understood by teachers and learners alike. First introduced in Chapter 2, the importance of this key dimension has been a recurring leitmotif in every chapter.

The second dimension is

- *Views of mind and knowledge*, and in Chapters 3 and 5 we explored the ways in which radically different views lead inevitably to radically different approaches to learners and the kinds and nature of knowledge seen as appropriate to learning.

Inextricably linked to this is the third dimension of

- *Views of learning and learners*, and how teachers and learners act in the classroom, as we explored in detail in Chapter 4, depends upon how they think learning takes place.

The fourth and fifth dimensions, exemplified particularly through the vignettes in Chapter 5 and Chapter 7, are

- *Learning and assessment activities*, as these define and structure classroom activity and are a manifestation of the other dimensions, but particularly the first three.

- *Roles and relationships*, and this dimension relates to both learners and teachers in any setting and includes such aspects as who controls the learning, the extent of collaboration and voice given to learners, and so forth.

Finally material and symbolic tools and artefacts have been presented as dimensions six and seven:

- *Discourse* (Chapter 4 and 7), as discourse is clearly inseparable from views of learning and is usually seen solely in terms of the language used in classroom and school. However, we have extended the notion to include the way subjects and classrooms are represented in the norms and behaviours developed within settings. We have emphasised that the way students act in the science lab is not the same as how they act in the drama classroom. Discourse in this sense is an expression of classrooms' micro cultures, part of a toolkit of practice inextricably related to our seventh dimension.

- *Tools and technologies*, as physical artefacts and technologies of all forms, we have argued in Chapter 6, are crucial to knowledge building. They extend our understanding and impact on the social context of our daily lives and activities and an explicit understanding of this aspect of human development is a critical dimension of pedagogy.

We know from our own experience that pedagogy can change people's lives. It has the power to transform. Each of us benefited from inspirational teachers who sowed the seeds that shaped our lives, not just 'in school' but later in life in situations where pedagogic excellence was less explicitly acknowledged. We know from books and films that the idea of such teachers feeds popular imagination. We want more teachers to feel and use the power of pedagogy. Such a commitment, however, requires a deeper knowledge of the frames of mind and the frames of practice than are generally allowed. And this, indisputably, is an intellectual process, not always easy but ultimately rewarding. Such a process requires us to lay open, at least to ourselves, the conceptual systems that play a role in defining our everyday realities. But our conceptual system is not something we are normally aware of, although it governs our everyday functioning down to the most mundane details. Our concepts structure what we perceive, how we move around the world and how we relate to other people. As George Lakoff and Mark Johnson[6] among others have noted, much of our conceptual world is organised around metaphors. In discussing pedagogy, notions of building loom large, most notably the way we construct knowledge, as this book repeatedly asserts, in a myriad of social contexts. Pedagogy is to teaching as architecture is to building. We need to know about the strength and properties of materials, we must understand the way different forces can impact in different settings and, above all, we need to know how a new configuration of resources, perhaps a new pattern of known ideas, can creatively offer and illuminate starkly new possibilities. Pedagogy, like architecture, should not be prosaic.

But pedagogy, like architecture, must respect the past. Italo Calvino captures this in his description of *Le Citta Invisibili:*

> Zenobia, a city in Asia, has houses made of bamboo and zinc, with many platforms and balconies placed on stilts at various heights, crossing one another, linked by ladders and hanging belvederes, with barrels storing water, weather vanes, jutting pulleys, fish poles and cranes.

> No-one remembers what need, command or desire drove Zenobia's founders to give their city this form, as the buildings are constructed on pilings that sit over dry terrain. But what is certain is that if a traveller asks an inhabitant of Zenobia to describe his vision of a happy life, it is always a city like Zenobia that he imagines, with its piling and suspended stairways, a Zenobia perhaps aflutter with banners and ribbons, quite different from the original but always derived by combining elements of that first model.

> However, it is pointless to try to decide whether Zenobia is to be classified among happy cities or among the unhappy. It makes no sense to divide cities into these two species, but rather into a different two: those that through the years and the changes continue to give form to their desires and those in which desires either erase the city or are erased by it.[7]

Zenobia, in representing the known and some of the new, provides a metaphor for one way of analysing the pedagogic settings that are at the heart of this book. This is the balance between the known and the new. The security that comes from knowing a place well provides the energy to change and innovate. A teacher who is confident in their pedagogic knowledge, understanding and expertise has the power to improve, innovate and reform. This places the teacher as an intellectual at the heart of the pedagogic endeavour.[8] Only in this way can we aspire to accord teachers a dignity, voice, autonomy, agency and self-esteem that command community approval and respect.

Our deliberations around pedagogy have not been linear. Between the first and the last, any sequence of chapters could be argued for. But it is enduringly human to search for patterns – this is a familiar process. You are listening to a piece of music and nothing seems to link one moment with the next. Sounds emerge without any before or after. You press for meaning. This is so with some reading. Passages accumulate, but in ways that test our understanding of what has gone before.

In a stimulating way, however, this creates a challenge to our perceptual capabilities. Perhaps the order behind the sounds is simply not being heard, perhaps the logic of the argument is not being understood. Paying attention to new, even alien, ideas can be like listening to a foreign language. There may be a logic latent in the sounds, but it is not evident to the untrained ear. This is the reason we persist so doggedly in trying to find order, even when it is not apparent.

It is almost a faith in science, psychology, religion even, that patterns will be found.[9] And so we believe is the case with pedagogy. But there is also a final proviso. Alberto Manguel, in his *History of Reading,*[10] writes that every act of reading is allegorical, the object of other readings. In that sense no reading can ever be final. Socrates argued that knowledge can only be acquired by dialogue, and reading alone is insufficient. The deliberations in this book are but preliminaries before the real work begins.

Endnotes

ACKNOWLEDGEMENTS

1   Seeley Brown, J.S., Collins, A. and Duguid, P. (1988) 'Situated cognition and the culture of learning' in *Educational Researcher*, 18: 132–42.

INTRODUCTION

1   Meta: at a higher stage of development, transcending, going above and beyond, change and transformation.

2   So much of this book owes a debt to our reading and re-reading of the work of Jerome Bruner. He introduces this expression 'going meta' on page 10 of his collection of essays *The Culture of Education* (1996) published by the Harvard University Press.

   An American psychologist, for the past 45 years he has been a leader in establishing cognitive psychology as an alternative to the behaviourist theories that dominated psychology in the first half of the twentieth century. His approach to childhood learning and perception has made him a key figure in educational reform in the United States and Britain.

   His public lecture entitled 'Cultivating the Possible', which he gave to mark the opening of the new Jerome Bruner Building at Oxford University Department of Education, gives a good sense of his approach to learning (listen at http://www. edstud.ox.ac.uk/). In this lecture he reflects on his early days at Oxford University and the beginning of theories about cognitive development in children. He goes on to talk about the use of story-telling as a way of 'cultivating a lively sense of the possible in the rising generation'.

   A prolific writer throughout his extensive career, Bruner lists two of his more recent publications as representative of his work: *Acts of Meaning* (Harvard University Press, 1991) and *The Culture of Education* (Harvard University Press, 1996).

CHAPTER 1

1   This quotation is taken from an article published in *La Repubblica* on 14 January 1996.

2   *La Stampa*, May 1993.

3   Taken from historical notes and information on the Municipal Infant Toddler Centres and Pre-schools of Reggio Emilia produced by the municipality of Reggio Emilia.

4   Montessori came into conflict with Mussolini and moved first to Spain and then to the Netherlands.

   The life of Dewey's prefigurative community was very brief and in the event a struggle over workers' control of the Laboratory School led to its demise. Dewey and his teachers did not own their workshop, the University of Chicago did. In 1904 its president sided with disgruntled teachers and administrators from the school and fired Alice. Dewey resigned and almost immediately accepted a position at Columbia University, where he remained for the rest of his long career.

5 For a more detailed exploration of the origins of this distinction see Yun Lee Too's analysis in Too (2001) *Education in Greek and Roman Antiquity* (New York: Brill Academic).

6 In Giroux, H.A. and McLaren, P. (1994) *Between Borders: Pedagogy and the Politics of Cultural Studies* (New York: Routledge).

7 Reproduced in Moon, B. and Shelton Mayes, A. (1993) *Teaching and Learning in the Secondary School* (London: Routledge).

8 In the USA 'instruction', rather than 'pedagogy' has been a dominant term in schools and in research into education, but this has changed in recent years with the work of people like Lee Shulman (see Chapter 7, p. 157) influencing a move to the use of the more broadly conceived term 'pedagogy'.

9 See Vygotsky, L.S. (1963) 'Learning and mental development at school age' in B. Simon and J. Simon (eds), *Educational Psychology in the USSR* (London: Routledge and Kegan Paul).

10 Simon's 1954 book, *Intelligence Testing and the Comprehensive School* (Lawrence and Wishart), was the first substantial publication to provide a critique of the post-Second World War 'selective' education system.

11 In making this statement Simon is drawing on the empirical work carried out at the University of Leicester in the late 1970s and early 1980s. This suggested that primary teachers who saw individualisation as the priority became so involved in the logistical and management lower order maintenance of the classroom that little opportunity for the higher order 'consistent challenge' of children was possible. See Galton, M., Simon, B. and Croll, P. (1980) *Inside the Primary Classroom* (London: Routledge and Kegan Paul).

12 An example here would be the Cyert Center for Early Education at the Carnegie Mellon University in Pittsburgh, USA.

13 For example, in Scotland Stirling Council have taken the idea of a documentary recording and displaying children's work as a policy aim explicitly attributed to the Reggio Emilia influence.

14 Kliebard, H.M. (1999). 'Constructing the concept of Curriculum on the Wisconsin frontier: how school restructuring sustained a pedagogic revolution' in B. Moon and P. Murphy (eds), *Curriculum in Context* (London: Paul Chapman).

15 There is, in Europe and North America, for example, quite a nostalgia for the small, one teacher school. The worldwide success of the French film *Être et Avoir*, which portrayed the life of a single teacher school in the Auvergne, is one example of this. In the UK the pedagogic advantages of the 'small scale' are being advanced by the group Human Scale Education at (www.hse.org.uk) which has the aim of promoting small, human-scale learning environments. An example of this in practice is reflected in the pioneering work of Mike Davies and the staff of Bishop Park College, Clacton, Essex. See Fielding, M. *et al.* (2006) *Less is More: The Development of a Schools-within-Schools Approach to Education on a Human Scale* (a report commissioned by the DfES Innovation Unit and available from Professor Fielding at the University of Sussex).

16 It is important to remember that in some parts of the world very large numbers of children still have to be provided with schooling, with many millions in Sub-Saharan Africa alone.

17 (i) Alexander, R. (2000) *Culture and Pedagogy* (London: Blackwell) distinguishes teaching from pedagogy. 'Teaching is an act while pedagogy is both act and discourse. Pedagogy encompasses the performance of teaching together with the theories, beliefs, policies and controversies that inform and shape it' (page 540).

(ii) Watkins, C. and Mortimore, P. (1999) 'Pedagogy: what do we know?' in P. Mortimore (ed.), *Pedagogy and its Impact on Learning* (London: Paul Chapman) pages

1–19. Note the tendency for discussions of pedagogy in the UK to dwell on the teacher and insist that any definition of pedagogy must also take the learner into account. They define pedagogy as 'any conscious activity by one person designed to enhance learning in another'.

(iii) Simon, B. (1999) 'Why no pedagogy in England?' in J. Leach and B. Moon (eds), *Learners and Pedagogy* (London: Chapman). Argues 'by pedagogy is meant the theory and practice of teaching'.

(iv) Watkins and Mortimore (1999) (op cit.) cite a Swedish definition of pedagogy as 'a discipline [which] extends to the consideration of health and bodily fitness, social and moral welfare, ethics and aesthetics, as well as the institutional forms that serve to facilitate society's and the individual's pedagogic aims'.

(v) Alexander, R. (2000) (op cit.) points out that in France 'didactics deals with the logical aspects of teaching while pedagogy covers the psychological aspects: on the one hand the disciplines, on the other hand children and learning' (page 543), while in the Central European tradition 'pedagogy is the overarching concept and didactics is that branch of pedagogy which deals with what is to be taught and how' (page 547).

18   For example, Bruner, J. (2006) *In Search of Pedagogy*, Vol. 1 (London: Routledge) and also Freire, P. (2000) *Pedagogy of the Oppressed* (London: Continuum).

19   Bruner, J. (1996) *The Culture of Education* (Cambridge: Harvard University Press).

CHAPTER 2

1   See Chapter 6 for more about CSILE software.

2   This insight is taken from Jerome Bruner (1996) *The Culture of Education* (Cambridge: Harvard University Press) page 21.

3   Beverley is now a teacher trainer attached to the Ontario Institute for Studies in Education (OISE) in their laboratory school.

4   Schools For Thought (SFT) was significantly influenced by the work of John Bruer (see his (1994) *A Science of Learning in the Classroom* (Cambridge: MIT Press)). SFT principles include:

- *Domain-specific learning* Students learn best when cognitive skills are taught in the context of a specific domain of knowledge rather than in contexts that are more general. An interpretation of this principle in terms of concepts suggests the importance of explicitly supporting students' acquisition of a deep understanding of the concepts, concept interrelationships, and the reasoning skills related to developing and using scientific representations of phenomena in any domain of scientific knowledge.

- *Case-based learning* Students learn best when cognitive skills are learned in the process of solving authentic problems rather than when pieces of information are presented as isolated facts to be learnt. A concept-based interpretation suggests the importance of constructing a learning environment in which specific problems are presented in ways that motivate the use of sets of concepts and interrelationships germane to the problems.

- *Scaffolded learning* Students learn best when the task difficulty is adjusted to meet their capabilities. The interpretation suggests providing students with subsets of concepts and concept representations appropriate to their level of knowledge.

5   See particularly Bruer, J.T. (1994) *Schools for Thought: A Science of Learning in the Classroom* (Cambridge: MIT Press).

6   This research is fully discussed in Chapter 4.

7   This insight comes in Simon Schama's (2006) analysis of Picasso's *Guernica* in *The Power of Art* (London: BBC Books), page 388. However, his analysis of 'great art' generally evokes many parallels with pedagogy, particularly its commitment to making a difference in how people see the world and relate to each other.

8   This is explored more fully in Chapter 4.

9   We originally developed this concept for an Open University MA Course 'Curriculum, Learning and Assessment' which was complemented by the (1999) book *Learners and Pedagogy* (J. Leach and B. Moon, London: Paul Chapman).

10   We explore this idea in more detail in Chapter 5.

11   Lave, J. (1988) *Cognition in Practice* (Cambridge: Cambridge University Press); Lave, J. and Wenger, E. (1991) *Situated Learning* (Cambridge: Cambridge University Press).

12   Bruner (1996) (ibid), Chapter 2.

13   Hanley, J.P., Whitla, D.K., Moo, E.W., and Walter, A.S. (1970) *Curiosity/Competence/Community: An Evaluation of Man: A course of study.* (Cambridge, MA: Educational Development Center, Inc).

14   Hanley *et al.* (1970) ibid; Cole, H.G. and Lacefield, W. (1980) *MACOS: Its empirical effect versus its critics.* Paper presented at the annual meeting of the American Educational Research Association, Montreal, Quebec, Canada.

15   See http://www.anthro.umontreal.ca/varia/beaudetf/MACOS/MACOS.html; http://crlt.indiana.edu/publications/duffy_publ5.pdf and http://www.nsf.gov/nsb/documents/2000/nsb00215/nsb00215.pd

16   Bruner (1996) (ibid), Chapter 2, especially page 63.

17   Bruner (1996) (ibid) calls this the 'instrumentalism' tenet that guides a socio–cultural approach to education (pages 25–9).

18   Found at http://www.communityplaythings.co.uk/c/resourcesuk/articles/educators/montessori.htm

19   Professor Tim Brighouse successfully sued the then Education Secretary John Patten for calling him a 'nutter' who wandered around the streets frightening children. Brighouse used the money to create a trust fund for one of his most innovative and highly successful reforms – setting up a University of the First Age at Aston University so that youngsters from deprived backgrounds could get a taste of university life and seize the chance to go on to higher education.

20   See Bruner's instrumentalism tenet (Bruner, 1996 (ibid), page 25).

21   Freire, P. (1972) *Pedagogy of the Oppressed* (Harmondsworth: Penguin).

22   Gandini, L. (1993) 'Fundamentals of the Reggio approach to early childhood ducation', *Young Children*, 49 (1): 4–8.

23   Martin, B. (1997) *Growing Trust in Public Services: Why Reggio Emilia's Pre-schools are World Class.* Available at http://www.publicworld.org/docs/italykids.pdf

24   This account is compiled from a variety of sources including:

   (i)   Howard Gardner (2000) 'The best preschools in the world', Chapter 5, in *The Disciplined Mind: Beyond Facts And Standardized Tests: The K-12 Education That Every Child Deserves.* Available at http://www.reggioinspired.com/gardneronreggio.html

(ii)   Dahlberg, G. and Moss, P. (2005) 'Introduction: our Reggio Emilia', in C. Rinaldi (ed.), *In Dialogue with Reggio Emilia* (London: Routledge Falmer).

(iii)   Surman, L. (2003) Available at: http://cmslive.curriculum.edu.au/leader/default.asp?issue ID=9691&id=4627

(iv)   Martin, B. (1997) *Growing Trust in Public Services: Why Reggio Emilia's Pre-Schools are World Class.* Available at: http://www.publicworld.org/docs/italykids.pdf

25   Gandini, L. (1993) 'Fundamentals of the Reggio Approach to early childhood education', *Young Children*, 49 (1): 4–8. In this article she sets out Reggio Emilia's ideas about the 'environment as a third teacher': the design and use of space encourage encounters, communication, and relationships. See also Chapter 4, page 78.

26   Gardner, H. (2000) *The Disciplined Mind*, (New York: Penguin Putnam), page 88.

27   These were banned in his home country of Brazil until 1974.

28   Freire, P. (1972) *Pedagogy of the Oppressed* (Harmondsworth: Penguin) page 46.

29   Liz Fusco, quoted in Rachal, J. R. (1998) 'We'll never turn back: adult education and the struggle for citizenship in Mississippi's Freedom Summer', *American Educational Research Journal*, 35 (2): 167–98.

30   See http://www.reflect-action.org/resources/ODAcomplete/ODA1.htm

31   See http://www.aldsa.org/themes/reflect/reflect.html

32   This is explored further in Chapter 5.

33   Hooks, B. (1989) *Talking Back: Thinking Feminist, Thinking Black* (Boston, MA: South End Press), page 51.

34   Freire, P. and Horton, M. (1990) *We Make The Road by Walking: Conversations on Education and Social Change*, edited by B. Bell, J. Ganavta and J. Peters (Philadelphia: Temple University Press).

35   See http://www.ptoweb.org/about/freire.php

36   Tochan and Munby discuss the distinction between didactics and pedagogy in 'Novice and expert teachers' time epistemology: a wave function from didactics to pedagogy', *Teachers and Teacher Education*, 9 (2): 206–7.

37   John Dewey, quoted in Hiebert, J., Carpenter, T.P., Fennema, E., Fuson, K., Human, P., Murray, H., Olivier, A. and Wearne, D. (1996) 'Problem solving as a basis for reform in curriculum and instruction: the case of mathematics', *Educational Researcher*, 24 (7).

38   Tim Brighouse discussed these ideas with colleagues at an invited lecture at the 1997 International Confederation of Principals in Boston, USA. *Transforming the great cities – leading schools to success against the odds* is available at http://www.aspa. asn.au/conbrig.htm

39   This student's name has been changed.

40   See also http://www.aspa.asn.au/conbrig.htm

41   Extract from conversation between Distance Education Programme Directors 1997–2001 and 2002–present.

42   The phrase Bruner uses when learners think about *how* they are thinking as well as what they are *thinking* about – 'metacognition' – see *The Culture of Education* (1996) page 10ff.

43   Permaculture (originally 'permanent agriculture') is often viewed as a set of gardening techniques, but it has in fact developed into a whole design philosophy. Its central theme is the creation of human systems that provide for human needs, but by using natural elements and natural ecosystems. Its goals and priorities coincide with what many people see as the core requirements for sustainability.

44   Schon, D. (1995) 'The new scholarship requires a new epistemology', *Change*, 27, 6.

CHAPTER 3

1   A very useful collection of documents and opinions can be found in Jacoby, R. and Glaulerman, N. (1995) *The Bell Curve Debate* (New York: Times Books). See also Moon, B. (1997) *A Curriculum Beyond the Bell Curve* (London: British Curriculum Foundation).

2   See Barber, M. (1994) *The Making of the 1944 Education Act* (London: Cassell).

3   We hope, in writing this book, to make explicit reflection on the appropriateness of such dispositions as a core part of teacher education and development. Anna Cianciolo and Robert Sternberg use the term 'frames of mind', which we think also captures the way in which we bring different socially and culturally created lessons to bear on the world (*Intelligence*: A Brief History (2004) Oxford: Blackwell).

4   From her diary for 30 August 1923.

5   We take this comparison from Alison Gopnick, who made this suggestion in a review for the *New York Review of Books*, 6 May 1999. Alison Gopnick is also the lead author of a fascinating (1999) study, *The Scientist in the Crib: Minds, Brains, and How Children Learn* (New York: William Morris).

6   Taken from his 1994 book *The Astonishing Hypotheses: The Scientific Search for the Soul*, (New York: Simon and Schuster).

7   It appears that at the core of our mental life are over one hundred billion nerve cells known as neurons. These make up what we know as the grey matter. Adjacent are the glial cells (perhaps a thousand billion in number) but these do not directly influence mental activity. The neurons, for the most part, appear to be set at birth. Each of these neurons has a trail (or axon) and a larger number of branching structures, the dendrites, which are the routers for passing messages from one neuron to another. The connectivity is not akin to a circuit diagram and connections are not switched on or off. Rather there is a continuous but variable connectivity, with the axon passing messages to the dendrites that may be in contact with any number of other neurons. Such connections are known as synapses and it is these that grow and fluctuate in number over time. The growth in the number of axons, dendrites and synapses that connect neurons is known as synaptogenesis. This growth is first in the womb and then in the early years of a lifespan and may vary from one part of the brain to another. Although growth may slow, this does not represent a falling away of mental activity, but rather the pruning away of redundant capacity as we become more experienced in performing certain forms of mental activity. In this context, therefore, the adult brain cannot be thought of as fixed. Neurons work in networks with groups becoming specialised in specific types of stimuli. Frequent connectivity builds long lasting changes in synaptic connections and it is these changes that appear to permit learning and memory. This description is in part derived from a very useful (2005) publication written by John Hall for the Scottish Council for Research in Education Spotlight series (No. 92) on 'Neuroscience and education: What can brain science contribute to teaching and learning?' See also Sarah-Jayne Blakemore and Uta Brith's *The Learning Brain: Lessons from Education* (Blackwell: Oxford) published in 2005, which provides a very accessible account of brain science.

8   Richard Dawkins points to the fallacy of presenting natural selection as just a 'weeding out' of the weak: see *The Blind Watchmaker* (London: Longman) published in 1986.

9   J.T. Bruner (1997), published in *Educational Researcher*, 26:8.

10 A conclusion not shared by some who are offering courses on the brain and education (for teachers and parents), with the promise that brain training can promote achievement.

11 As do others – see, for example, the journal *Mind, Brain and Education*, founded in 2007.

12   This was part of a comprehensive review of education: parallel reports looked at elementary schooling (the Newcastle Commission) and the public schools (the Clarendon Commission).

13   Schools Inquiry Royal Commission, *The Taunton Report, 1868*, page 15–21.

14   Two very thorough accounts include Harry Torrance's (1981) 'The origins and development of mental testing in England and Wales', in *The Journal of Sociology of Education*, 2 (1), and Paul Davis Chapman's *Schools as Sorters: Lewis M. Terman, Applied Psychology and the Intelligence Testing Movement 1890–1930*, published in 1988 by the New York University Press.

15   Burt's story is told in detail by his biographer L.S. Hearnshaw, who started out as a Burt adviser and then, with great personal disappointment, discovered how invalid some key aspects of the work were.

16   *Spens Report on Secondary Education*, 1938, pages 357–81.

17   Burt contributed to the so-called Black Papers produced by the *Critical Quarterly* publication in the late 1960s and early 1970s that asserted the need for a more traditional and selective approach to education in Black Paper Two. Burt continued his defence of the testing system which allocated pupils to different types of schooling at age 11. Any injustice in the tests he saw as a minor concern. We quote:

> ... about 1 in 20 of the candidates [for the 11+] were rejected and subsequently did better (or were ultimately judged capable of doing better) than an equal number who had been accepted ... The important point, however, is this: none of the 'errors' were bad errors; the majority were confined to borderline cases. (Cyril Burt, *Black Paper Two*, page 18)

Given the widespread use of such tests for over 30 years, such errors would have impacted on the lives of many millions of children as well as their parents, family and friends.

18   See the discussion in Chapter 4 of Paul Davis Chapman's (1988) *Schools as Sorters: Lewis M. Terman, Applied Psychology and the Intelligence Testing Movement 1890–1930* (New York: New York University Press).

19   One of the most interesting analyses of this period is by John White, Emeritus Professor of the Philosophy of Education at the Institute of Education in London: see White, J. (2006) *Intelligence, Testing and Education: The Ideological Roots of Intelligence Testing* (London: Routledge).

20   An interesting example comes from a mid-1990s Conservative Party election briefing:

> While ABC 1s can conceptualise, C2s and Ds often cannot. They can relate only to things they can see and feel. They absorb their information and often views from television and tabloids. We have to talk to them in a way they understand. (Leaked Tory party election proposals by former minister John Maples – reprinted in the *Financial Times*, 21 November 1994, page 10)

21   Robin Alexander in his (2000) book *Culture and Pedagogy* (Oxford: Blackwell) provides an insightful analysis of Bruner's repositioning of educational psychology more firmly in the cultural domains – see Chapter 17; see also Mortimore, P. (ed.) (1999) *Understanding Pedagogy and its Impact on Learning* (London: Paul Chapman) Chapter 1, pages 7–8 for a review of perceptions of learners as thinkers.

22   Gardner, H. (1993) *Frames of Mind: Theory of Multiple Intelligences* (London: Fontana).

23   A criticism that Gardner refutes in his later book.

24   OECD (2002) *Understanding the Brain: Towards a New Learning Science* (Paris: OECD).

25   Blackmore, S.J. and Frith, U. (2005) *The Learning Brain: Lessons for Education* (Oxford: Blackwell).

26   This section of the argument draws on the seminal work of John T. Bruer, in particular his 1997 article in *Educational Researcher* (26:8) 'Education and the brain: a bridge too far', and more recently *The Myth of the First Three Years: A New Understanding of Early Years Development and Lifelong Learning* (New York: Free Press).

27   9 March 2000.

28   *Neuroscience and Education: Issues and Opportunities. A Commentary by the Teaching and Learning Research. Programme* London: ESRC TLRP.

29   This argument is taken from Blackmore, S.J. and Frith, U. (op cit.).

30   The journal, *Mind, Brain and Education* (first published in 2007) had an opening editorial, 'Why Mind, Brain and Education? Why Now?'. The editors suggest that society has high expectations, often unrealistic, about what neuroscience and genetics can bring to education. The explosion of new knowledge in biology has led to expectations that can distort the connections between research and practice in education. Educators, scientists, and journalists energetically pursue the connections, often in the form of sound bites and overly simple messages about what 'research shows', but it is a trap to assume that scientific research by itself will answer important questions in education. New findings on brain functioning, for example, require judicious interpretation, followed up by research that tests their application to the classroom. Equally important, decisions about how to educate require not only scientific information about what is effective but also decisions about what is valuable, including both what should be taught and how communities, schools, and teachers should organise the institutions that support learning and development.

     Scientists sometimes argue that relating biology to education is premature. They say that science first needs to answer the deep questions about how the mind/brain works. To the contrary, we affirm that research in educational settings will shape the great discoveries to come concerning basic biological and cognitive processes in learning and development. Research in practice settings is essential for the field of mind, brain, and education, in the same way that research in medical settings is essential for knowledge about medical practice.

31   From Perkins, D. (1995) *Outsmarting IQ: The Emerging Science of Learnable Intelligence* (New York: Free Press).

32   Bruner, 1996 (ibid.) pages 37 and 38.

CHAPTER 4

1   At the time of writing Albania is the poorest country in Europe. In 2007 an estimated 5 per cent of the Albanian population lived on an income of less than $1 a day and 25 per cent lived below the national poverty line of $2 a day. It is estimated that 40 per cent of the population have no access to basic services such as education, water, sanitation and heating.

2   See http://www.unicef.org/albania/RE_ext_eval_Engl_version.pdf

3   Reggie Emilia's ideas are discussed in Chapter 1.

4   Drita is fictional but this case study generalises the experiences of Albanians being educated under these circumstances and guided by a quite explicit philosophy of learning. It has been jointly authored with Zana Lita, a specialist in Albanian education, who also contributed to the broader commentary on Albania in this chapter. See Lita, Z. (2004) 'Teacher Education in Albania: past – present – future', unpublished PhD thesis.

5   Examples are Bransford, J.D., Brown, A.L. and Cocking, R. (eds) (2000), *How People Learn: Brain, Mind, Experience, and School,* London: Commission on Behavioural and Social Sciences and Education National Research Council; Murphy, P. (1999) *Learners, Learning and Assessment* (London: Paul Chapman); Wood, D. (1998) *How Children Think and Learn,* 2nd edition (Oxford: Blackwell).

6   Berryman, S. (2000) *Albania's Education Sector: Problems and Promise.* Published by the Human Development Sector Unit, Europe and Central Asia Region, World Bank.

7   Science teacher, Shales, Albania.

8   Berryman, S. (2000) *Albania's Education Sector: Problems and Promise.* Published by the Human Development Sector Unit, Europe and Central Asia Region, World Bank.

9   See Leach, J. and Lita, Z. (1996) *Regenerating Teacher Professional Development through Open and Distance Learning: the Albanian Kualida Project,* Poitiers: EDEN.

10   Recent research carried out by Professor Ronald Sultana, at the University of Malta, shows that this will be a long-term problem to be faced by Albanian educators; see Sultana, R.G. (2006) *Facing the Hidden Drop-Out Challenge in Albania* (evaluation report piloted in basic education in six prefectures of Albania from 2001 to 2005. Available at: http://www.unicef.org/albania/HDO_new_eng_2006.pdf)

11   A small number of experimental kindergartens, for instance, based on neighbouring Italy's Reggio Emilia model have been developed in different areas of the country and are currently being evaluated. These schools 'must assume the form of a live organism' the reformers write. 'The old educative theory of the individual must give way to the educative theory of participation. If a child is a carrier of theories, interpretations, questions and she is an active protagonist, the education dimension changes radically, not simply as an act of transmission of knowledge and competences, but as a complex self construction.' A few secondary schools inspired by the controversial Turkish pedagogic thinker Fetullah Gulen have similarly been encouraged to develop, despite their Islamic foundation, because of a dual focus on state-of-the-art science and technology teaching together with human values such as honesty, humility, justice, integrity and responsibility to others. Educators have also looked at approaches to the assessment of learning within the Scottish educational system, have visited experimental schools in South Africa, and have examined the Coalition of Essential Schools in the USA.

12   Article 26 of the Universal Declaration of Human Rights.

13   Core values:

   • ensure that Fenway continues to be a school that offers physical, cultural and intellectual safety and that stresses the ideas of social commitment and moral responsibility;
   • provide structures and experiences that encourage teachers to take a 'whole student' approach in content teams and across disciplines;
   • ensure that addressing the issues of race, class, gender and other differences is central to Fenway life;
   • ensure that students are vital participants in school decision making;
   • support the health and wellness of staff;
   • ensure that faculty members are vital participants in school decision making;
   • provide opportunities for staff and students to learn and grow together and to sustain deep intellectual and personal relationships;
   • ensure that every Fenway student participates in some form of physical activity.

14   Fenway High School was founded in 1983 as a school-within-a school. Its first students were 10th through 12th graders who were failing at other high schools. From the start,

the Fenway programme was a pioneer in the small schools movement. Fenway values personalised relationships between teachers and students, curricular integration and flexibility, school site autonomy, and collaborative relationships with outside organisations. In 1994 Fenway won charter status from the state. To stay within the school system, the school's co-directors worked with system officials to create the Boston Pilot School model, which gave Fenway greater control over its educational programmes, staffing, and budgets. Like other Boston Pilot schools, Fenway has an open enrolment admissions policy and draws students from middle schools across the city. Many of its 280 students come from Dorchester, Roxbury, Hyde Park, and East Boston, but all neighbourhoods are represented. The racial mix is about 55 per cent African-American, 20 per cent Hispanic, 20 per cent Caucasian, and 5 per cent Asian. More than 60 per cent qualify for free or reduced lunches. About 20 per cent receive services for documented learning issues. Over 20 per cent speak English as a second language, with Spanish, Haitian Creole, Russian, Portuguese, Polish and Italian among the native languages represented at the school. It is now a full 9th–12th grade high school, widely recognised for its success with urban students, many of whom enter the school near the bottom of the academic ladder and then go on to college after graduation. It was one of the first 'New American High Schools' named by the US Department of Education and has been designated an 'exemplar' and a 'lead school' by other educational organisations, including the Coalition of Essential Schools. Teachers and school administrators from around the world come to observe Fenway in action.

15   The advisory also involves developing personal relationships with other students and with teachers; sharing/supporting each individual in the group; discussing community issues; co-parenting; debating/speaking skills; a teen issues forum; town meetings; study skills and time management; violence prevention; preparing for portfolio deadlines and exhibitions; motivational speakers; Facing History and Ourselves case studies. See http://fenwayhs.org/advisory.htm

16   K–12 teachers; higher education; science/business/professionals in the field; programme or policy developers; K–12 leaders/administrators; students; education assessment specialists.

17   This case study is based on author observations and conversations with staff, especially Eileen Sullivan Shakespear, Fenway's humanities curriculum co-coordinator and Director of the Teacher Education Programme with Tufts, Harvard and Fenway students between 1998 and the present. See also http://www.fenwayhs.org/

18   Bruner, J. (1996) (ibid) 'The complexity of educational aims' (Chapter 3), pages 67–8.

19   Rashid, M. and Dorabawila, V. (1999) *Poverty, the Labor Market, and Public Programs: Household Welfare in Pre-Crisis Albania*. Washington, DC: World Bank.

20   It is important to note that this approach assumed that the majority of children possessed a common ability or potential. The expectation was that all could become literate.

21   Sfard, A. (1998) 'On two metaphors for learning and the dangers of choosing just one', *Educational Researcher*, 27(2): 4–13.

22   Freire writes about banking education thus: 'The teacher talks about reality as if it were motionless, static, compartmentalized, and predictable. Or else he expounds on a topic completely alien to the existential experience of the students. His task is to 'fill' the students with the contents of his narration – contents which are detached from reality, disconnected from the totality that engendered them and could give them significance. Words are emptied of their concreteness and become a hollow, alienated, and alienating verbosity.'
     The outstanding characteristic of this narrative education, then, is the sonority of words, not their transforming power. 'Four times four is sixteen; the capital of Para is Belem.'The

student records, memorises, and repeats these phrases without perceiving what four times four really means, or realising the true significance of 'capital' in the affirmation 'the capital of Para is Belem', that is, what Belem means for Para and what Para means for Brazil. Narration (with the teacher as narrator) leads the students to memorise mechanically the narrated content. Worse yet, it turns them into 'containers', into 'receptacles' to be 'filled' by the teacher. The more completely she fills the receptacles, the better a teacher she is. The more meekly the receptacles permit themselves to be filled, the better students they are. Education thus becomes an act of depositing, in which the students are the depositories and the teacher is the depositor. See Freire, P. (1972) *Pedagogy of the Oppressed* (Harmondsworth: Penguin, Chapter 2).

23 Bruner (1996) ibid, page 1.

24 Bruner (1996) ibid.

25 Chaiklin, S. and Lave, J. (1993) *Understanding Practice: Perspectives on Activity and context* (Cambridge: Cambridge University Press).

26 McDermott, R.P. (1993) 'The acquisition of a child by a learning disability'. In *Understanding Practice*, S. Chaiklin and J. Lave (eds) (New York: Cambridge University Press) page 292.

27 The school owes a lot of its thinking to the work of Ted Sizer, a leading educational reformer in the United States. In 1984, he founded the Coalition of Essential Schools (http://www.essentialschools.org/) and is author of Horace's *Hope: What Works for the American High School* (1997). Also to Deborah Meier, teacher, educational reformer, writer and activist, who set out the idea of habits of mind (see http://www.essentialschools.org/pub/ces_docs/about/phil/habits. html) in her (1995) book, *The Power of their Ideas: Lessons for America from a Small School in Harlem* (Boston: Beacon Press) pages 50–1.

28 Cobb, P. (1999) 'From representations to symbolizing: Individual and communal development in the mathematics classroom'. Paper presented at the Annual Meeting of the American Education Research Association, Montreal, Canada.

29 Bruner (ibid) 1996.

30 Claxton, G. (1990) *Teaching to Learn: A Direction for Education* (London: Cassell).

31 Hendry, G.D. and King, R.C. (1994) 'On theory of learning and knowledge: Educational implications of advances in neuroscience', *Science Education*, 78(3): 223–53.

32 Drawn from Wenger, E. (1998) *Communities of Practice: Learning, Meaning, and Identity* (Cambridge: Cambridge University Press).

33 In a lecture given at University of Oxford on 13 March 2007, Jerome Bruner suggested that three principles – the *multiplicity, perspectival* and the *comparative* – are key for pedagogy. We have intentionally used these principles throughout the book in our exploration of the notion of pedagogy.

34 Simon, B. (1994) 'Why no pedagogy in England?', in B. Moon and A. Shelton-Mayes (eds), *Teaching and Learning in the Secondary School* (London: Routledge).

35 McDermott, R.P. (1993) 'The acquisition of a child by a learning disability', in *Understanding Practice*. S. Chaiklin and J. Lave (eds) (New York: Cambridge University Press) page 292.

36 McDermott, R.P. (1993) ibid, page 293.

37 Leach, J. (2001) 'One hundred possibilities: creativity, community and new technologies', in A. Craft and B. Jeffrey (eds), *Creativity in Education* (London: Cassell).

38   DfEE (1999) 'All Our Futures: Creativity, culture and education', report to the Secretary
     of State for Education and Employment and the Secretary of State for Culture, Media and
     Sport, May 1999, page 28.

39   Sloboda, J., Howe, M.J.A. and Davidson, J.W. (1998) 'Innate talent: reality or myth?',
     Behavioural and Brain Sciences, 21(3): 399–442.

40   Howe, M.J.A. (ed.) 'Encouraging the development of exceptional gifts and
     talents', in V. Lee, *Giftedness* (Milton Keynes: The Open University) pages 1–16.

41   Messenger, J.C. (1962) Anang Art, Drama, and Social Control *African Studies Bulletin*,
     Vol. 5, No. 2, Arts, Human Behavior, and Africa (May, 1962), pp. 29–35

42   Green, L. (2002) 'Gender identity, musical experience and schooling', in G. Spruce (ed.),
     Aspects of Teaching Secondary Music: Perspectives on Practice (London and New York:
     Routledge).

43   Green (2002) ibid, page 106.

44   Simon, B. (1994) ibid, 'The demise of the elementary school [where, he argues, the devel-
     opment of pedagogical thinking might have taken root], combined with an emphasis on
     selection and preoccupation with the measurement of ability and psychometric theory set
     this process in motion'. Such a process was further fuelled, he suggests, by the emergence
     of child-centred approaches to teaching in the 1960s, which drew on Piagetian theories
     of learning that focused on individual difference.

45   Sen, A. (1999) *Development as Freedom* (Oxford: Oxford University Press); Bruner, J. (1996)
     ibid.

46   Simon, B. (1994) ibid, page 39. Simon argues that the introduction of a national curricu-
     lum into the English education system in the late 1990s created just the conditions for
     identifying effective pedagogy, by attempting to define common learning objectives for all
     students across the main domains of both primary and secondary phases. Sadly, he argues,
     this opportunity to make something of a breakthrough has in the event marginalised ped-
     agogy. Questions about how the development of *all* children might be achieved have been
     sidelined and research about the kinds of learning activities that move understanding for-
     ward has been largely disregarded. Pedagogy has been confined to 'effective teaching'
     issues, notably *classroom organisation* (e.g. choice of groups, individual and whole-class
     teaching, and fitness for purpose of such strategies) and discrete *teaching skills* (e.g. use of
     explanation, questioning and so forth). Such approaches, Simon argues, take no account
     of underpinning pedagogical means and learning principles.

47   See educational research by Resnick, for example.

48   Both old and more recent philosophical theories have generated the conceptual body of
     ideas, which could be termed *philosophical constructivism* (i.e. that our beliefs and percep-
     tions of the world are purely human constructs). The roots of philosophical constructivism,
     going back to Aristotle and the ancient Greek instrumentalist philosophy, can be found in
     Kant's philosophy and Berkeley's philosophy of science. Thomas Kuhn's *Structure of
     Scientific Revolutions* (1962) provided a theory of scientific development, in which 'anom-
     alies' and 'crises' in the established research tradition necessitated the acceptance of a new
     paradigm to be extended by the practices of prevailing science. Scientists need to construct,
     not discover, 'what is really there' he argues, by means of persuasion and social justifica-
     tion in order to arrive at a sort of consensus around the emerging new research tradition.
     The philosopher Richard Rorty has also contested traditional realist views about the
     nature of knowledge and has adopted a constructivist view. In his book *Philosophy and the
     Mirror of Nature* (1979) he tried to deconstruct the dominant metaphor in modern post-
     Cartesian western philosophy of the human mind as a 'Mirror of Nature'. According to
     this metaphor, the human mind is equipped with two working elements, a 'mirror',

reflecting reality, and an 'inner eye,' contemplating and comprehending that reflection. In the realist tradition, the captured reflection together with the accompanied contemplation constitute the processes of learning and the acquisition of knowledge. Rorty, drawing on the work of Wittgenstein, Heidegger and Dewey, attacks these metaphysical abstractions. His pragmatist thesis (shared by constructivism) is that 'we understand knowledge when we understand the social justification of belief, and thus have no need to view it as accuracy of representation' (Rorty (1979) ibid, page 170).

49 Dewey, J. (1966) *Democracy and Education* (New York: Free Press).

50 Piaget, J. (1973) *To Understand is to Invent* (New York: Grossman).

51 To be intentionally aware of one's thoughts and actions.

52 Reciprocal teaching refers to an instructional activity based on research by Palincsar and Brown (1985) that takes place in the form of a dialogue between teachers and students regarding segments of text. The dialogue is structured by the use of four strategies: summarising, question generating, clarifying, and predicting. The teacher and students take turns assuming the role of teacher in leading this dialogue. The purpose of reciprocal teaching is to facilitate a group effort between teacher and students as well as among students in the task of bringing meaning to the text. Each strategy was selected for the following purpose: *Summarising* provides the opportunity to identify and integrate the most important information in the text. *Question generating* reinforces the summarising strategy and carries the learner along one more step in the comprehension activity. When students generate questions, they first identify the kind of information that is significant enough to provide the substance for a question. They then pose this information in question form and self-test to ascertain that they can indeed answer their own question. *Clarifying* is particularly important when working with students who have a history of comprehension difficulty. When students are asked to clarify, their attention is called to the fact that there may be many reasons why text is difficult to understand (e.g., new vocabulary, unclear reference words, and unfamiliar and perhaps difficult concepts). They are taught to be alert to the effects of such impediments to comprehension and to take the necessary measures to restore meaning (e.g., reread, ask for help). *Predicting* invites students to hypothesise what the author will discuss next in the text. In order to do this successfully, students must activate the relevant background knowledge that they already possess regarding the topic. The students have a purpose for reading: to confirm or disprove their hypotheses. Furthermore, the opportunity will have been created for students to link the new knowledge they will encounter in the text to the knowledge they already possess. In summary, each of these strategies is selected as a means of aiding students to construct meaning from text, as well as a means of monitoring their reading to ensure that they are in fact understanding what they read.

53 Benchmark Instruction is a genre of teacher instigated, full-class discussions aimed at promoting conceptual changes in students' thinking. These are designed to draw out and engage students' own ideas in a context of communal inquiry. Students typically participate in three primary phases of discussion: (1) presenting an initial response to the problem or idea and a justification; (2) critiquing and discussing the ideas drawn out by the lesson; (3) reflecting on what has been learnt and its generalisabilty. A goal of the benchmark is not simply solving a particular problem, but learning how to solve problems in general. Students are encouraged to be aware of and to identify the key concepts of a problem and to develop their communication skills while answering the questions and providing understanding to the rest of the group.

54 Bauersfeld, H. (1995) '"Language games" in the mathematics classroom: Their function and their effects', in P. Cobb and H. Bauersfeld (eds), *The Emergence of Mathematical*

Meaning: Interaction in Classroom Cultures (Hillsdale, NJ: Lawrence Erlbaum Associates) pages 271–91.

55   Di Vesta, F.J. (1987) 'The cognitive movement and education', in J.A. Glover and R.R. Ronning (eds), *Historical Foundations of Educational Psychology* (New York: Plenum Press) pages 203–33.

56   von Glasersfeld, E. (1995) 'A constructivist approach to teaching', in L. Steffe and J. Gale (eds), *Constructivism in Education* (New Jersey: Lawrence Erlbaum Associates) pages 3–16.

57   von Glasersfeld, E. (1996) 'Introduction: aspects of constructivism', in C. Fosnot (ed.), *Constructivism: Theory, Perspectives, and Practice* (New York: Teachers College Press) pages 3–7.

58   The Plowden Report (1967) *Children and their Primary Schools: A Report of the Central Advisory Council for Education (England)* (London: HMSO) drew heavily on Piaget's theories of cognitive development, especially his concepts of activity, discovery learning, and readiness. Many primary schools tried to take the notion of the individualisation of learning to its logical limits ('at the heart of the educational processes lies the child'), constructing individual tasks for each child in the school with teachers managing this complexity by 'leading from behind'.

59   Needham, R. and Hill, P. (1987) *Teaching Strategies for Developing Understanding in Science: Children: Learning in Science Project*, University of Leeds.

60   Vygotsky studied in Moscow in the early twentieth century and his psychological theories were developed throughout the 1920s until his death in 1934. His work is therefore interpreted by others in the field, including Bruner, who studied with Vygotsky in his early career.

61   Vygotsky's influence on thinking about learning came after Piaget, even though they were contemporaries. This reflects in part the length of time taken for books that translated his work to be published in the West.

62   Rogoff, B. (1990) *Apprenticeship in Thinking: Cognitive Development in Social Context* (New York: Oxford University Press).

63   Bruner, J. (1986) *Actual Minds, Possible Worlds* (Cambridge, MA: Harvard University Press) page 129.

64   Bruner (1996) ibid.

65   Scardamalia, M. and Bereiter, C. (1985) 'Fostering the development of self-regulation in children's knowledge processing', in S.F. Chipman, J.W. Segal and R. Glaser (eds), *Thinking and Learning Skills: Research and Open Questions* (Hillsdale, NJ: Lawrence Erlbaum Associates).

66   Extract from Collins, A., Brown, J.S and Holum, A. (1991) 'Cognitive apprenticeship: Making things visible'. *American Educator* 15(3) 6–11.

67   May, W. (1991) 'Constructing history in a graduate curriculum class', *Curriculum Inquiry*, 21, 2: 163–91.

68   Belenky, M., Clinchy, B., Goldberger, N. and Tarule, J. (1986) *Women's Ways of Knowing* (New York: Basic Books); Gilligan, C. (1982) *In a Different Voice* (Cambridge MA: Harvard University Press).

69   Rutenberg, T. (1983) 'Learning Women's Studies', in G. Bowles and R.D. Klein (eds), *Theories About Women's Studies* (New York: Routledge & Kegan Paul); Kenway, J. and Modra, H. (1992) 'Feminist pedagogy and emancipatory possibilities' in C. Luke and J. Gore (eds), *Feminisms and Critical Pedagogy* (New York: Routledge); Haraway, D. (1988)

'Situated knowledges: the science question in feminism and the privilege of partial per-spective', *Feminist Studies*: 575–91.

70   Robinson, B.D. and Schaible, R. (1993) 'Women and Men Teaching "Men, Women, and Work"', *Teaching Sociology*: 363–70.

71   Du Bois, B. (1983) 'Passionate scholarship: notes on values, knowing, and method in fem-inist social science', in G. Bowles and R.D. Klein (eds), *Theories of Women's Studies* (New York: Routledge & Kegan Paul) page 112.

72   e.g. Seeley Brown, J.S., Collins, A. and Duguid, P. (1988) op cit.

73   Lave, J. and Wenger, E. (1991) *Situated Learning* (Cambridge: Cambridge University Press) page 45.

74   Cobb, P. (1999) 'Where is the mind?', in P. Murphy (ed.), *Learners, Learning and Assessment* (London: Chapman).

75   Lave, J. (1988) *Cognition in Practice* (Cambridge: Cambridge University Press); Putnam, R.T. and Borko, H. (2000) 'What do new views of knowledge and thinking have to say about research on teacher learning?', *Educational Researcher*, 29(1): 4–15.

76   Lave and Wenger (1991) ibid.

77   Pedder and McIntyre (2006) ibid.

78   This case study is drawn from a research project carried out by the City of Edinburgh EAL Service and the Black Community Development Project, January–September 2005 and a personal interview with Ms Eileen Simpson, EAL co-ordinator, August 2006.

79   Weil, C. and Southerland, L. (eds) (1991) *Theory and Practice in Social Group Work – Creative Connections* (London: Haworth Press).

80   Simpson, E. (2005) 'Juggling Two Cultures', A report into individual support and group work with S5 Muslim boys in the James Gillespie High School, carried out by the city of Edinburgh's EAL Service and the Black Community Development Project, July–September 2005.

81   Eckert, P. (1997) 'Gender, race and class in the preadolescent marketplace of identities'. Paper presented at the 96th Annual Meeting of the American Anthropological Association. Washington, DC.

82   Lave and Wenger propose that newcomers to any culture of practice should, in the first instance, be encouraged to observe on the boundaries of the practice, a process they term 'legitimate peripheral participation'. Legitimate peripheral participation, they argue, can enable learners to progressively piece together the culture of the group, what it means to be a member, and what roles and responsibilities they can take. 'To be able to participate in a legitimately peripheral way entails that newcomers have broad access to arenas of mature practice.' As learning and involvement in the practice increase, so the learner moves from the role of observer to gradually becoming a more fully functioning participant.

83   This case study appears in Banks, F., Leach, J. and Moon, B. (1999) 'New understandings of teacher pedagogic knowledge', in J. Leach and B. Moon (eds), *Learners and Pedagogy* (London: Paul Chapman.)

84   Lave and Wenger (1991) ibid, page 116.

85   This is a pseudonym.

86   Lave and Wenger (1991) ibid.

87   Lave and Wenger (1991) ibid.

88   Tochan, F. and Munby, H. (1993) 'Novice and expert teachers' time epistemology: a wave function from didactives to pedagogy', *Teacher and Teacher Education*, 9(2): 205–18.

89   McDiarmid, G., Ball, D. L. and Anderson, C.W. (1989) 'Why staying one chapter ahead doesn't really work: subject-specific pedagogy', in M.C. Reynolds (ed.), *Knowledge Base for the Beginning Teacher* (Oxford: Pergamon Press).

90   The concept of distributed cognition emphasises the interaction among the individual, the environment, and cultural artefacts. It claims that the development and cognitive growth of individuals should not be isolated events, rather the changes should be a reciprocal process. Three sources emerge from the theory of distributed cognition: first, the increasingly important role that technology plays in handling intellectual tasks: second, the re-emphasis on Vygotsky's sociocultural theory; third, the shifting of attention to cognitions that are situated dependent and distributed in nature.

91   Dede, C. (1996) 'Emerging technologies and distributed learning', *American Journal of Distance Education*, 10(2): 4–36.

92   Wenger, E. (1993) ibid.

93   'Meet the team', *Addenbrooke's Matters*, Winter 2007, pages 4–5.

94   *Te Aorangi* is also the name of Mount Cook, the highest mountain in New Zealand and therefore also a place in the literal sense.

95   *Hawaiki* is the Maori name for the land to which some Polynesian cultures trace their origins and the place to which they return after death. It is a common thread throughout the Polynesian Pacific. The future is always contained in the past and the past leads to the future – indeed the way verbs are constructed in the Maori language emphasises this.

96   It is of great importance that the placenta is literally buried on the land. The child is therefore symbolically planted on the ancestral land and belongs to it. Nowadays hospitals are careful to return the placenta to the parents for planting, but it was a cause of great distress in previous years when this was derided as a practice.

97   This means literally *whare* (house) and *kura* (school) – the learning or school house.

98   This information is drawn in part from Pere, R.T. (2003) *Te Wheke*, published by Ao Ako Global Learning New Zealand Limited, Wairoa. However, Phillida Bunkle also provided the authors with invaluable insights into Maori education and culture.

99   e.g. Fuhrer, U. (1993) 'Behavior setting analysis of situated learning: the case of newcomers', in S. Chaiklin and J. Lave (eds), *Understanding Practice Perspectives on Activity and Context* (Cambridge: Cambridge University Press). The adults in Fuhrer's study were attempting to locate job listings in a job centre that none of them had previously visited. As part of this study Fuhrer analysed in detail how the layout of the centre, including the furniture and the placing of notice boards and notices, the information desk and the photocopier, played a part in their ability to negotiate this activity.

100   See, for example, T. Gordon and E. Lahelma (1996) '"School is Like an Ant's Nest": spatiality and embodiment in schools', *Gender and Education*, 8(3): 301–10.

101   Gordon, T. (2003–2005) *Research Study Agency and Power in Young People's Lives: Boundaries and Limitations* (University of Helsinki).

102   Ceppi, G. and Zini, M. (eds) (1988) *Children, Spaces, Relations: Metaproject for an Environment for Young Children* (Reggio Children: Reggio Emilia, Italy).

103   See, for example, Vecchi, V. (1998) 'What kind of space for living well in school?', in G. Ceppi and M. Zini (eds), *Children, Spaces, Relations: Metaproject for an Environment for Young Children* (Reggio Children: Reggio Emilia, Italy).

104   Hardy, B. (1968) 'Towards a poetics of fiction: an approach through narrative', *Novel*, 1: 5–14.

105 Hardy (1968) ibid, page 5.

106 Bruner, J. (1986) *Actual Minds, Possible Worlds* (Cambridge, MA: Harvard University Press). Bruner, J. (1987) 'Life as narrative', *Social Research*, 54: 11–32. Bruner, J. (1991) 'The narrative construction of reality', *Critical Inquiry*, 18: 1–21. Bruner (1996), ibid.

107 Douglas, M. (2007) *Thinking in Circles: An Essay in Ring Composition* (London: Yale University Press).

108 Bruner (1996) ibid.

109 A longer version of this case study appears in Leach, J. and Moon, B. (1999) *Learners and Pedagogy* (London: Chapman).

110 Nearly all researchers agree on the following format: introduction to setting and characters; explanation of a state of affairs; initiating event; emotional response or statement of a goal by the protagonist; complicating actions; outcomes; reactions to the outcome. Narratives that conform to the above schema all have their basis in oral tradition, e.g. Propp, V. (1968) *Morphology of the Folktale* (Austin/London: University of Texas Press).

111 The Xhosa are a group of peoples of Bantu origins living in southeast South Africa, and in the last two centuries throughout the southern and central southern parts of the country, particularly in the Eastern Cape.

112 This work which has been ongoing since the mid-1990s (see http://www.open.ac.uk/deep and Dladla, N. and Moon, B. (2002) *Challenging the Assumptions about Teacher Education and Training in Sub-Saharan Africa*, published by the Pan-Commonwealth Forum on Open Learning, International Convention Centre, Durban, South Africa.

113 Wiske, M. S. (1994) 'How teaching for understanding changes the rules in the classroom', *Educational Leadership*, 51(5): 19–21; Perkins, D. and Blythe, T. (1994) 'Putting understanding up front', *Educational Leadership*, 51(5): 4–7; Wiske, M. S. (ed.) (1998) *Teaching for Understanding: Linking Research with Practice* (San Francisco, CA: Jossey-Bass).

114 Gardner, H. and Boix Marsella, V. (1994) 'Teaching for understanding within and across the disciplines', *Educational Leadership*, 51(5): 14–18.

115 A generative topic or theme is one that is central to the discipline, that is accessible to students, and that can be connected to diverse topics both inside and outside of the discipline. In a study of biology, for example, the themes of health, growth, sickness, or ecological balance might be used to organise a unit of study that would reach beyond the boundaries of biology textbooks.

116 Several key understanding goals for each topic must be identified and stated. These goals serve to focus instruction.

117 Performances which support the understanding goals must be part of each unit from beginning to end.

118 Assessment is an integral part of instruction, not a summary statement of adequacy. The key factors are shared and public criteria, regular feedback, and frequent reflection during the learning process.

119 Newmann, F.M. and Archbald, D.A. (1992) 'The nature of authentic academic achievement', in H. Berlak, F.M. Newmann, E. Adams, D.A. Archbald, T. Burgess, J. Raven and T.A. Romberg (eds), *Toward a New Science of Educational Testing and Assessment* (Albany, NY: State University of New York Press) pages 71–84.

120 Newmann and Archbald (1992) ibid, pages 73–5.

121   Wiske, M.S. (ed.) (1998) *Teaching for Understanding: Linking Research with Practice*. (San Francisco, CA: Jossey-Bass).

122   Overarching goals, or throughlines, describe the most important understandings that students should develop during an entire course. The understanding goals for particular units should be closely related to one or more of the overarching understanding goals of the course. Examples of throughlines: *for an American history course:* 'How does our historical past make us who we are today'?; *for a general science course:* 'Students will understand that "doing science" is not the process of finding facts but of constructing and testing theories'; *for an algebra course:* 'How can we use what we know to figure out what we don't know'?; *for a literature course:* 'Students will understand how metaphors shape the way we experience the world'.

123   Restating questions using sentence stems like 'Students will understand and appreciate …' or 'Students will begin to understand …' helps to remind us to focus instruction on understanding and not on some other active verb, like 'examine' or 'explore' or 'describe'. Those are great, thoughtful actions, but the GOAL is understanding, not a behaviour such as exploration. Exploration is something we do to develop and/or demonstrate understanding.

124   *Senior Portfolio Guidelines*

1.   A senior must include a cover letter that outlines the whole portfolio. This cover letter should introduce each piece and should comment on your personal journey towards creating a high quality senior portfolio.

2.   PERSONAL/STORIES: Write a short story or a persona in which you explore your chosen person/event in a creative way. A senior must be able to write a story that has structure and tension, and that uses vivid, well chosen language to create clear characters and settings. A senior's story must make explicit connections to his/her issue. A senior must submit evidence of a writing process: brainstorming, outlining, several drafts, several peer/adult edits, significant revision and a polished final copy. All outlines and drafts must be saved and filed with the final story.

3.   RESEARCH: Research a question about your person/event and write a 7–10 page research paper. A senior must show the ability to write a 7–10 page research paper. A senior research paper should demonstrate deep investigation of a specific question about an historically significant person or event. It must be thoroughly researched, carefully structured, and well edited. It must have an appropriate format and all the correct conventions. It must have citations within the paper from a bibliography of not less than five sources. A senior must submit evidence of having followed a writing process as outlined above. All note cards, outlines and rough drafts must be saved and filed with the final research paper.

4.   ANNOTATED BIBLIOGRAPHY READER'S LOG: Assemble an Annotated Bibliography that includes at least ten articles, chapters, or whole books that you read while researching your person or event. Use the correct bibliographic format to identify each reading. For each source, summarise the reading and evaluate its usefulness (3–4 paragraphs). A senior's Annotated Bibliography must show evidence of regular and varied reading with good comprehension. A senior's Annotated Bibliography must demonstrate critical reading skills such as applying the Habits of Mind to a reading, distinguishing fact from opinion, evaluating the usefulness of a source, evaluating author's bias, purpose and reliability. A senior's Annotated Bibliography must show variety of reading and cannot include more than three Internet entries. It must include at least one whole book.

5. POSITION PAPER: Write a final senior position paper related to your person or event. A senior must independently write, revise, and edit a 500–word paper arguing a position that is related to his/her person or event. A senior must be able to use his/her own voice to persuasively argue that position. The paper must show that a senior can: identify a key issue and a personal position; gather information from at least three sources; logically argue for the position; use supporting evidence from three sources; and acknowledge opposing perspectives. A senior's position paper must have the appropriate format, a clear structure, paragraph unity and coherence, and the correct conventions for citations and bibliography, and for spelling, grammar, and mechanics. As in other writing pieces, a senior must show evidence of having followed a writing process and of revising and editing independently. All note-cards, outlines, and drafts must be filed with the final position paper.

6. LISTENING: Include notes taken during an interview or a lecture given by an expert on your person/issue. A senior must demonstrate the ability to take useful and complete notes. A senior must write a cover letter for this piece that evaluates the content, bias, style and delivery of the speaker and that offers personal comment on the usefulness of the interview.

7. INTERDISCIPLINARY: Create a visual or musical representation that responds to or illustrates your person/event. A senior must demonstrate the ability to respond artistically to the life of a person or to the details of an event.

125 *Academic Courses:* In order to graduate from Fenway, a student who begins in ninth grade must take and pass the following courses: 4 years of Math, 4 years of Humanities, 4 years of Science Spanish I and II; *Portfolios:* Seniors must complete a portfolio in Math, Humanities and Science that demonstrates their mastery of competencies defined by each academic department. In addition, seniors must complete an internship portfolio; *Internship:* Before graduation, seniors must complete a six-week internship, providing a total of 60 hours; *Position Paper:* Each student must complete a position paper that is approved by the head of school; *Science Fair:* Each student must pass science fair for each year they attend Fenway (the science fair is recorded as Science Project on the student's transcript); *Community Service:* Each student must complete a total of 40 hours community service (this is usually completed in the sophomore year); *Standardised Tests:* In order to receive a Diploma from Boston Public Schools, all students must take and pass the ELA and Math MCAS.

126 HyperStudio is computer software that facilitates project-based learning, collaborative learning and tools to create rubrics, portfolio pieces, and other assessment components. It enables brainstorming tools, visual organisers, project planners, desktop publishing features, and multimedia presentation.

127 *Assessment for Learning: Beyond the Black Box* (Cambridge: Cambridge School of Education) and Black, P. and Williams, D. (1998) *Inside the Black Box: Raising Standards Through Classroom Assessment* (London: School of Education, King's College).

128 Sadler, R. (1989) 'Formative assessment and the design of instructional systems', *Instructional Science,* 18: 199–44.

129 Professor at the Centre for Activity Theory and Developmental Work Research, University of Helsinki, Finland. Major proponent of activity theory and developmental work research in general. Engestrom works within the framework of cultural-historical activity theory and is best known for his theory of expansive learning. He studies transformations in work and organisations, combining micro level analysis of discourse and interaction with the historical analysis and modeling of organisations as activity systems working through developmental contradictions. His research groups use intervention

tools such as the Change Laboratory, inspired by Vygotsky's method of dual stimulation, to facilitate and analyse the redesign of activity systems by practitioners. His current research is focused on health care organisations, a bank, and a telecommunications company striving toward new forms of co-configuration and knotworking. Recent works include *Cognition and Communication at Work* (edited with David Middleton, 1996), *Perspectives on Activity Theory* (edited with Reijo Miettinen and Raija-Leena Punamäki, 1999), and *Between School and Work: New Perspectives on Transfer and Boundary Crossing* (edited with Terttu Tuomi-Gröhn, 2003).

130   In 1969, Gregory Bateson (see Bateson (1972) *Steps to an Ecology of Mind: Collected Essays in Anthropology, Psychiatry, Evolution, and Epistemology*, University of Chicago Press) developed a sophisticated version of learning theory which, rather than seeing cognitive and cultural views of learning as being separate and distinct, suggested a complex hierarchy of stages which he called Learning I, Learning II, and Learning III (Bateson (1972) ibid, page 287). According to Bateson, Learning I comprises those forms of learning that encompass behaviourism, habituation, conditioning and rote learning. Learning II or learning to learn (deutero-learning) is the acquisition of context or structure to Learning I. The outcomes of Learning II, habits or 'character', he argues, save individuals from 'having to examine the abstract, philosophical, aesthetic, and ethical aspects of many sequences of life' (1972, ibid, page 303). Learning III, on the other hand, is essentially conscious: it 'throws these unexamined premises open to question and change' (page 303). Learning III, he argues, is a rare event, produced by contradictions in Learning II. The inner contradictions in Learning II that generate Learning III Bateson named the *double bind*.

131   See Moscovici, S. (1984) 'The phenomenon of social representations', in R. Farr and S. Moscovici (eds), *Social Representations* (Cambridge, Paris: Cambridge University, Editions de la Maison des Sciences de l'Homme) pages 3–69.

132   Engestrom, Y. 'Learning by expanding'. Available at: http://lchc.ucsd.edu/MCA/Paper/Engestrom/expanding/toc.htm; Bartlett, F. (1958) *Thinking: An Experimental and Social Study* (London: Allen & Unwin).

133   Engestrom, Y. 'Learning by expanding'. Available at: http://lchc.ucsd.edu/MCA/Paper/Engestrom/expanding/toc.htm. See also Schön, D. A. (1983) *The Reflective Practitioner: How Professionals Think in Action* (London: Temple Smith) and Seidel, R. (1976) Denken – *Psychologische Analyse der Entstehung und Lösung von Problemen* (Frankfurt am Main/New York: Campus).

134   Chaiklin, S. and Lave, J. (1993) *Understanding Practice: Perspectives on Activity and Context* (Cambridge: Cambridge University Press) page 13.

135   Engestrom, Y. (1996) '*Non scolae sed vitae discimus:* Towards overcoming the encapsulation of school learning', in H. Daniels (ed.), *An Introduction to Vygotsky* (London: Routledge).

136   This vignette is drawn from Leach, J. (1998) 'Beyond reflection: reconceptualising practice in professional development for education', in *Supporting Learners in Open and Distance Learning* (Johannesburg, South Africa: SACHED).

137   The *acquisition* metaphor.

138   The *participatory* metaphor.

CHAPTER 5

1   Published in 2005 by Dover Publications in a series on books on Western philosophy.

2   Here I am drawing on the still very persuasive analysis of Richard Pring in his 1976 publication *Knowledge and Schooling* (London: Open Books).

3   Gilbert Kyles's *The Concept of Mind,* published in 1949, provided a seminal exploration of these two dimensions of knowledge.

4   See Hurst, P. (1974).

5   Freire, P. (1998) *Teachers as Cultural Workers: Letters to Those Who Dare Teach,* translated by Donald Macedo, Dale Koike and Alexandre Oliveira (Boulder: Westview Press) page 93.

6   See for example Bereiter, C. and Scardamalia, M. (1993) *Surpassing Ourselves: An Inquiry into the Nature and Implications of Expertise* (Chicago: Open Court).

7   Michael Polanyi's work has been seen as particularly influential in promoting the importance of the concept of tacit knowledge. In his book *The Tacit Dimension,* published in 1967, he argued that in looking at problems we should start from the position that 'we can know more than we can tell'.

8   Scardamalia, M. (2002) 'Collective cognitive responsibility for the advancement of knowledge' in Smith, B. (ed.), *Liberal Educators in a Knowledge Society* (Chicago: Open Court).

9   See Young, M. (2007) *Bringing Knowledge Back In* (London: Routledge).

10 Here we are drawing on the work of Michael Young. See Young, M. (1999) 'The curriculum as socially organised knowledge' in R. McCormick and C. Paechter (eds), *Learning and Knowledge* (London: Paul Chapman).

11 In England, in the 1980s, Margaret Thatcher's government insisted that research on economics should be given much more importance in the funding of social science research. Thus the Social Science Research Council (SSRC) became the Economic and Social Science Research Council (ESRC), as it is today.

12 Spruce, G. (1999) 'Music, music education and the bourgeois aesthetic: developing a music curriculum for the new millennium' in McCormick, R. and Paechter, C. (eds) *Learning and Knowledge,* (London: Paul Chapman).

13 In the early part of the 1980s a Technical and Vocational Educational Initiative (TVEI) was introduced to England and Wales with funding to persuade schools to adopt a more vocational orientation in the curriculum. This was phased out following the introduction of the National Curriculum.

14 See Moon, B. (1990) 'The national curriculum: origins and context', in T. Brighouse and B. Moon (eds), *Managing the National Curriculum: Some Critical Perspectives* (BEMAS).

15 Young (1999) op cit, page 155.

16 Our own organisation of knowledge is often incomplete; in the week that we wrote the first draft of this chapter we were puzzling over the differences and overlaps between anthropology and ethnology – a process that sent us scuttling to the reference books and for the 'web'.

17 Bruner (1996) op cit, page 56.

18 And so it follows that we are rather impatient with the fruitless, quasi ideological debates that try to pitch subject-based and child-centred approaches to pedagogy as being in opposition to each other.

19 See his essay, 'Knowledge and Teaching: Foundations of the New Reform' in Shulman, L. (ed.) (2004) *The Wisdom of Practice: Essays on Teaching, Learning and Learning to Teach,* San Francisco, Jossey-Bass.

20 We return to this issue and the relationship of knowledge to pedagogic practice in Chapter 8.

21   Simon, B. (1994) 'Why no pedagogy in England?', in B. Moon and A. Shelton-Mayes (eds), *Teaching and Learning in the Secondary School* (London: Routledge).

22   See Van Der Veer, R. and Valsiner, J. (1991) *Understanding Vygotsky: A Quest for Synthesis* (Oxford: Blackwell).

23   See Basil Bernstein's analysis of this in Bernstein, B. (1971) 'On the classification of educational knowledge', in M.F. Young (ed.), *Knowledge and Control: New Directions for the Sociology of Education* (New York: Collier Macmillan).

24   This issue is usefully explored by a range of specialists in Goodson, I. (1985) *Social Histories of the Secondary School Curriculum: Subjects for Study* (London: Falmer Press).

25   Bruner, J. (1996) See the chapter on 'Folk Pedagogy' in *The Culture of Education* (Cambridge, MA: Harvard University Press).

26   This is at the core of Lee Shulman's highly influential (1987) article 'Knowledge and teaching: foundations of the new reform', in the *Harvard Educational Review*, 57 (1): 4–14. Howard Gardner, in a series of articles, also espouses the importance of allowing well established communities of scholarship to have an important place in pedagogic practice:

> Organised subject matter represents the ripe fruitage of experiences … it does not represent perfection or infallible vision; but it is the best at command to further new experiences which may, in some respects at least, surpass the achievements embodied in existing knowledge and works of art.

(Gardner, H. and Boix-Marsella, V. *Intelligence Reframed*, New York: Basic Books, page 198)

27   The Teaching and Learning Research Programme (TLRP) has, however, given attention to this in a seminar series organised by Bob McCormick and Bob Moon, entitled 'Curriculum, Domain Knowledge and Pedagogy'. A special edition of *The Curriculum Journal* 18 (4) in 2007 published the papers presented at this seminar.

28   There is a long European tradition in the study of didactics, the ways in which the structure of knowledge can be made accessible to learners. The work we have quoted here draws on Chevellard, Y. (1991) *La Transposition Didactique: Du Savoir Savant au Savoir Enseigné* (Paris: La Pensee Sauvage) and Verret, A. (1975) *Le Temps des Études* (Paris: Librarie Honoré Champion).

29   See, for example, Wolf-Michael Rok (1995) *Authentic School Science: Intellectual Traditions* (Amsterdam: Kluwer).

30   Such an appropriation, Vygotsky argued, in a much analysed phrase, took place in the zone of personal development where (usually) adults could, through pedagogic expertise, help learners internalise in an individual sense the fruits of collective endeavour.

31   Here we are drawing on the ideas of Jean Lave and Etienne Wenger (1991) *Situated Learning: Legitimate Peripheral Participation* (Cambridge: Cambridge University Press).

CHAPTER 6

1   This information is drawn from Hadingham, E. (1979) *Secrets of the Ice Age* (New York: Walker and Company) and Charroux, R. (1970) *One Hundred Thousand Years of Man's Unknown History*, translated from the French by Lowell Bair (Berkley: Berkley Publishing Corporation).

2   From Williams, R. (1976) *Keywords* (London: Collins); see also the new edition published by Oxford University Press in 1984.

Culture in William's sense encapsulates both:

- the *traditions* (meanings and values expressed and mediated by the artefacts, tools and technologies handed down and learnt in families, workplaces, schools, places of worship and so forth);

- and *selections* (the arranging, living, challenging and changing of such meanings, ideas and artefacts in everyday life).

3   See http://en.wikipedia.org/wiki/Font-de-Gaume and www.drakensberg-tourism.com/bushman-rock-art.html

4   'Forms of life' were critical to Wittgenstein's philosophy – what matters to you depends on how you live (and vice versa), and this shapes your experience. See Wittgenstein, L. (1953) *Philosophical Investigations (PI)*, G.E.M. Anscombe and R. Rhees (eds), G.E.M. Anscombe (trans.). Published by Blackwell, Oxford.

5   For Vygotsky, symbolic tools of the mind encompassed language, various tools for counting, mnemonic techniques, algebraic symbol systems, works of art, writing schema, diagrams and maps, and mechanical drawings – all sorts of conventional signs. See Vygotsky, L.S. (1978) *Mind in Society: The development of higher psychological processes* (Cambridge, MA: Harvard University Press) page 137.

6   Bruner, J. (1996) *The Culture of Education* (Cambridge, MA: Harvard University Press).

7   This insight also comes from Bruner (1996) ibid, p.2 and 115.

8   See also Swidler, (1986) 'Culture in action: symbols and strategies', *American Sociological Review*, 51: 273–86.

9   See May, W.T. (1999) 'Constructing history in a graduate classroom', in J. Leach and B. Moon (eds), *Learners and Pedagogy*, (London: Paul Chapman) page 188.

10 See Stredder, J. (1999) 'The north face of Shakespeare: practical approaches to the teaching of Shakespeare's narratives', in J. Leach and B. Moon (eds), *Learners and Pedagogy* (London: Paul Chapman) page 171.

11 Bruner (1996) ibid, page 39.

12 Stredder, K. (1999) 'Cultural bridging and childrens' learning', in P. Murphy (ed.), *Learners, Learning and Assessment* (London: Paul Chapman) page 171.

13 Rosaldo, R. (1989) *Culture and Truth: the remaking of Social Analyses* (Boston: Beacon Press); Gertz, C. (1983) *Local Knowledge* (New York: Basic Books).

14 Brown, A.L. and Campione, J.C. in *Communities of Learning and Thinking, or a Context by Any Other Name*, discussed by Bruner (1996) ibid, page 132.

15 Wenger, E. (1999) *Communities of Practice: Learning, Meaning and Identity* (Cambridge: Cambridge University Press) Pages 82–3.

16 Shared repertoire is one of three key dimensions of a community of practice together with joint enterprise and mutual engagement, according to Wenger, E. (1999) ibid, pages 82–3.

17 Norman, D. A. (1988) *Things That Make Us Smart: Defending Human Attributes in the Age of the Machine* (Cambridge, MA: Perseus Publishing).

18 Saljo, R. (ed.) (1999) *Learning Sites: Social and Technological Resources for Learning* (Oxford: Pergamon).

19   See Marcia Anne-Dobres' fascinating (2000) book, *Technology as Social Agency: Outlining a Practice Framework for Archaeology* (Oxford: Blackwell) for more on this, and particularly Chapter 1 ('Of Black Boxes and Matters Material: the State of Things') page 14.

20   Freire, P. (1970) *Cultural Action For Freedom* (Harvard Educational Review and Center for the Study of Development and Social Change, Cambridge, Massachusetts).

21   Vygotsky, L.S. (1978) *Mind in Society* (Cambridge, MA: Harvard University Press); Luria, A.R. (1981) *Language and Cognition* (Washington, DC: Winston); Leont'ev, A.N. (1981) *Problems in the Development of Mind* (Moscow: Progress Publishers). Western interpreters: Cole, M. and Wertsch, J.V. (1996) 'Beyond the individual-social antinomy in discussions of Piaget and Vygotsky', *Human Development*, 39: 250–56, and Bruner (1996) ibid.

22   Engestrom, Y. (1987) *Learning by Expanding* (Helsinki: Orienta-Konsultit).

23   Wartfosky, M. (1973) *Models* (Dordrecht: D. Reidel). Wartfosky makes a distinction between primary and secondary artefacts. According to him primary artefacts, such as a word, a knife or a telephone, are artefacts which directly mediate between humans and reality; the critical features of primary artefacts are that they always 'stand for' an entity in the physical world (like a word), mediate the interaction among humans and the physical world itself (like a knife), or mediate human interaction (like a telephone). Unlike primary artefacts, secondary artefacts do not mediate the interaction between humans and the physical world. Instead, they represent primary artefacts and mediate the interaction of humans with them. Secondary artefacts (algorithms, rules, norms, procedures) are representations of modes of interaction with primary artefacts. A procedure, such as a checklist or a recipe, is a representation of a sequence of actions that one should apply to reach a particular goal by using a set of primary artefacts; as a secondary artefact, the procedure can be conceived as a representation of the sequence of actions one could perform using primary artefacts, that is a representation of objects in the world. Secondary artefacts are therefore second-level representations – they represent modes of actions using first-level representations of the real world.

24   Noss, R. and Hoyles, C. (1996) *Windows on Mathematical Meanings: Learning Cultures and Computers* (Dordrecht: Kluwer Academic Press).

25   The reference is Bruner, J. (1996) *The Culture of Education* (Cambridge, MA: Harvard University Press). However, the phrase was first used in a letter written by Isaac Newton to fellow scientist Robert Hooke on 5 February 1676, where he very modestly claimed that his success had been built on the achievement of others: 'What Descartes did was a good step. You have added much in several ways, and especially in taking the colours of thin plates into philosophical consideration. If I have seen further it is by standing on the shoulders of giants.'

26   Google Scholar uses the invitation on its home page 'Stand on the Shoulders of Giants' (http://scholar.google.com/).

27   Discussed in a video conference at the Open University's Faculty of Education in 1996. See also Saljo, R. (ed.), (1999) *Learning Sites: Social and Technological Resources for Learning* (Oxford: Pergamon).

28   Cole, M. (1996) *Culture in Mind* (Cambridge, MA: Harvard University Press).

29   The Psalter map is so called because it accompanied a thirteenth-century copy of the Book of Psalms. It is one of the earliest maps with Jerusalem at the centre, reflecting the medieval worldview. Although tiny (15cm × 10cm), it contains a wealth of information and is characteristic of mediaeval *mappae mundi*, or world maps, that elucidated the writings of the Church fathers rather than geography. Jerusalem is indicated in the centre of the map (and of the world) and around it appears, relatively much enlarged, the 'Holy Land'. The world is depicted

with an encircling sea and three important waterways: the rivers Dan and Nile and the Mediterranean. They divide the land into three continents, with Asia at the top, Africa bottom right, and Europe in the bottom left quarter. The map has East at the top; just below Christ is a depiction of Adam and Eve in the Garden of Eden. If the map is rotated so that North is at the top it becomes much easier to understand.

30 Multimap is an Internet site that provides detailed maps of any part of the United Kingdom.

31 Saljo, R. (ed.) (2005) *Discourse, Tools, and Reasoning: Essays on Situated Cognition* (Berlin: Springer Verlag).

32 Salomon, G., Perkins, D. and Globerson, T. (1991) 'Partners in cognition: extending human intelligence with intelligent technologies', *Educational Researcher*, 20(4): 2–9.

33 Professor Ara Darzi in 'Trust Me I'm A Robot: Medical robots set to transform our hospitals' from *Science and Space CNN*, 26 April 2006. Posted: 1057 GMT (1857 HKT) http://edition.cnn.com/2006/TECH/science/04/19/robmedical/index.html

34 Lave, J. and Wenger, E. (1991) *Situated Learning* (Cambridge: Cambridge University Press).

35 Lave and Wenger, (1991) ibid.

36 Manguel, A. (1997) *A History of Reading* (London: Flamingo).

37 Schmandt-Basserat, A. (1996) *How Writing Came About* (Austin, TX: University of Texas Press).

38 See other examples in Leach, J. (2000) 'Breaking the silence: the role of technology and community in leading professional development', in B. Moon, L. Bird and J. Butcher (eds), *Leading Professional Development* (London: Paul Chapman).

39 For those fascinated by the historical development of cultural tool and artefacts see Ciolec's 'Global Networking: A timeline 30,000BCE-999CE' at http://www.ciolek.com/GLOBAL/early.html. This electronic document is intended as a electronic reference tool, providing a timeline for three types of human developments and milestones: (1) advances in long distance person-to-person communication; (2) advances in the storage, replication, cataloguing, finding, and retrieval of data; (3) standardisation of concepts and tools for long-distance interaction. The advancements, Ciolec states, may have involved: a **T** echnical (hardware), a **C** onceptual (software), or an **O** rganisational aspect, or represent an important **M** ilestone in the history of a given invention, and are annotated as such in the timeline.

40 Bruner (1996) ibid, pages 21–2.

41 Wenger (1998) ibid, page 74.

42 Wenger (1998) ibid, uses the term 'points of focus'.

43 Wenger (1998) ibid, uses the term 'reification' to emphasise the process of giving form to our experience by producing objects that crystallise the experience into 'thingness'. See page 58.

44 Deaney, R., Ruthven, K. and Hennessy, S. (2006) 'Teachers developing 'practical theories' of the contribution of information and communication technologies (ICT) to subject teaching and learning: an analysis of cases from English secondary schools', *British Education Research Journal*, 32 (3): 459–80.

45 Seeley Brown, J.S., Collins, A. and Duguid, P. (1988) 'Situated cognition and the culture of learning', *Educational Researcher,* 18: 132–42.

46 From the 'butterfly effect' beloved by chaos theory (if sufficient butterflies whirr their wings in the Amazonian rainforests, they can cause a significant climatic change in North

America). So these are small things, preferably requiring not too much effort, that can still have a disproportionate impact.

47   'Butterflies for school improvement' by Tim Brighouse and David Woods. See http://www.teachernet.gov.uk/docbank/index.cfm?id=9354

48   Another example is the strategy of encouraging staff members in rotation to introduce a new book, journal article, or idea for practice at monthly staff meetings.

49   Lave, J. and Wenger, E. (1991) *Situated Learning* (Cambridge: Cambridge University Press) and see also Chapter 3.

50   This vignette was developed in conversation with Tom Leach, Project Director of the Brent Teaching Primary Care Trust.

51   She was given the following list to consider, drawn from an OECD definition of ICT: *computers and computer software; telecommunications* including cable, satellite and telephone networks; *information* such as data bases, film and audio-visual products, music, photographs.

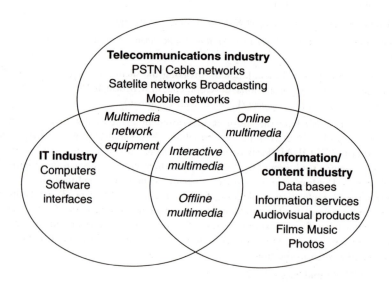

Taken from OECD (2000) *Schooling for Tomorrow: Learning to Bridge the Digital Divide* (Paris: OECD); see also Office for National Statistics (2001) 'Internet Access' (London: The Stationery Office).

52   Streibel, M.J. (1993) 'Instructional design and human practice: what can we learn from Grundy's interpretation of Huberman's Theory of Technical and Practical Human Interests?', in R. Muffoletto and N.N. Knupfer (eds), *Computers in Education: Social, Political and Historical Perspectives* (Cresskill, NJ: Hampton Press) pages 114–62. McCormick, R. and Scrimshaw, P. (2001) 'ICT, Knowledge and Pedagogy', *Education, Communication and Information*, 1 (1).

53   Leach, J. and Moon, R.E. (2000) 'Pedagogy, information and communication technologies and teacher professional knowledge', *Curriculum Journal*, 11 (3): 385–404.

54   Malaguzzi, L. (2000) at http://www.itd.ge.cnr.it/augusto/elevator/html

55   The Knowledge Forum, called CSILE (Computer Supported Intentional Learning Environment), was developed by the Ontario Institute for Studies in Education of the University of Toronto.

56   See http://www.uni.edu/darrow/reference/csile.html

57   Lodi, M. (1970) *Il Paese Sbagliato* (Turin: Giulio Einaudi).

58   Tonucci, F. (1981) *Viaje Alrededor de 'El Mundo' : Un Diario de Classe de Mario Lodi y sus Alumnos*, M. Vassallo, trans. (Barcelona: Editorial Laia). Original work published in 1980 as *Un Giornalino di Classe* (a classroom newspaper) Roma Bari: Guis, Laterza and Figli Spa.

59   Cummins, J. and Sayers, D. (1995) *Brave New Schools* (Toronto: OISE Press).

60   Cummins, J. and Sayers, D. (1995) ibid, page 42.

61   See http://www.enlaces.cl/; http://learnlink.aed.org/Publications/Sourcebook/chapter4/chile_casestudy.pdf

62   The Virtual Identities Digital Arts Project Case Study, Learning Schools Programme, Open University, 1999.

63   Leach, J. (2001) 'Teaching, long revolution: from ivory towers to networked communities of practice', in F. Banks and A. Shelton Mayes (eds), *Early Professional Development for Teachers* (London: David Fulton).

64   Drawn from Leach, J. (1997) 'English teachers "on line": developing a new community of discourse', in *English in Education*, 31 (2): 61–9.

65   See also Leach, J. (2000) 'Breaking the silence: the role of technology and community in leading professional development', in B. Moon, L. Bird and J. Butcher (eds), *Leading Professional Development* (London: Paul Chapman) pages 303–27. Research included questionnaires to participants, follow-up interviews, and a transcribed group discussion with six participants.

66   e.g.: 'Just had the "paper" through the post . . . will do a mini summary over the weekend'./'Is this what you mean? I'll attach the other ones I designed tomorrow, but they are a little harder'./'Having scanned the first couple of sentences, I know I need to read this closely off line'./'Wow! S-, talk about taking the horse by the bit! I will get back to you when I have time to digest this – there is a lot of food for thought there. . .'.

67   'Sounds brilliant I will scour the library tomorrow'./'I've read everyone's comments with interest. I've also made a note of the book you recommend, A-'.

68   Time of postings varied widely across the 24-hour period from 7 am to 2 am (with 8.30–10.30 as the busiest time).

69   Terminology drawn from Lave and Wenger (1991), ibid.

70   Meyerson has argued that community activity creates joint 'oeuvres', and that these '... produce and sustain solidarity, help to make a community of learners ... promote the sense of division of labour that goes into such a product', from Bruner, 1996, ibid.

71   From participant interviews.

72   Lave and Wenger (1991), ibid, distinguish 'talking about' and 'talking within' a practice. Talking within, they argue, embraces both talking within (e.g. exchanging information, discussing concepts) and talking about (e.g. stories, community lore). In a community both forms of talk fulfil important functions: they include engaging and focusing attention but also the supporting of communal forms of memory and reflection.

73   e.g. any other suggestions?; ... do you have this for each class?; ... but how does he introduce clauses and phrases? ... this is an area of the NC I've never seen taught and it is an area that the

new test will focus on?; ... what texts are used in MFL teaching?; ... how could we apply this strategy to younger students? There lies the challenge?

74   e.g. 'I'm finding my feelings about grammar to be ambiguous; one of my targets is to improve the way I keep tabs on such things. I will invest in a notebook.'

75   e.g. 'Oh . . . what a good idea ... ; Interesting, I-! ; Sounds brilliant.'

'I now have the courage to try out all sorts of things I was absolutely terrified of. I'm amazed. If you had told me last year that I would have been doing [those things] I would have laughed at the inanity of the suggestion ...'

76   19 June (one of the final messages from an English specialist): 'Just to let you know that as a result of this conference, I have begun to liaise with our MFL department at my place-ment school (where I have a job for September) in the hope that we can produce some kind of unified approach to language.'

77   Drawn from Leach, J. (2006) *DEEP IMPACT: An investigation of the Use of Information and Communication Technologies for Teacher Education in the Global South* (London: Department for International Development).

78   Global Campaign For Education, at http://www.campaignforeducation.org/index.html

79   In the drift to urban centres over the next decade this figure is likely to fall to 50 per cent.

80   These data are drawn from: www.devinfo.org; Mulkeen, A. (2005) 'Teachers for Rural Schools: A Challenge for Africa', Ministerial Seminar on Education for Rural Peoples in Africa: Policy Lessons, Options and Priorities, Addis Ababa, 7–9 September; Hedges, J. (2000) 'The importance of posting in becoming a teacher in Ghana', *International Journal of Educational Development,* 22: 353–66.

81   Sen, A. (1999) *Development as Freedom* (Oxford: Oxford University Press).

82   Nelson Mandela Foundation (2005) *Emerging Voices* (Johannesburg: HSRC).

83   Milward-Oliver, A. (ed.) (2006) *Maitland +20 – Fixing the Missing Link* (Bradford on Avon: Anima Press) page 136.

84   Leach, J., Klaas, N., Mnqgibisa, M. and Power, T. (2002) 'ICT and the building of profes-sional knowledge: experience in different African contexts'. Paper presented to the Commonwealth of Learning Conference, 'Transforming Education', Durban, South Africa, 30 July – 1 August 2002.

85   The majority of participating teachers and their communities had no prior experience of using information and communications technology (ICT).

86   See Leach, J. (2006) *DEEP IMPACT: An Investigation of the Use of Information and Communication Technologies for Teacher Education in the Global South* (London: Department for International Development).

CHAPTER 7

1   Loris Malaguzzi (translated from the Italian by Lella Gandini).

2   Jerome Bruner, *The Culture of Education,* 1996, page 43.

3   Paulo Freire, quoted in hooks, 1994: page v.

4   Bruner, (1996) ibid, page 37.

5   Bruner (1996) ibid, page 93.

6   Freire uses the word 'oppressors'.

7   See Rudduck, J. and Flutter, J. (2003) *How to Improve Your School: Listening to Pupils* (London: Continuum).

8   See 'Pupil Voice is Here to Stay!'. Professor Jean Rudduck, Director of the ESRC/TLRP Project: Consulting Pupils about Teaching and Learning, University of Cambridge, http://www.qca.org.uk/downloads/11478_rudduck_pupil_voice_is_here_to_stay.pdf

9   See ESRC project '*Consulting Pupils about Teaching and Learning*' by John MacBeath, Helen Demetriou, Jean Rudduck, Kate Myers, Michael Fielding, Sara Bragg, Madeleine Arnot, Donald McIntyre, David Pedder and Diane Reay, http://www.pearsonpublishing. co.uk/education/catalogue/SCHCPL. html

10   Pedder, D. and McIntyre, D. (2006) 'Pupil consultation: the importance of social capital', *Educational Review*, 58 (2): 145–57. See also Pedder, D. and McIntyre, D. (2004) 'The impact of pupil consultation on classroom practice', in M. Arnot, D. McIntyre, D. Pedder and D. Reay (eds), *Consultation in the Classroom* (Cambridge: Pearson), and Rudduck, J. and Flutter, J. (2004) *How to Improve Your School: Giving Pupils a Voice* (London: Continuum).

11   Their ideas as well as their readiness to share them reflect the opposite of what Onora O'Neill referred to as a passive culture of rights ('A Question of Trust', Annual BBC Reith Lecture, 2002).

12   The HertsCam Network consists of teachers from all phases of schooling, some of whom are employed by the local authority as teaching and learning consultants or advisers. All members of the network have participated in a programme that began in 1999 and includes the 'Herts. MEd in Teaching and Learning' and the linked, school-based 'Teacher Led Development Work' (TLDW) groups (Frost *et al.*, 2006, ibid). The network is supported through the alliance of the University of Cambridge Faculty of Education and the local education authority in Hertfordshire, now known as CSF (Children, Schools and Families).

13   Apple, M. (2006) 'Markets, Standards, and Inequality – Keynote Address to ICSEI', (International Congress on School Effectiveness and Improvement) Fort Lauderdale, Florida. USA audio recording retrieved from the Web on 10 March 2006 at http://www.leadership.fau.edu/icsei2006/archive.htm

14   Pedder, D. and McIntyre, D. 'Pupil consultation: the importance of social capital', *Educational Review* 58 (2): 145–57.

15   The Herts/Cams network produces the journal *Teacher Leadership* that publishes teachers' accounts of their professional development activities.

16   e.g. Caswell, B. and Bielaczyc, K. (2001) 'Knowledge forum: altering the relationship between students and scientific knowledge', *Education, Communication, Information*, 1(3).

17   e.g. Simpson, E. (2005) 'Juggling two cultures: a report into individual support and group work with S5 Muslim boys in James Gillespie High School'. Carried out by the City of Edinburgh EAL Service and the Black Community Development Project, July–September.

18   e.g. *Preparing urban teachers: uncovering communities a community curriculum for interns and new teachers*, by Eileen Shakespear (Fenway High School), Linda Beardsley, (Tufts University), Anne Newton (Jobs for the Future), September 2003. A joint publication of the Urban Teacher Training Collaborative and Jobs for the Future, prepared with funding from MetLifeFoundation. See http://ase.tufts.edu/education/projects/documents/project UTTC.pdf

19   Hubbard, R. and Power, B. (1999) *Living the Questions: A Guide for Teacher Researchers* (York, ME: Stenhouse).

20   Hubbard and Power (1999) ibid.

21   See Coleman, G. (1996) *Emotional Intelligence* (London: Bloomsbury).

22   See Croall, J. (1983) *Neil of Summerhill – The Permanent Rebel* (London: Routledge and
      Kegan Paul) and Vaughan, M. (2006) *Summerhill and AS Neil* (Maidenhead: Open
      University Press).

23   Pedder and McIntyre (2006) ibid.

24   Eckert, P. (1995) 'Adolescent trajectory and forms of institutional participation', in L. Crockett
      and A. Crouter (eds), *Pathways Through Adolescence: Individual Development in Relation to Social
      Contexts* (Hillsdale, NJ: Lawrence Erlbaum) pages 175–96.

25   See   http://www.futurelab.org.uk/resources/other_resources/video/Video282   and
      http://www.futurelab.org.uk/projects/mudlarking_in_deptford/details/

26   Nieto, S.M. (2003) 'What keeps teachers going?', *Educational Leadership*, 60: 15–18.

27   *MetLife* (2002) *The MetLife Survey of the American Teacher, 2002* (New York and Atlanda,
      GA: MetLife).

28   *MetLife* (2002) ibid.

29   Hollins, E.R. (2002) *Crossing Over to Canaan: The Journey of New Teachers in Diverse
      Classrooms* (San Francisco, CA: Jossey-Bass).

30   Delpit, L.D. (1995) *Other People's Children: Cultural Conflict in the Classroom* (New York:
      The New Press).

31   *Preparing Urban Teachers: Uncovering Communities A Community Curriculum for Interns and
      New Teachers*, by Eileen Shakespear (Fenway High School), Linda Beardsley (Tufts
      University), Anne Newton (Jobs for the Future), September 2003. A joint publication of
      the Urban Teacher Training Collaborative and Jobs for the Future, prepared with funding
      from MetLifeFoundation. See http://ase. tufts.edu/education/projects/documents/
      projectUTTC.pdf

32   Shakespear *et al.* (2003) ibid.

33   These include observations such as regardless of an intern's race or ethnicity, many of us live
      in middle-class neighbourhoods, and that the public facilities in the students' neighbourhoods
      are not as well maintained as those in our communities, yet there are many more youth activ-
      ities and institutions in students' neighbourhoods.

34   Steiner, G. (1975) *After Babel: Aspects of Language and Translation* (London: Oxford
      University Press).

35   Based on DES (1989) *English for Ages 5–16* (London: Department of Education and
      Science).

36   See Leach, J. (2000) 'Mother tongue teaching', in S. Brown, R. Moon and
      M. Ben-Peretz (eds), *International Companion to Education* (London: Routledge) pages
      771–98.

37   Bakhtin, M.M. (1981) 'Discourse in the novel', in M. Holquist (ed.), *The Dialogic
      Imagination: Four Essays by M.M. Bakhtin* (Austin: University of Texas).

38   Swales, J.M. (1990). *Genre Analysis,* (Cambridge: Cambridge University Press).

39   Cobb, P., McClain, K. and Yackel, M. (2000) *Symbolizing and Communicating in Mathematics
      Classrooms: Perspectives on Discourse, Tools and International Design,* (New Jersey: Lawrence
      Erlbaum).

40   National Advisory Committee on Creative and Cultural Education (NACCCE) (1999)
      All Our Futures: Creativity, Culture and Education, page 28.

41　Shulman, L.S. (1986). 'Those who understand: knowledge growth in teaching', *Educational Researcher*, 15 (5), 4–14, page 5.

42　e.g. Leinhardt, G. and Smith, D. (1985) 'Expertise in mathematical instruction: subject matter knowledge', *Journal of Educational Psychology*, Vol. 77(3): 247–71.

　　Grossman, P.L., Wilson, S.M. and Shulman, L.S. (1989) Teachers of substance: subject matter knowledge for teaching, in Reynolds, M.C. (ed.) *Knowledge Base for the Beginning Teacher* (Oxford: Pergamon Press) pages 159–99. 94, no. 2, pp. 397413. Books, New York.

　　Wilson, S.M. and Wineberg, S.S. (1988) 'Peering at history through different lenses: the role of the disciplinary perspectives in teaching history', *Harvard Educational Review*, Vol. 89(4): 527–39; McDiarmid, G., Ball, D.L. and Anderson, C.W. (1989) 'Why staying one chapter ahead doesn't really work: subject-specific pedagogy', in Reynolds, M.C. (ed.) *Knowledge Base for the Beginning Teacher*, (Oxford: Pergamon Press).

43　McKewan, H. and Bull, B. (1991) 'The pedagogic nature of subject matter knowledge', *American Educational Research Journal*, 28(2): 319–34.

44　Shulman, L.S. (1987) 'Knowledge and teaching: foundations of the new reform', *Harvard Educational Review*, 57: 1–23.

45　Gardner, H. and Boix-Marsella, V. (1994) 'Teaching for understanding in the disciplines and beyond', *Teachers' College Record*, 96(2): 19.

46　Egan (Egan, K. (1992) 'An exchange', *Teachers College Record*, 94(2) led this critique arguing that Gardner's work:

> appears to assume that effective human thinking is properly more disciplined, more coherent and more consistent than seems to me to be the case. This is not an argument on behalf of greater in-discipline, incoherence and inconsistency, but a speculation that human thinking operates very effectively with a considerable degree of those characteristics, and that attempting to reduce them to greater conformity with what seems like rules of disciplinary understanding – whose provisionalness and unclarity should not be underestimated – will more likely reduce our humanity or enhance it. (page 405)

He goes on:

> the danger of letting disciplinary understanding call the educational tune was, for Dewey, no less than an attack on democracy itself. It inevitably led to an aristocracy, or meritocracy, and so to the kinds of social divisions America was founded to prevent. (page. 405)

47　Project Zero; Gardner, H. (1991) *The Unschooled Mind*, (New York: Basic Books) page 161; See also Sizer, T.R. (1992) *Horace's School*, (New York: Houghton Mifflin).

48　Lave, J. (1988) *Cognition in Practice* (Cambridge: Cambridge University Press); Lave, J. and Wenger, E. (1991) *Situated Learning: Legitimate Peripheral Participation* (Cambridge: Cambridge University Press).

49　Shulman's category of *subject content knowledge* we retained, but we denoted it simply as subject knowledge. In doing so we wished to emphasise the dynamic, process-driven nature of 'subject knowledge' which encompasses 'essential questions, issues and phenomenon drawn from the natural and human world, methods of inquiry, networks of concepts, theoretical frameworks, techniques for acquiring and verifying findings ... symbol systems, vocabularies and mental models' (Gardner (1994) ibid). School knowledge we suggested as an analytic category in its own right, subsuming the *curricular knowledge* of Shulman. We therefore split the category of pedagogic content knowledge as defined by Shulman to gain a greater hold on this important epistemological construct. By 'school knowledge' we do not mean knowledge of the school context. Rather we viewed it as the transposition of subject knowledge referred to above. Our third category which we called *pedagogical knowledge* we saw as going beyond the generic set of beliefs and practices that inform teaching and learning. Although these exist, and rightly form an important part of the development of teacher expertise, we would argue they are insufficient unless integrated into an understanding of the crucial relationship between subject knowledge and school knowledge. One might initially see 'school knowledge' as being intermediary between subject knowledge (knowledge of technology as practised by different types of technologists, for example) and pedagogical knowledge as used by teachers ('the most powerful analogies, illustrations, example, explanations and demonstrations'). This would be to underplay the dynamic relationship between the categories of knowledge implied by the diagram. For example, a teacher's subject knowledge is transformed by his or her own pedagogy in practice and by the resources that form part of their school knowledge. We would argue it is the active interaction of subject knowledge, school knowledge and pedagogical understanding and experience that brings teacher professional knowledge into being.

50   Banks, Leach, and Moon (1999), ibid.

51   Shulman, L.S. and Shulman, J.H. (2004) 'How and what teachers learn', *Journal of Curriculum Studies*, 36, 2 March-April. The new model incorporates teacher vision, with motivation alongside understanding and practice embedded in communities of practice (page 265).

52   Giroux, H.A. (1988) *Teachers as Intellectuals: Towards a Critical Pedagogy of Learning* (New York: Bergin and Garvey).

53   Quote from Lave and Wenger (1991) ibid, page 116.

CHAPTER 8

1   A number of documents explore the themes of this paragraph in more detail. Two examples would be the 2005 UNESCO Education for All Global Monitoring Report 'The Quality Imperative', and the Report of the Commission for Africa (also published in 2005) 'Our Common Interest'. See also the chapter on Women's Agency and Social Change in Sen, A. (1999) *Development is Freedom* (Oxford: Oxford University Press).

2   'We must do more to make sure education meets the needs of our children and the demands of the future. First and foremost we must continue to hold students, teachers and schools to the highest standards. We must ensure students can demonstrate competence to be promoted and to graduate. Teachers must also demonstrate competence, and we should be prepared to reward the best ones, and remove those who don't measure up, fairly and expeditiously.' Taken from *Between Hope and History* published in 1996 (page 44).

3   Advance notice of this was given in Peter Mandelson and Roger Liddle's book *The Blair Revolution: Can New Labour Deliver?*, published in 1996 by Faber and Faber.

4   More accurately we should say English schools because rather different political strategies were pursued in the more independent systems of Northern Ireland, Scotland and Wales.

5   *Emerging Voices: A Report on Education in South African Rural Communities* (2005), Cape Town: Nelson Mandela Foundation (see Chapter 6).

6   See Lakoff, G. and Johnson, M. (1980) *Metaphors We Live By* (Chicago: The University of Chicago Press).

7   We are indebted to Nabeel Hamdi for alerting us to this reference in his (2004) book *Small Change* (London: Earthscan).

8   We are aware that the dominant philosophical traditions that shape ideas in parts of the West (particularly in England and the USA) find the concept of the intellectual difficult to handle. However, in a learned profession like teaching 'possessing a high level of under-standing' (an *Oxford English Dictionary* definition) seems entirely appropriate to teachers' mission.

9   We take these assertions from an article in the *New York Times* of 26 March 2007 by Edward Rothstein, 'Tests that Run Rings Around Everyday Linear Logic'.

10   Published by Harper Collins in 1996 – see especially 'The Missing First Page', pages 85–94.

Index